THE ACCOMPANIST. . . and friends
An Autobiography of Andre Benoist

Edited by John Anthony Maltese.

Albert Spalding   Andre Benoist   Jascha Heifetz

Published by PAGANINIANA PUBLICATIONS, INC.
211 West Sylvania Avenue, Neptune City, N.J. 07753

ISBN –0-87666-614-4

TABLE OF CONTENTS

Notes & Acknowledgements

André Benoist evidently had the thought of writing an auto-biography on his mind for many years. No doubt the idea of being able to write about the world's greatest musicians first hand and from "the other side of the footlights," so to speak, intrigued him. The earliest manuscript that could be found from among his papers dated from the 1920's. From that point forward he frequently revised and added to the present work.

Benoist never lived to see his book published, but in 1965, his son, Albert Spalding, mimeographed a few copies of the final manuscript as a gift for his family. In 1977, one of those copies came into the hands of Dr. Herbert R. Axelrod and Paul Paradise of Paganiniana Publications. After consultation with Albert Spalding Benoist it was decided that this book should be published as a living document of the career of the greatest of the great accompanists. It is these men, therefore, who must be credited for letting this book see the light of day.

Once the publication of the book was definitely decided upon, I was called in to serve the general duties of the book's editor. With the very kind assistance of my father, John, and of Joan and Albert Spalding Benoist, various pictures and documents were chosen to be included in the book. I am, however, solely responsible for the placement of those pictures in the text, and for the captions which accompany them. With few exceptions, the pictures are from the collection of the Benoist family.

The manuscript used here is based upon that which was distributed privately by Albert Benoist. Nevertheless, in numerous instances I have added material from some of Benoist's earlier manuscripts. The writing itself has, however, been left untouched so as to preserve Benoist's style and also to catch some of the flavor of the times during which it was written.

5

To add further to the documentation of this work, I have also included a complete discography of Benoist, as well as a list of his compositions.

A special word of thanks must go to my father and Dr. Herbert R. Axelrod for their patient and generous assistance with the preparation of this book.

My thanks must also be given to Bertha Beekman, Faye Valerio, and Jim Bailiff for their valuable suggestions, corrections, and help with the translations. Of course, we are all indebted to the Benoists for their preservation of the materials which constitute this book, and also for their help in identifying various personages in the many photographs.

I hope that this work will serve as a valuable, as well as an interesting and informative documentation. If so, this project was well worth the effort involved.

John Anthony Maltese
Wells, New York

Introduction

by John Anthony Maltese

This book recalls the experiences of an accompanist. He is more correctly remembered as "The Accompanist," for in his time he was truly one of the greatest. This remarkable man was André Benoist.

He was born in Paris in 1880, where he later studied at the Conservatoire with Saint-Saens, Franck, Massenet, Godard and Thomas. He graduated in his teens and was then taken to the United States by his parents.

Benoist sought, at first, the role of soloist. As such he toured for a time with the Callamarini-Repetto Grand Opera Company. His programs with them usually consisted of two or three works intermingled between the many operatic selections.

His dislike of solo work soon led him to become an accompanist. He collaborated first with the great Hungarian violinist, Edouard Remenyi, around 1900, and over the next two years he worked with several lesser musicians who are now almost totally forgotten.

Benoist's career truly began to blossom when he accompanied the French violinist, Jacques Thibaud, for his first recital at Carnegie Hall and for a subsequent tour in 1903-04. Critics began taking notice of the young accompanist in their accounts of those recitals. The *Boston Times* of November 14, 1903, for instance, described him as having *"much talent,"* although *"a talent not yet entirely under his control. . . He has great resources, however, and his accompaniments were exquisite—sympathetic and soundly musical. It was a pleasure, too, to hear that Liszt Polonaise given without forced tone. . ."*

That same season he accompanied the great American woman violinist, Maud Powell, for several concerts. Included among these was the United States premiere of the Sibelius Violin Concerto. An engagement with the singer, Emma Eames, followed, as well as a tour with Fritz Kreisler and Josef Hofmann in 1905.

The next year, 1906, included a major tour with the 'cellist, Jean Gerardy, as well as a program with the violinist, Henri Marteau. Ensuing programs with the baritone, Emilio di Gogorza; the mezzo-soprano, Ernestine Schumann-Heink; the 'cellist, Pablo Casals; the baritone, Charles Gilibert; and the American soprano, Lillian Nordica; served to complete his acceptance as *The Accompanist* by the musical world.

Benoist's tours with Luisa Tetrazzini and Mary Garden in 1910-11, ended the first phase of his career as an accompanist. This, because in 1912 he began a life-long collaboration with the American violinist Albert Spalding. The remainder of Benoist's life was devoted, almost without exception, to the services of the violinist. A rare personal and musical friendship sprung up between them which is nearly unparalleled in the history of soloist-accompanist relations.

Together they toured the United States, Europe, Russia, and Egypt, with great success. There was a brief interlude to their collaboration, however, when Spalding joined the Armed Services after America's entry into World War I in 1917.

It was during this time that Benoist accompanied the young violin master from Russia, Jascha Heifetz. They toured extensively together with tremendous success. Reviews were typically ecstatic, such as this one by Dudley Glass from Atlanta, Georgia: *". . . With Schubert's* Ave Maria *the Strad became a human voice with a pipe organ dimly in the background. It did not seem possible that only one violin was being played. Heifetz was singing, and somewhere a celestial choir was chanting an accompaniment. And no less beautiful than this dream music was the rippling piano accompaniment by André Benoist, as clear and silvery as tiny bells might be. It was the first time we had remembered the piano, and it may be said here that no better accompanist than Mr. Benoist ever played in Atlanta."*

In the meantime, Spalding and Benoist kept up a friendly correspondence. In his letters, Spalding accounted his activities in sharp and often moving detail. He expressed pleasure at Benoist accompanying Heifetz in his absence, as shown by this letter, postmarked February 2, 1918: *". . . I am always enchanted to have your news and after all it was a great piece of luck, your falling in with the 'sheep of five legs.' He must be an extraordinary boy from all accounts and, of course, as a child he was a wizard. . . Alas!—my poor violin. I scarcely ever see it or touch it, and yet when I do (quite alone and for myself) I am astonished that I lose very little in facility. But, of course, my memory is all to pieces for I have to concentrate on such different things—statistics, spare parts, and other (confidential) matters which can not be mentioned. However, the work is exceedingly interesting and engrossing and my officers are all enthusiastic and appear anxious to push me in every way possible. In short, one does what one can. This is my job now, and though I do not love it, at this moment I can not and will not be interested in anything else. It is for this very reason that I fear to play too often in the evening with my violin—and so I trudge back often to the Barracks for a few hours more work—and there is always plenty of work to be done. I am hoping for more active work when Spring comes, but fear that they will keep non-flying officers as pen-pushers as long as they can. Well, old man, this must go off as it is—or it won't go at all. . . Always your 'Captain', A.S."*

With the end of the war, Benoist returned to his full time collaboration with Spalding, although he still continued to see Heifetz occasionally on an informal basis.

Many tours, recordings, and broadcasts continued for the next twenty years. But then, once again, war broke out and Spalding went off to serve his country. They met on occasion, nonetheless, and the two gave several concerts for servicemen.

But, by now, Benoist was feeling the strain of tours, and he bowed out of full time concert work to devote his time to teaching at his home in Monmouth Beach, New Jersey. Notwithstanding, the two remained indefatigable companions.

They both became ill in 1953, and in one of Spalding's last letters to Benoist, he remarked wistfully: *"Beautiful days pass and never return!!!!!"* Shortly afterwards Spalding had a stroke and died. Benoist was never told, but he sensed it and lost all will to live. Within a month he, too, was dead.

On Monday, June 22, 1953, the *New York Times* published his obituary. It was entitled simply and lovingly with the familiar phrase *The Accompanist,* and it read:

"*The life and career of André Benoist, who died on Friday at the age of 74, illustrate strikingly how important can be the role of those whose function is to help others without seeking the limelight for themselves. Mr. Benoist was one of the most gifted pianists of our generation, but he was known and loved not as the solo performer, but in his supporting capacity. To musicians all over the world his name meant* The Accompanist.

"*His marvelous skill added to the luster of some of the most famous instrumentalists. The three most outstanding violinists of our time, Fritz Kreisler, Jascha Heifetz, and the late Albert Spalding; and the greatest 'cellist, Pablo Casals, had the benefit of his magnificently sympathetic understanding at the keyboard. Each was better for his assistance.*

"*In other walks of life, similarly, there are many persons who voluntarily take the second role, gratified in their contribution to the success of others. It requires rare skill and deep human sympathy to do this well. Some, like André Benoist, do it supremely.*"

Chapter
I

The place of his birth was Paris of the early eighteen eighties, when Paris was still the heart and core of France. After the turn of the century, Paris became as extra-territorial to France as New York is extra-territorial to the United States.

While a small crust of the City, such as the Batignolles, Montmartre, La Chapelle, Clichy, etc., remained strictly French, the center of cosmopolitan activity existed around the Rue de la Paix, the Place de la Concorde, the Madeleine, the Opera and the American Express Company. Also the Hotels, Meurice, Ritz, Continental, Regina and Grand, where, when you heard French spoken, the language seemed incongruous and out of place. What you heard was generally uttered by English-speaking people, Spaniards, Russians, Germans, Argentinians, Algerians, Americans, and sometimes even by some Dahomisians, princes all, but coal black anyway.

No, the Paris of these early eighties was not the Paris of today. It was the most straight-laced city in the world. And the people who inhabited it had highly-corseted minds. Next to them, Puritans were real sinners! Young ladies never went out without Mama and Papa, or, in rarefied circles, a governess or two. There were no night clubs or cinemas. As for theatres, children (and girls were considered children until they were married) were confined to seeing a very boring tragedy by Racine or Corneille at the Comedie-Française or the Odeon. Even Moliére was looked upon askance! Sometimes on a special occasion you were allowed to witness the performance of a "faerie" at the Chatelet, (something on the order of Jules Verne's *"Twenty Thousand Leagues Under the Sea")*, or *"Michael Strogoff."* If you had been unusually good or "sage" as it was called in French, you were allowed to accompany the cook, who did all the buying of victuals, for each item of which she was allowed to retain a commission of one penny out of every franc. And what a blissful walk that was, through streets still damp from a recent rainfall, looking in at the little shop windows, behind which some friendly face would nod a look of kindly recognition. There was no *"Hi, Dick"* or *"Hello, Tom."* It was *"Good Day, Monsieur Richard"* or *"Bonjour, Monsieur Thomas."* There was not the easy familiarity of the so-called "democracy." But on the other hand, there was a good deal of self-respect and courtesy.

Thus Paris, of which Americans spoke in hushed tones and with a leer in their eyes, saying, *"Ah, those French, they are such an immoral nation!"* As Max O'Rell once so aptly said, *"If they found immorality, they must have gone looking for it!"* Of course they found it. For the Parisian, in spite of any faults attributed to him, worshiped true liberty and shunned hypocrisy. Consequently, nothing was forbidden, except annoying your neighbor, and anything you wished for was to be found, from the heights of the Sorbonne to the dregs of human behavior. You could drink all you desired behind closed doors and with shades drawn, but if you were caught intoxicated in public you were sent to jail for being a bad influence on the general weal. Discipline was strictly enforced, especially among children, though not in an unkindly manner, with the result that pesty children were conspicuous by their absence. Children were given everything they needed, and, when obedient, all they wished. Their lives were really happy ones, for all they had to do was behave, and the world was theirs. There was never a question of petty jealousy in schools, for all were made to wear the same kind of uniform, rich and poor alike. No matter what clothes they wore, they were covered by a knee-length black alpaca apron held tight at the waist by a brown leather belt. In a fight, both parties were punished as being uncivilized. Physical strength, in those days, did not overshadow justice.

One day, our little boy jumped off his bicycle. (This new contraption had succeeded the machine with the high front wheel trailing a very little one in the rear, which, up to then, had enjoyed the name *bicycle*). The new machine did not tip forward to let you fall on your nose. No, this one was steady, owing to the fact that both wheels were of one size, and its new name was *bicyclette*. It had been given the boy in reward for exceptionally good behavior. Little did he think that this thing, his pride and joy, would also serve to chalk up marks against him!

Having jumped off his wheel, a bit breathless and with a self-conscious assumption of bravado, he approached the mustachioed "guardien de la paix" (in American slang, "cop"). He had never feared the guardians; quite the contrary, he had always admired them for their well-known bravery, for had they not been instituted for his special protection? Their kindness too, as well as their interest in little children was proverbial in his world of ease and comfort. It must be admitted that this world narrowed down to Papa, Mama, Gouvernante, Cook and Maid. There was also François who came once a week to wax the immaculate "parquet," beat rugs and do the things the weaker sex were not supposed to do. In the boy's eyes, François was wonderful! For as he waxed the floors and polished the wax with a brush attached to his foot, he seemed to do a dance more graceful than a fairy's.

Papa, too, was wonderful, for he had a beautiful, curled-up moustache. When he sallied forth, clad in a fine Prince Albert coat, (which he called his redingote), topped by a shining silk hat dubbed "haut-de-forme," he looked very "distingue." He impressed the little boy deeply. Mama, he took for granted, for she was always around, either catering to his comforts, or trying to arrange some kind of settlement when punishment was at hand for infringement of local discipline.

His little world also comprised the "salon;" that mysterious room used only on special occasions, which contained, in addition to the Pleyel grand piano, innumerable standing oil lamps, which, with their huge silk shades, seemed like so many tents in an alien camp. And what a thrill it was, when a party was at hand, to be allowed within its sacrosanct purlieus (sacred walls) to play on that lovely piano, in place of the plain little upright in one's own room. But first one had to wash one's hands, and take off one's muddy shoes and replace them with clean slippers. What a bore!

Going farther afield, his world embraced the Tuilerie Gardens, (The jardin d'acclimatation with its wealth of strange and fascinating animals), the Eiffel Tower, (that had just been completed), and finally the bicyclette from which he had alighted. But this bicyclette, while a precious possession, was of little use to him unless he could ride it; and, unfortunately, he was not allowed to ride it on the streets. For, though there were as yet no automobiles to be dodged, there were carriages with horses, the latter being feared as potential runaways! The only place youngsters belonging to "nice" families were supposed to ride was the Velodrome Terron. This was a huge barn of a place, of a size and shape not unlike our Madison Square Garden. It contained a wide, banked track, over which one could ride around and around until one got tired or dizzy, or both.

On this particular day, the boy had been taken to this place of amusement by his grand-pére, owing to its being a day off for Gouvernante. As he rode around the track over and over again, the boy watched his grandfather from the corner of his rather shrewd eye, hoping against hope the latter might doze off. Suddenly he noticed that the old gentleman's chin was resting on his chest and his eyes were closed. Thereupon, he steered his wheel straight for the exit door and joyfully found himself out in the open. He rode and rode blissfully on, until he came to the nearby Bois de Boulogne where everything was in full-scented bloom. . . then, all at once, he was lost! Panic-stricken, he turned to the policeman.

After all, why should one be afraid to speak to an unusually tall uniformed officer? Nameless fears kept creeping into the boy's consciousness. (One's conscience was a terribly bothersome commodity!) Thus the following dialogue:

"Pardon me, Monsieur," the boy spoke in his most polite and dulcet accents, "would you please show me the shortest way to the Velodrome Terron?"

The law looked down and was intrigued; and seeing the distance separating his own head from the little boy's, he squatted to reduce this distance to its minimum.

"Do you mean to tell me," he gently asserted, "that you've traveled on that thing," pointing to the boy's pride and joy, "through that carriage and horse traffic all the way from Terron's to the Bois de Boulogne?"

The boy thought he detected understanding in the officer's voice, and feeling a bit reassured, timidly replied:

"Yes, Monsieur; but alas, Monsieur, in my haste to try to get

14

back to the Velodrome before Grand-pére wakes up, I lost my way, and here I am."

Benevolence suddenly left the officer's face, and voice. Looking sternly at the boy he growled:

"So. . . you're the little scalawag that's put half the police force on alert." He was no longer squatting, but standing erect in all the majesty of the law.

"Ah me," thought the little boy, "what have I said? Now, surely I am undone. No theatre, no allowance, no long rides through the Bois in the old family caleche (coach), and no delicious goute (sweet or nosh) on return from school, for at least two weeks. And hours of extra practice on the darned old piano. Well, I'll just have to take my medicine."

Continued the law: "And now, my little one, I shall have to walk you home, for obviously, we cannot get this dirty machine of yours in a cab. Even if the 'cocher' (coachman) wouldn't object, the horse would, owing to the extra weight. So, walk it is."

WALK! . . . Horrors! . . . the one stupid exercise the boy loathed more than any other. To put one foot before the other, and get nowhere slowly. . . ever so slowly and boringly. Oh well, there was nothing else to do, so with trepidation in his heart, he walked home. There, against all expectation, he was greeted with "my darling," "my lost one," "my loved one," ad nauseam. Then and there he decided never again to try a runaway act. It entailed too many emotional and physical disturbances, two things to which, even today, he is thoroughly allergic!

This was the world in which the small boy grew. He was no different from other small boys; he was inquisitive, lazy, and loved having a good time.

Who shall blame him?

As I have hinted, his family was what is commonly called "nice," and, being brought up with "nice ways," one had to learn to play the piano. You will ask, "Why the piano?" The psychology of this was as follows: If you learned to play the violin, the violoncello, the clarinet or their ilk, you might end by acquiring a taste for playing in an orchestra. . . not in a trio or a quartet, but a real symphony orchestra, which was decidedly not "nice," but thoroughly vulgar. That way you became a musician and not an artist. . . shades of Debussy, who later signed his works "Musicien

Français" instead of "Compositeur"!

And so the little boy was given into the hands of an old lady who, having fallen on evil times, and needing to eke out her budget, taught piano at three francs a lesson. It so happened that this little boy had often been charmed by the sounds issuing from the old grand piano that stood, mysteriously hidden by a screen, in a corner of the hallowed precincts of the family salon, when his mother would regale the family and guests with some waltzes by Waldteufel, or accompany his father when the latter would sing, in a pleasing baritone, sentimental ballads of bygone days. All this would give the child ecstasies of pleasure, upon seeing which, it was suddenly decided that the child had talent bordering upon genius! Ah, Talent! What crimes have been committed in thy name! No one thought of the fact that talent is a benign disease, curable only by hard work. But the going was not too hard at the beginning. Many times, when Mama thought that scales were being practiced diligently, (as many repetitions of the same one seemed to indicate) the young scalawag in reality had a book of *La Fontaine's Fables* or even a newspaper in front of him, while mechanically going over and over the same scale. These he quickly slid behind the music sheet at the first suspicious sound of footsteps approaching the salon. And with an innocent air, he received the maternal kiss given as reward for his diligence! Thus are hypocrites created!

But in spite of all this, the child seemed to progress amazingly. The only drawback was that he detested playing solo, or, as he would put it, "tout seul" (all alone). His greatest joy was when some visiting friend would bring a violin, or just his voice, and permit André to accompany him. That was bliss! Just like an interesting conversation between two people! Music wasn't made to show off how clever you were, or what wonderful dexterity you had attained. It was something to be shared, to be a complete experience.

Finally convinced of his talent, his family decided that André had outgrown the lady teacher and that it was time to send him to that hallowed institution of art, the Conservatoire de Musique et de Declamation. But that was not as easy as it sounds. There was an entrance examination to go through, and to the child, that seemed quite superfluous. Consequently, during the year of preparation, he stopped by the wayside to smell flowers, eat delicious

Rosalie and Emile Benoist, parents of Andre. Circa 1890, Paris.

grass, and create other silly amusements like the proverbial hare. So that when the time came for the examination, being utterly unprepared, he flunked flatly and flatulently, as nervousness as well as disappointment turned his poor little stomach upside-down! But it had been a salutary lesson and at the next trial, he entered the great school with flying colors. Ah, those entrance exams! What a cruel ordeal for a child! In this case, it was the first time the little boy realized that he was an entity. That he did not have Papa and Mama to stand by him and help his morale. He suddenly realized that he was "I" and "me." And so I became myself. . .

The composer Ambroise Thomas, who lived from 1811 to 1896.

Chapter
II

I walked down the long, dark corridor that led to the examination hall, escorted by an indifferent usher, and feeling like a lamb being led to his slaughter. The usher opened a door and gently pushed me through. I found myself on a stage, facing a dark, gloomy, rather small concert hall. The stage displayed a concert grand piano, on the music stand of which stood, on opposite sides, a lighted candle. I could think of nothing else but a wake! Through the gloom of the hall, from which the usual "fauteuils" (easy chairs) had been removed, I could discern a long green baize-covered table, at which sat a number of solemn-looking gentlemen, some bearded, some mustachioed, all facing the stage. This, I thought, was the jury. And what a jury! I only found out later who the members were: the president was the Director General of the Conservatoire, Ambroise Thomas, composer of *Mignon* and other operas. On his right sat Camille Saint-Saens, of the sardonic tongue and pronounced soprano lisp. On the left, sat the venerable Cesar Franck, already rather feeble, but ever kind and benevolent. Further down the table sat Jules Massenet, at that time in the middle of his mad love affair with the gorgeous American soprano, Sybil Sanderson, who was the antithesis of the popular conception of the conventional prima-donna. For she had the face of an angel, the figure of a Venus and a voice of melting and unparalleled beauty. Massenet also was the romantic type, so favored by novelists when they write about an artist-musician; with his delicate, Grecian features surmounted by a mane of iron-grey hair, which he wore shoulder length. Consequently, despite its illegitimacy, the romance had the complete blessing of Paris.

It was fortunate for me that at the time I had no knowledge of the world celebrities who were to pass on my worthiness as a student.

As it was, I wobbled onto the stage completely forlorn, until I spied, in an unobtrusive corner, the one face I knew; my beloved teacher, Emile Decombes, in whose classes I had been allowed to be a "listener," or as the French put it, "auditeur," during my year of probation after flunking my first entrance exams. As I went past him, he patted my shoulder, saying, "Ca ira, mon petit" (it will go alright, my little one).

Suddenly all seemed bright once again, and since my bearded and benevolent professor had confidence in me, I would justify it. With the disappearance of my nervousness and fear, I picked my way through the several works I had to play and did not do too bad-ly. Then came the sight reading test, which had to be done from manuscript, to make it more difficult. To make it worse, the

Jules Massenet wrote the sight reading test which Benoist took as his entrance examination to the Conservatoire in Paris.

Seated in the center is Cesar Franck. He audited the program played by Benoist for his entrance to the Paris Conservatoire. Immediately behind Franck is his good friend, Eugene Ysaye. The other musicians from left to right: Leon Van Hout, Joseph Jacob, Mathieu Crickboom, and in the window, the pianist Paul Braud. Circa 1890.

manuscript was written for the occasion by Massenet who proverbially wrote fly specks! By that time, instead of being nervous, I was angry! Consequently, I plunged in the best way I knew how and read the two pages more glibly than I could have done under normal conditions. (For passing marks, you were allowed three mistakes on a page, but it seems I only made two). When I arose from the piano chair, I thought I could detect some nodding of heads among the critical heads sitting in judgment. Again, a pat on the shoulder from dear Decombes, and back to Papa and Mama, who were waiting with trepidation in the outer vestibule.

Jules Massenet at the age of 35. His musical penmanship is described by Benoist as *flyspecks*.

My father, as usual, looked terribly impressive, wearing his Prince Albert coat and high silk hat under which a carefully, upward-curled moustache made him look like the Frenchmen of whom we still see pictures in old story books. All this did not prevent him from possessing a devastating sense of humor, which he was not averse to using even against himself. But this time he thoroughly puzzled me, for he gravely examined my neck, front, back and sides, then looked at me quizzically and said, "Well, the guillotine did not do such a thorough job after all today." Upon this, Mother and I went into peals of laughter and the day was saved!

It took three days of waiting before the verdict came. Three days of fingernail biting and heart fluttering. At last the official looking document arrived and there it was: "One Benoist (André) is accorded the honor of becoming a student of the Conservatoire National de Musique et de Declamation at the expense of the Republique Française (Liberté, Egalité, Fraternité)." To say we were elated would be an understatement. I was for buying a cane at once, but my father remarked that, being in my first year, it might be wise to wait until I saw what the customs were in the classes. After all, this was not the time to show off one's sartorial magnificence!

At last came the day when classes opened, and, with a black, moroccan leather attaché case filled with sheet music under my arm, I started for the shrine of music, accompanied by the ever-present Gouvernante. I must admit that, in spite of my apparent jauntiness, my heart was going pit-a-pat. We finally arrived at the great door in the Faubourg Poissoniere and I was at last alone. The haughty concierge, upon reading my name on a list, condescendingly told me where to go. The old, gloomy building was full of

Camille Saint-Saens with his Shih Tzu dog. Saint-Saens was one of Benoist's examiners and professors in Paris.

dark corridors, which smelled musty and dank. (From what I learned later, it had been a military barracks before being turned into its present use). From the room next to the one to which I had been directed, issued forth brazen sounds, and to my horror, I found that it was the class of Monsieur le Professeur Cerclier, who taught (of all things) the trumpet! The class I entered consisted of about twenty boys. Naturally, they were all talented! But they were not all angels. Far from it! (Although one of them did look like one.) His name was Armand Ferte. He wore his very blonde hair shoulder length in what you would call a boyish bob, but this bob had been carefully curled 'round a curling stick. The front was cut in bangs. A rosy complexion and beautiful, regular features completed his appearance. He also enjoyed the distinction of being the illegitimate son of the great playwright Victorien Sardou, which earned him quite a degree of respect in the class. He was usually accompanied by his mother, a gorgeous blonde, who was Sardou's mistress of the moment. When I last saw this ethereal being (who in reality was one of the worst he-devils) in 1923, he was conducting opera at the Comique. He was short, obese and quite bald!

As everyone knows, a class in any institution of learning always contains an imp of some kind, and our class was no exception. The imp in this case was called Camille Decreus and, without being deliberately mischievous, he either was, or got someone else into trouble. (Nevertheless, he was, without a doubt, the most gifted boy of all.) He looked at a composition, played it over a couple of times, and it was imbedded in his brain and hands. Of course, it did not stay there long, but whatever he touched reflected grace and charm without effort. He was lazy and slow to concentrate on any given subject, and for that reason was always *near* the top of the class instead of being number one, as his great gifts would have entitled him to be.

What pranks dear old Camille could play! He was about seventeen and was THE lady killer of our group, which I can assure you, was precocious, to put it mildly! The young ladies of Papa Saint-Saens' piano classes looked with undisguised approval on Decreus' sturdy, athletic figure, surmounted by classic features and golden locks. Whenever he was missing from our class, one could be sure to find him in some neighboring empty class room, immersed in an interesting téte-a-téte with a similarly missing talent from the female class. This part of his life remained, until the end, a deep secret from the powers that were, for no one would turn informer on so fine a pal. But Decreus almost came to grief one day. He loathed the solfege and harmony classes which entailed a good deal of midnight oil burning, and where one had to show in concrete form what one had really accomplished. There, charm of manner and fascinating ways were useless. He had warned us that when the next class took place, he would not only see that *he* got out of it, but that we *all* got out of it! He explained that he had a rendezvous which could not be broken, for the young lady in question was not only beautiful, but carried, along with her undoubted pulchritude, a thoroughly satisfactory dot, or dowry. Of course we all sympathized with him, but what to do? We were soon to find out.

This particular class began in the prescribed orthodox way. Suddenly, we noticed the professor had stopped examining papers and was sniffing the air suspiciously. Thereupon, those of us who were not afflicted by a head cold, also began to sniff just as suspiciously as had the professor. What was that infernal smell? We opened all the windows in spite of the bitter cold, but the foul air persisted and in fact grew worse. One could hardly breathe. I had dropped a paper on the floor and owing to the draft caused by the open windows, it had flown under the grand piano. On reaching to pick it up, I noticed tiny pieces of glass lying about the floor, and eureka! The mystery was explained. Someone had thrown some Chinese stink balls under the piano so that the room became uninhabitable! And who had thrown them? I leave it to you to guess! The next moment, the professor dismissed classes for the day, and Camille, with the most innocent face, expressed his mournful regrets at being deprived of further learning! I was, up to that time, the only one who knew the truth; and I was honor bound not to divulge it. But, thought I, if the concierge comes in to clean up before we can do away with the evidence, we are all lost, for such a prank would be considered open rebellion. The consequences: dismissal from the school for the whole class, unless a traitor were found. So I shared the secret, and sometime later, on the excuse that in the hurry of leaving, some of us had left some books behind, we sneaked back and cleaned up the mess without anyone becoming the wiser.

Decreus eventually became one of the most sought after piano teachers in Paris and in the last years of his life was Director General of the Conservatoire of Fontainebleau. He died in that position, loved and missed by all who had come in contact with him.

The real cock-o'-the walk was a chap called Alfred Cortot. He was about the same age as Decreus, and there the resemblance ended. For, where the latter was lazy, the first was indefatigable. He would have lengthened his day to twenty-eight hours of practice, if he could. Where Decreus, in spite of his apparent flightiness, was loyalty personified, Cortot would have used any means to arrive at his ends, which in his case were fame and power. He was also the "Beau Brummel" of our group. When he wore his hair "a la Bressant'" (pompadour), all the boys would wear it that way. When he began to sport a cane, we all bought canes. When he wore certain clothes, we all tried to be similarly attired. And there the imitations ended. We just could not keep up the pace of his work, nor did any of us care to. Is it any wonder that Cortot, in the end, graduated ahead of everyone? And this, in spite of the fact that he was not endowed with the talent of the least of us. But a worker he was, and that won the day for him. How he strutted! One of the professors who understood his character thoroughly was old "Saint-Saens of the caustic tongue." It was a part of his duties to go through the solfege and harmony classes to see how the students got along. The usual procedure would be to ask the student what instrument he was studying, and the answer would generally be, "Master, I play the violin," (or flute, or 'cello, or whatever he was majoring in). When Saint-Saens came to Cortot that day, he asked, "And you, my little one, what do you play?" "Master," came the reply from a slightly inflated ego, "I am a pianist!" Came in a dulcet lisp from the Master, "Oh, do not let us exaggerate, my little one!"

It is certain that Cortot achieved fame as a conductor and pianist, though not as composer, which had always been one of his goals. He did for a while, also achieve some degree of power, but that was during the Nazi occupation.

Another personality of that period that fascinated all who came in contact with him was Reynaldo Hahn. He was a real clown by nature, and despite the fact that he was quite a bit older than any of us, having left the Conservatory two years before my entrance, he liked to continue his acquaintance with the younger students. I

26

Alfred Cortot was Benoist's indefatigable classmate in Paris. By coincidence, Paul Paradise and Dr. Herbert R. Axelrod were members of the Cortot String Trio in the mid-1940's.

well remember a rather stuffy party given by one of the professors (I think it was Louis Diemer, one of the greatest pianists of that time). Of course, tea was served along with cookies. The ladies present kept their knees close together, (though their skirts reached the floor) and their eyes cast down when a man addressed them. We had heard that Hahn, whose rather ribald mind couldn't bear such goings-on, had been invited. We knew that he would scarcely make an appearance, for he loathed such parties. Suddenly a commotion was heard in the front vestibule, and into the room burst a toreador, clad in full Spanish regalia! In his hand, he had the tea tray, which he used as a tambourine, shaking it in the air with a couple of spoons rattling against it, or knocking it against his heels, in the maddest fandango ever seen! Imagine what pandemonium broke loose, especially when he went to the piano and started a polka, and we boys began asking the tightly-corseted females to dance. They were too flabbergasted to refuse. The professor's wife thereupon thought it best to swoon and was carried out, which gave us complete liberty. It was one grand party!

Of the many celebrities I failed to appreciate in my childhood days, several stand out in my memory. There was of course, our Director-General, the venerable Ambroise Thomas. We knew he had composed the operas *Mignon* and *Hamlet,* and the fact that a man had composed an opera, already entitled him to a certain amount of respect in our childish brains. So we respected him. But he was so old and decrepit that this respect was, in reality, mere lip service. To us he was just a rather nice old gentleman, none too clean nor well-groomed, who once in a while would come to the classes to see how things went. He did not say much, and what he did sounded more like senile doddering. So we dismissed the great Thomas with "Un grand compositeur, et c'est tout" (A great composer, and that's all)!

The real romantic figure, to us, was Jules Massenet. He was verging on old age, for was he not thirty-six or thirty-seven? He was very handsome, with classic features and graying hair which he wore in a long mop, "a la Liszt." His innumerable love affairs, culminating in his "liaison" with the reigning queen of song and beauty, Sybil Sanderson (la belle Americaine), had made him the hero "par excellence" of the Conservatoire, to both the male and female students. He also taught harmony and counterpoint for the

Georges Bizet, the Jewish genius who was forced to do such chores as writing the piano part for Saint-Saens' Introduction and Rondo Capriccioso, died when his opera, *Carmen*, failed in Paris.

usual stipend the great French Republic granted its civil servants, aside from a pretty purple or red ribbon you could wear in your lapel!

The veneration of everyone went to the kindly and benevolent old gentleman, whom all affectionately called "Papa Franck." Yes, it was Cesar Franck who was considered by most students the real genius of French music. We would follow him for blocks through the streets as he trudged along, his green umbrella tucked under his arm; a short, squat figure with hands folded together behind his back, and his little grey head, ornamented by white side whiskers, tilted forward, lost in reverie, like a gentle bird. He was of Belgian extraction, and this was one of the reasons the chauvinistic French government had been slow to recognize his great genius. So to eke out a living, he was compelled to play the organ at the Church of St. Sulpice and give private lessons in piano and organ at ten francs each!

One morning, on arriving at the Conservatoire, we noticed him scanning the bulletin board, and, just to be near him, we did the same. My companions, Camille Decreus, Armand Ferte, and I watched his every move with loving interest. Suddenly we saw him put his hand to his head, reel a little and settle down to the ground like a deflated balloon. Panic-stricken, we ran for an usher who reverently carried the frail little body to a room and lay him on a couch. A doctor, hurriedly summoned, pronounced him dead from a heart attack. To say we were grief-stricken would be an understatement. Musical Paris went forthwith into mourning. When I think back on the struggle for recognition this modest and self-deprecating little man had during his long career, it is a wonder that he had the courage to write the magnificent works he left behind as a real monument to his memory.

It is a parallel to the life of Georges Bizet, who died of a broken heart when his great opera *Carmen* failed with the French public. Imagine such a genius being compelled by poverty to do hack arranging of piano parts for the orchestrations of Camille Saint-Saens! Yes, it was he who wrote the piano part, arranged from the orchestra score, for the celebrated *Introduction et Rondo Capriccioso* by Saint-Saens. The story goes that he received the munificent sum of twenty-five francs for this work. He had, besides his poverty, another great handicap. There was great rivalry between himself

30

Charles Francois Gounod, the devout Catholic who always
wore a skullcap, took every opportunity to remind people of
"the little Jewish upstart, Bizet." He was a powerful anti-
Semite in those years when his opera *Faust* was a success
and Bizet's *Carmen* was a failure. Of course history changed
their roles and today *Carmen* is the most popular opera in
the repertoire.

and Charles Gounod, who had just had an enormous success with
his *Faust*. Gounod was a devout Catholic, and in his case "more
royalist than the king." He was known to be bigoted in the extreme. His influence in musical circles was limitless. On the other
hand, Bizet was of Jewish origin, and according to all reports of the
period, Gounod was none too happily disposed toward what he
called "the little Jewish upstart." One need go no further in guessing as to the why's and wherefore's of Bizet's end.

Chapter
III

And so time went by in a happy-go-lucky manner, while none of us realized we were dancing on a volcano until catastrophe was upon us. Of course, we had all heard some rumblings of the forthcoming storm, but what do young fellows of from fourteen to eighteen care about rumblings? Neither do they believe in storms. Maybe a few showers to cool off the atmosphere, and then clear and comfortable. We rather looked with good-natured humor upon Ravachol and his gang of anarchists, until they began throwing bombs in cafes and killing inoffensive passers-by. Then the students of the Sorbonne and the Conservatoire started marches on the Prefecture of Police to urge them to do something about it.

But nothing was done, and things went from bad to worse until the culminating crime: the assassination of the poor, hapless President Sadi Carnot. Horrible riots began to take place all over Paris. Enmities sprang up among students who took sides. The Stock Exchange, or Bourse, was forced to close. Due bills were cancelled by the suicides of those who owed others, and inside of two weeks my father, whose importing business of fine art objects was his pride and joy, was ruined completely. His fortune went with it, and when the dust cleared, all that was left was some nice jewelry and some fine furniture. This, once liquidated, left just enough to leave France in a modest but decent fashion. Both father and mother could not, in an inferior position, face the world they had lived in so long, so they decided to go to the "promised land" of America.

No one can realize what it meant to my parents to take this drastic step. For a French family to uproot itself from its cherished surroundings, its friends and acquaintances, and its daily routine, must have been a heartbreaking decision to make, and must have been a matter of heroic courage and fortitude for my parents to carry through. At the time I did not realize all this. All I could think of was the great adventure. Imagine, going to America! A great, big steamer! The ocean! Settling in the fabulous city of New York! And if you didn't like it there, why you could run over to San Francisco or Chicago! I had heard all those magic names in school, and the question of distance did not exist for me. In fact, I didn't know anything about distances. I spent most of the intervening days to sailing time, bragging to my friends about the "Great Adventure," and watching their envious expressions.

At last came the great day when we embarked at Boulogne-sur-Mer (to distinguish it from Boulogne-sous-Bois, a suburb of Paris) on the steamer *Amsterdam*, and we were off! Whether it was an omen or not, we sailed on the Fourth of July, which, though we didn't know it at the time, is the American national holiday, and arrived at New York on the 14th, the French National Holiday. I could not help thinking of that, when in December, 1912, I proudly became an American citizen.

Our arrival in America was a disappointment; for instead of landing in New York City proper, as we thought we would at the time, we debarked in Hoboken, New Jersey, of all places! And though it was midsummer of the year of Our Lord, 1894, it was a drizzly and chilly morning. Fortunately we had traveled first-class, for had we not done so, we would have been sent to a place called Ellis Island, there to remain until the powers-that-be judged us fit to associate with the free and independent citizens of the United States of America. As it was, we were asked innumerable questions, all through a rather efficient interpreter, who seemed quite impressed by our credentials (which at first we thought would not be needed and which fortunately had been carefully packed with our luggage anyway). These had to be unpacked after a diligent search, and after exhibiting them, we found to our intense relief that the impression they made on the interpreter was contagious; so that the severe official who was probing us for a reason for our coming to this country, turned suddenly mild and lamb-like.

I was having a marvelous time observing the queer way the Americans had of dressing, never dreaming of the incongruity of my own attire! As I look back upon it, I must have been quite a sight. With the idea in mind that we were going to an Anglo-Saxon country, my parents had thought it wise to outfit me in the appropriate style. Consequently, I was taken to a shop bearing the suggestive name of *Old England* (written in English so as to impress the French customers). There I was given the clothes which, in Paris, passed as authentically English or American. I will pass over the suit, which was loud enough in pattern to be seen miles away, and very tight indeed. But the overcoat! Oh, that overcoat! Even with all the effrontery that was mine, I must confess I felt self-conscious while wearing it. But it was American, and that was enough for me to undergo any sort of torture. Its color was a violent yellow traversed by pale pink plaid. There were no lapels. Only a flat turned-down collar which looked as though it needed a necktie to fill in a gap. Under this collar, began a cape of the same material which fell way below my hands. All this was surmounted either by a double visored cap a la Sherlock Holmes, (for the steamer), or by a bowler or derby hat (for the land), which looked on my mop of very long hair as if the slightest breeze would blow it off. Thus attired, I decided that the "aborigines" I looked upon for the first time looked funny!

At long last the formalities were over, and we were allowed to go about our business in peace. "Ah," thought I, "at last we shall see the fabled New York.!" But no. We were placed on another boat, and went. . . to Brooklyn, where, it seemed, we had some friends who would guide our further steps. I must confess, with apologies to its denizens, that Brooklyn was not edifying to my hungry eyes. But that was of no importance, it appeared. After a few days of rest and looking around for a place to live, and having as yet no furniture to place in a permanent home, it was decided to "board." It is useless to try to describe a New York boarding house of the gay nineties, for it has been done many times by better pens than mine. Suffice it to say that we were not too unhappy in our new surroundings.

My dear father, after many vicissitudes and with indomitable courage, found a remunerative position, and after a while it was judged the time to see what to do with the family offspring. And so, with fear and trepidation, we arrived at the day when we took ourselves to the great House of Steinway and Sons to present the

William Steinway of the piano firm was Benoist's first real friend in America.

credentials I had obtained from the Paris Conservatoire. The gentleman to whom I was to present these credentials was William Steinway, the president of the firm in 1895. He was undoubtedly one of Nature's noblemen. He was benevolent, kindly, tolerant and generous to a fault. He received us graciously, read over the several documents submitted to him, and then and there asked me to play something. In spite of my fear and nervousness, I must have acquitted myself not too badly of my task, for he smiled and said, "Fine talent! But oh Youth! What impulsiveness! And at the same time, what fire! Nevertheless young man, we'll soon have all that balanced together and put in good order." Whereupon he suggested a course to follow: I was to continue my studies with Ferdinand von Inten or Raphael Joseffy or both, as I pleased; prepare a suitable repertoire and come back to see him in a few months. All this seemed reasonable and right, but, we questioned, what about the financial remuneration to which these great stars of the teaching world were entitled? "That," he replied, smiling sweetly all the while, "is something you are not to worry your young head about, nor mention to anyone, for I have some special arrangements with these gentlemen, which will enable you to study with them without your parents having to spend anything. But," he continued, "if you divulge to anyone what is taking place, the benefits you are to enjoy in this manner will cease immediately. In addition to this I will send you a grand piano on loan, and some day when you are able to, you may wish to own one of our glorious instruments." It was the first time he spoke with anything like pride, and well he had a right to that feeling! I left his presence feeling like a male Cinderella!

The following week I began my studies with Ferdinand von Inten, one of the finest gentlemen I have ever known, and a great teacher. I also went to Joseffy for some special advice, and found him to be not only a superlative artist, but patient and gentle in his teaching. Whenever a special difficulty would turn up, he would say, "How well I remember how I slaved to master that passage!" Months went by in this manner, and again I went to play for Mr. Steinway, who delightedly turned me over to Mr. Tretbar, the good-will ambassador and liaison officer between the Steinways and any artist they were interested in. Mr. Tretbar told me the story of the first arrival in this country of Ignaz Jan Paderewski.

Ferdinand von Inten, the first American teacher of Andre Benoist.

An early publicity photograph showing the young Benoist in a typical romantic pose of the period. Circa 1898.

He had come to the main office to meet the heads of the firm, and, as was customary, was taken across the street to Luchow's for lunch (that was the time when Steinway Hall was still on Fourteenth Street). At the door of this celebrated restaurant, stood a resplendent gentleman covered with gold braid. He was huge and most imposing. Upon entering, Mr. Tretbar jokingly said to him, "Hans, this is our new piano artist who has just arrived from abroad. What do you think of him?" Hans, beholding the tall spare figure clad in a Prince Albert coat, flowing black Windsor necktie, and silk top hat atop burnished golden locks (truly the romantic type), uttered this Delphic prophesy: "Er wird schon Erfolg haben," ("He's bound to be a success")! "And," added Tretbar, "that was before he had ever heard him play one note! Not that it would have made any difference," he added under his breath.

One evening I was invited to a party where very distinguished company was to be present. I had made up my mind that nothing on earth would induce me to play for this distinguished group, which I naturally expected to include some great musicians. (By that time modesty had become my middle name.) Upon arrival, I found a very mixed gathering. I was introduced, in turn, to a fussy, short, bald old gentleman; a tall Beethoven-like Viking; and an academic bespectacled person sporting hair *a la Liszt.* Respectively, their names were Edouard Remenyi, Otto Lohse, and Anton Seidl. These names made no more impression on my youthful mind than did Liszt, Wieniawski, or Saint-Saens. So I began to wonder who the "distinguished company" was to be. So nonthreatening was this group that I concluded that I had been deceived, and I decided that maybe I could play a few pieces without too much danger of criticism.

After my performance, I heard the fussy gentleman say to a lady in a tone of quiet authority, "Mais il joue tres bien ce jeune homme, fort bien." ("He plays well, this young man; especially well.") And no matter who said it, it was pure honey to my ears! So I was beginning to like the old gentleman, when I observed him taking a violin out of its case and walking over to me.

"Would you mind," he asked, "playing a Beethoven sonata with me?"

I was so taken aback that I hardly knew what to answer, but I finally demurred, saying that I did not know those sonatas, and

Edouard Remenyi, the Hungarian violinist whose first accompanist was Johannes Brahms, and who later was accompanied by Benoist. Remenyi was in his eighties when he
met Benoist. Benoist's private diaries indicate that Remenyi
was a terrible violinist, unable to play in tune or in time. He
was just too old. Eventually Remenyi couldn't make it on the
concert stage so he tried vaudeville where he died of a heart-
attack.

would rather not attempt to read them before company. "Oh," said he, "Quand on joue comme vous on s'en tire toujours!" ("When one plays as you do, one always complies!") So we tried the Fifth! That performance sealed my fate, for it was with the keenest pleasure that I went through my first experience in ensemble-playing, (though, while Remenyi's tone was one of utmost beauty, his rhythym was such as to upset even an experienced ensemble player, and, much more, a neophyte like myself).

However, I pulled through somehow, and was rewarded with the most complimentary responses. Remenyi embraced me; Lohse clicked his heels, bowed stiffly and shook hands; and Seidl grunted approvingly (at least I think so!). Toward the end of the evening, having been informed of these men's fame, I became quite overwhelmed, and very glad I had not learned of this earlier, or nervousness and self-consciousness would have hampered me dreadfully.

From that evening, a great friendship began between Mr. Remenyi and myself. I had received a note, not long after that evening, stating that he wished to engage me to play at his home, where he was giving a large party at which he was going to perform a first audition of a new Hungarian national hymn he had composed. The evening was a great success, and Mr. Remenyi proved to be not only a most genial and witty host, but the most kindly and patient artist it has been my lot to play with. His fund of anecdotes and humorous stories was inexhaustible, and the reminiscences of his connection with Brahms, when the latter was his accompanist, were most interesting. I had the honor of playing for Mr. Remenyi many times, until he drifted into vaudeville and our connection ended.

It was during these early years in America that I was made to realize the true feeling of hospitality that existed in this country. No one cared who you were nor why or where you came from. So long as you behaved yourself, you were welcome. Your ancestry was of no consequence. But your behavior was! My first true and lasting friendship was formed when some mutual friends insisted that I meet a young musician of great promise. Strange to say, I was told that he played the cornet. My curiosity was aroused, for I had never thought of the cornet as a "musical instrument." I knew, of course, that it was played in military bands, but I was told that this

Ignaz Jan Paderewski concertizing at St. James's Hall, London, circa 1892.

young man did not play in bands, though he did play in the Metropolitan Opera House Orchestra sometimes. But he played mostly as soloist, being the most brilliant pupil of the great cornet virtuoso, Jules Levy. Finally came the day we met, and from the first moment, we became fast friends. After playing with him I realized at once his reputation was justified. Not for him those brazen sounds that had so often hurt my ears in my Conservatoire days. His were velvety notes that charmed and took on the color and character of any composition he played. The young man's name was Edwin Franko Goldman; today he is the worthy suc-

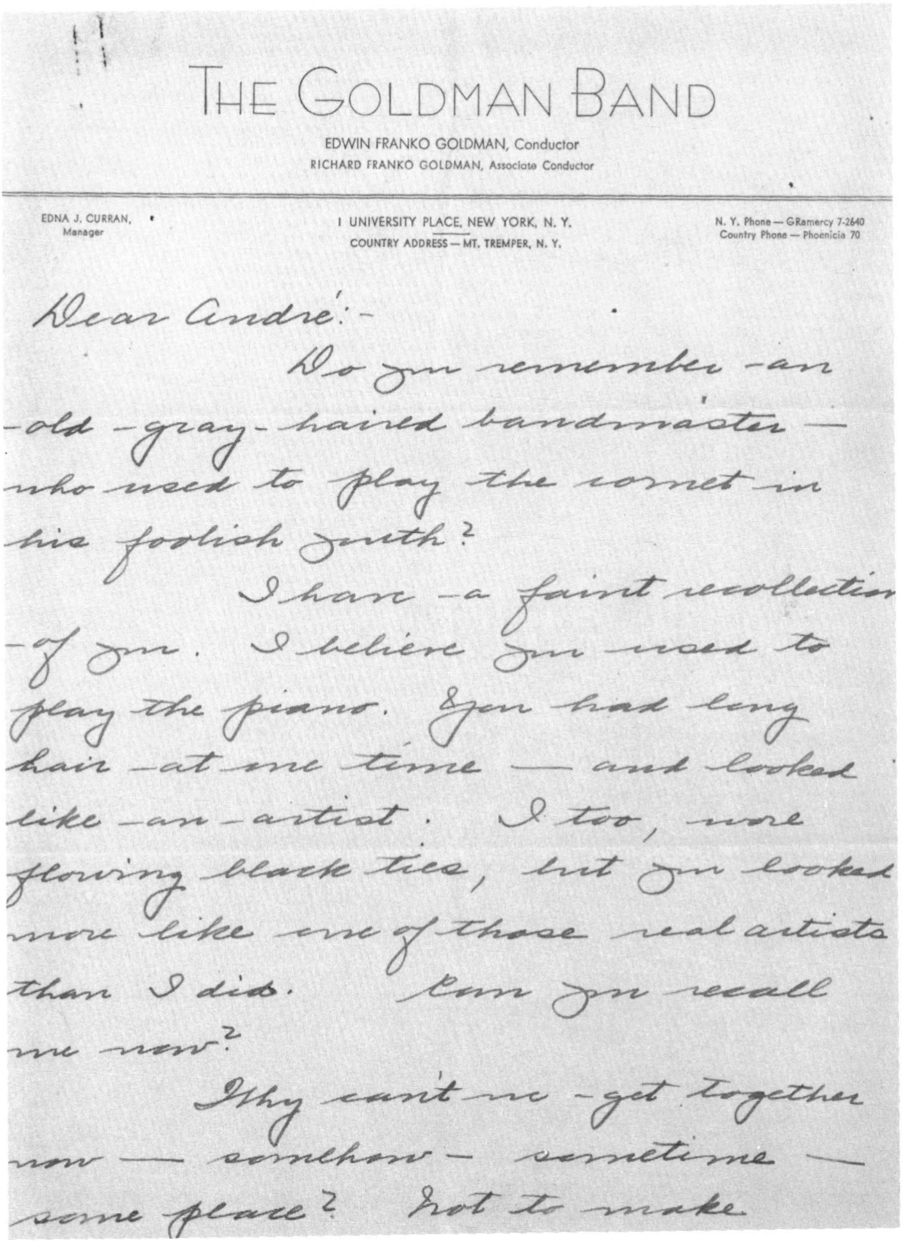

THE GOLDMAN BAND

EDWIN FRANKO GOLDMAN, Conductor
RICHARD FRANKO GOLDMAN, Associate Conductor

EDNA J. CURRAN, Manager

1 UNIVERSITY PLACE, NEW YORK, N. Y.
COUNTRY ADDRESS — MT. TREMPER, N. Y.

N. Y. Phone — GRamercy 7-2640
Country Phone — Phoenicia 70

Dear André:—

Do you remember —an —old —gray-haired bandmaster — who used to play the cornet in his foolish youth?

I have —a faint recollection —of you. I believe you used to play the piano. You had long hair —at one time — and looked like —an —artist. I too, wore flowing black ties, but you looked more like one of those real artists than I did. Can you recall me now?

Why can't we —get together now — somehow — sometime — some place? Not to make

A letter from Edwin Franko Goldman to Benoist at a time when Benoist needed a friend most.

43

make music. Heaven forbid.

Can't you arrange to come to Mt. Tremper with Alice for a few days or a week? Just think of the vast number of people we would talk about _____ and how we would settle all the affairs of the world.

Love to you and Alice.

Your old "forester"

Damn

Sept. 13/43.

John Philip Sousa's autographed picture.

Andre Benoist in the 1890's. Note his moustache. He shaved
it off that year and never grew one again.

The 1890's saw Benoist with cellist Walter Henry Rothwell and two unidentified musicians as they entertained on the porch of a large summer resort hotel in New Jersey.

cessor of the great John Philip Sousa, in whose footsteps he walked towards national popularity.

Eddie, as we affectionately called him, became my mentor and pilot, steering me among his friends with a kind of proprietory pride. And in musical circles he knew, music seemed a passport of unlimited potency. That friendship is this year fifty years old! Goldman's career needs no comments, for who today doesn't know of the Goldman Band?

Sometime later, an opportunity arose for me to go to the Pacific Coast where I had been offered a tour. I played several solo recitals during that period, but I never again had the keen sense of pleasure I had derived from playing either with an instrument or with the voice. I hungered so much for an opportunity to resume this line of work that I decided to return East to see what could be done. . .

This was Jacques Thibaud's favorite photograph of himself. He used it in all his promotional literature and gave it to his best friends.
This inscription, dated 1904, attests to the closeness of his "friend
and collaborator" Andre Benoist.

Chapter IV

Upon my return to New York, I had the pleasure of becoming acquainted with the greatest musical manager I have known in America. He was Henry Wolfsohn and to him I am indebted for the real beginning of my professional career as an accompanist. Wolfsohn was a type which has, alas, died out in our country. He was a genuine impresario. He had two inherent qualities which made him ideal for his profession. He adored music in any form, and he had a passionate belief in any artist he selected for promotion.

In the meantime, one had to keep the pot boiling, and when legitimate engagements were few and far between, I took any job that might prove remunerative (a practice that could have proved my undoing had it become known.) One of these jobs took me to the Café Martin, one of the finest and most brilliant restaurants of that period. It was patronized, not alone by the wealthiest class, but by the most famous artists.

During my engagement there, Wolfsohn telephoned one day, and told me that he had been in Paris and had engaged the great French violinist, Jacques Thibaud to come to the United States for a coast-to-coast tour. How would I like to play for him? That was in 1903 and I could hardly contain myself for joy at the thought. But, I reasoned, should I not better confess what I was doing at the Café Martin? For, suppose Thibaud found out that I was playing for a small weekly stipend; how could I claim the fee a legitimate accompanist was entitled to? It sounds like snobbishness, but this sort of thing comes up in real life and cannot be wiped away by all the philosophy in the world. My heart was set upon obtaining this engagement at any cost. I hated the very thought of more solo tours. The hours traveling alone; the lonely time waiting in a dreary hotel room, again alone, for the hour of doom, concert time, to sound. The fluttering of the stomach from stagefright and nervousness. The going through program after program with a blank mind from sheer fright! No, no! The career of the soloist was not for me! Let some one else have the limelight with all its attendant responsibilities; I would play "second fiddle" for the rest of my life, but I would try to be the finest "second fiddle" that could be found!

All these thoughts were whirling through my mind, and on the impulse of the moment I decided to tell all to my friend Wolfsohn, including my present occupation. He looked at me for a long time without speaking. Then he arose from his chair, came over to me, shook my hand and said, "Young man, you have been blessed with wisdom beyond your years; yours is a wiser decision than you realize at present. Fine accompanists are rare because of the fact that people do not realize that to be a really fine one, it is necessary, first of all, to be a fine pianist with a perfect technique and sound musical training. Most of the people who wish to be accompanists, feel that the slightest accomplishment on the piano is good enough to play accompaniments. When in reality, the repertoire is one of the most difficult and largest that can be found. For it embraces not alone the music for one instrument, but the whole realm of ensemble playing, be it voice, violin, 'cello or combinations of several instruments." Having made this rather sentimental speech, Wolfsohn reverted to the businessman and said, "All this is very well, but no one must know what you are doing at present. So much is certain. Consequently I shall call Jean-Baptiste Martin and tell him he must put a screen in front of the orchestra gallery, so you won't be seen. For the Thibauds are bound to land in a French café sometime, and it would not do if they saw you. But I don't want you to give up any position from which you gain an assured income, a thing you cannot afford to neglect. By the way, go and buy a copy of the sonata by Cesar Franck, which is the piece which I am sure Thibaud will judge you by, and the principal number on the program for his first recital at Carnegie Hall. Practice and have it ready." With deep gratitude in my heart I took my departure, thanking my Maker for the existence of men like William Steinway and Henry Wolfsohn.

To say I practiced would be putting it mildly, and my absorption in my work made me forget the passage of time. I did not in fact realize that Mr. and Mrs. Thibaud were due in America almost any time. One evening, while hearing me finger a bit of the Franck sonata on the piano, the first violinist in the little orchestra suggested that we play one movement then and there to see what sort of reaction the café public would show towards such serious music. At first I demurred, but upon his insistence I agreed. No sooner was the last note ended, when we beheld Mr. Martin in person, quite out of breath, and we thought, "Now we're in for it." We were sure he was furious and hated it. But what he said was, "There's a customer down there who wants to meet the piano player, so come on, you!" I asked who the "customer" was. He said: "It's a fellow named Jacques Thibaud, I think." Whereupon I turned white and tried to explain that I was not feeling too well, and begged to be excused for the night; some other time perhaps. Martin, seeing my pallor, said that indeed I wasn't looking any too well and that he would explain it to the "customer." He had no sooner departed than I grabbed my coat and hat and fled the premises! This episode cost me my job. For had I not deserted under fire? All the explaining I tried to do the next day was to no avail. Orchestra musicians could not understand what it was all about, so there was nothing to do but think of a rosy future, even if the present were black!

My optimistic feeling was justified, for shortly thereafter I was called by Mr. Wolfson, who asked me to meet him at Mr. Thibaud's apartment in the old Belvedere Hotel. It is difficult to explain what a thrill it was for a young man of 23 to meet so distinguished an artist as Thibaud. He was fairly tall and graceful in his bearing. He wore his hair almost shoulder length, as was the mode for any artist worthy of the name, and a rather flowing moustache. He received me with true French courtesy, more in the manner of greeting a colleague than a flowering accompanist. His manner put me at ease immediately and quieted the budding nervousness I felt. After a few moments of conversation, in which he asked a few diplomatically put questions as to my background, we found we had many acquaintances in common; a fact that created

CARNEGIE HALL

Friday Afternoon, **Nov. 20**

at three o'clock

JACQUES
THIBAUD
VIOLIN RECITAL

ANDRÉ BENOIST AT THE PIANO

PROGRAMME

1 Sonate . . . . *Cesar Franck*

        Allegretto ben Moderato—Allegro Recitative—Fantasia—Allegretto
MESSRS. THIBAUD AND BENOIST

2 *a)* Prelude
  b) Fugue } First Sonate, G Minor . . . . *Bach*
THIBAUD

3 Piano Solo — Polonaise E Major . . . . *Liszt*
ANDRÉ BENOIST

4 *a)* Rondo Cappriccioso . . . . *Saint-Saens*
  b) Serenite . . . . *Vieuxtemps*
  c) Scherzando . . . . *Marsick*
  d) Melodrame . . . . *Guiraud*
  e) Polonaise . . . . *Wieniawski*
THIBAUD

Management, HENRY WOLFSOHN

Reserved Seats, **75**cts. to **$2.00**—at Box Office of CARNEGIE HALL,
and DITSON'S, 867 Broadway

Jacques Thibaud's debut recital program, 1903.

an immediate bond. Then we began to play. From the first moment, I felt there would be no difficulty in assimilating myself to so musical an artist. His tone was not large. He never forced an issue. There were no temperamental exaggerations. It was the loveliest quality imaginable — velvety, warm and pure.

We played a great many engagements together, but two stand out in my mind. The first was the debut appearance at Carnegie Hall, on which occasion, both Wolfsohn and Thibaud insisted I play a group of soli, against my own wishes. (I think I did not do too badly with the "big" number on the program, the sonata by Cesar Franck. Of course Thibaud was superb in it.) But when my solo group came, I felt more like committing suicide than marching all alone onto that huge bare stage and facing the cavernous space filled with curious and inimical human beings! What horrible fate awaited me there? However, I went on like a sleepwalker and must have gone through the pieces somehow. My last number was the rather exacting *Polonaise* by Liszt towards the end of which I felt, in a frenzy of panic, that my memory was going to play me false; but through rigid concentration I somehow reached the end. To my intense surprise a good deal of applause rewarded my efforts. I walked off the stage, where my friends told me it had been fine. But I knew better, and resolved then and there that I would not go through such torture again for anything in the world! The rest of the program was uneventful and Thibaud's success was assured. Besides, while his unmistakable and brilliant gifts brought him swift recognition, he was such a romantic figure that the fair sex overwhelmed him with attention, which was most inconvenient, as his charming wife Marguerite (nick-named Didi) traveled everywhere with him, and they had left two baby sons, Roger and Philippe, in Paris.

The day after this memorable concert we were all curious to see the reaction of the press, and it was most favorable for Thibaud. As for me, I shall quote only one of the gems of reviling that was done by a William J. Henderson in the *New York Sun*: "*It was an affront to the musical public of our city to foist such a nonentity upon it. He played with a hard, dry, hammering touch, like a nice new pianola, and with an abysmal ignorance of line, phrasing or pedaling. This young man had better cease his endeavors for he is utterly devoid of anything approaching talent.*" As I think back, Mr. Henderson was

Mrs. Jacques Thibaud, Didi, inscribed this photograph to Mrs. Benoist at the time their two husbands were working together. February, 1904.

Translation of the Thibaud letter: "*Didi is coming, she leaves on the "DeGrasse" January 14th. She will be here nine days later. I don't know where she will stay. Quickly, a telephone call. Thousands of affections. Jacques Thibaud.*" Not only did Didi safely arrive and stay at the Benoists' home in Monmouth Beach, but they left several trunks in the attic—and they are still there, filled with lovely mementos.

right, except for his last phrase, which I set out to belie. I must have been in some small way successful in this too, for in later years his opinion changed completely, and a personal friendship sprang up between us that lasted until his lamented death. He was at heart one of the fairest critics it has been my lot to encounter, and he often retracted in print, a too hastily expressed opinion. In other words, all this justified the old saying that, "Talent is a disease for which the only cure is work and more work."

The next Thibaud concert that stands out in my mind is one we played in Buffalo, New York. It was midwinter, and everything was covered with snow and ice. Our train was late in arriving, so that we barely had time to snatch a bite to eat and dress. (I had just had a new dress suit made in New York and this was the first occasion on which I could wear it). When we were ready, a large four-wheeled landau stood at the door, ready to drive us to the Convention Hall. The concert was scheduled for eight-fifteen, but it was eight twenty-five when we finally reached the stage door, as the amount of snow and ice in the streets precluded anything but a snail's pace. Arriving at the stage door, we found it impossible to alight from the carriage, owing to the accumulation of snow. So we had to wait until some of the stagehands scurried about for a board to lay over the snow, reaching from the carriage to the door. This was at last found and I was the first to alight. Madame Thibaud followed, helped on each side by one of us to steady her on the precariously balanced and slippery plank. But impulsive Thibaud, not waiting for help, and realizing how late we were, took it upon himself to try the perilous descent unaided, and to our dismay we saw him fall sideways, landing on his right arm. Now, everyone knows that the right arm of a violinist is his most vulnerable member and one can imagine our concern when he arose and said he could hardly move it! Once inside, we immediately called for hot water and towels with which to bathe the injured arm, and after about fifteen minutes of this treatment, Thibaud declared himself ready to go on. Then began a search for a music stand, as in those days ensemble music, like the Sonata, was played with both artists using the printed notes. Another precious five minutes! By the time the stand was found, it was nine-fifteen and with the audience already quite justifiably restless, at long last we began. The Sonata over, it was my turn to go on alone. Just as I was about to pass through the

Jacques Thibaud with his two sons Phillippe (left) and Roger. Thibaud developed a close friendship with Benno Rabinoff because he looked so much like his son Roger who was killed in the war.

door leading to the stage, feeling finally at ease in my new dress suit, I stretched my arms full length, bringing them forward and backward a few times. At the second try I suddenly heard a frightful tearing sound and realized in a panic that the entire back seam had opened up. I couldn't go forward. So I had to go back to the green room to exhibit the catastrophe! What to do? Finally Madame Thibaud suggested that for my solo group I borrow her husband's suit, and while I was playing she would see what could be done to repair the damage, if only temporarily. The suggestion was accepted. But Madame had not considered that her husband was a good five inches taller than I, and built in proportion! So when I slipped on the coat I had to roll up the sleeves, and the tails trailed on the ground! But there was nothing for it, and in the laughter that followed, I forgot all about getting nervous and went through my numbers with greater ease than ever before. Now came the crucial time when the repaired dress suit made its appearance. The best that could be done was to gather the seam with safety pins, which made it tighter than ever, and to prevent the audience from noticing its back, I walked on the stage crabwise, sidling on, facing the audience, which must have thought I went suddenly crazy. We had many a laugh over this incident, which came near being tragic.

Shortly after that, Mr. Wolfsohn organized a concert which he expected would create a sensation. He had at that time under his management, besides Jacques Thibaud, the conductor Felix Weingartner, and the 'cellist Pablo Casals. Having heard that Weingartner, besides being a great conductor, was also a fine pianist, Mr. Wolfsohn conceived the idea of presenting these three artists at Carnegie Hall in a concert of standard trios. Consequently, rehearsals were begun and everything progressed swimmingly, until two days before the concert. A difference regarding financial arrangements sprang up between the great Spanish 'cellist and his manager, with the consequence that the artist refused point blank to appear. The impresario, undismayed and setting out to remedy the situation, found he could not replace Casals, but could give a new artist an opportunity of appearing at his best and in distinguished company. To Paul Kefer, the French 'cellist, went this splendid chance to display talents before an elite audience. As accompanist for Thibaud, I had volunteered to turn the pages for

58

A 1904 photograph of Pablo Casals, the cellist, given to Benoist when they played together in 1904.

A mon cher ami
André Benoist
Souvenir de

PABLO CASALS

Pablo Casals

André Benoist

Andre Benoist, circa 1904.

Weingartner. So being in the artist room just before the concert, what was my surprise to see the great conductor come to me and pale, perspiring, and trembling as with the flu, saying, "I am so glad you will play those piano parts for me, for I should have died of fright had I had to do so myself. You know I am not a pianist at all and only play the piano enough to read through my scores!" I thereupon assured him that, in spite of my wish to be courteous, and to try to please him in any possible way, I had never contemplated such an eventuality, and even had I the wish to do so, no audience nor manager would, for one moment, tolerate such a substitution. This he could not understand. "But," said he, "Thibaud assures me that you play the piano uncommonly well, and what possible difference can it make to anybody whether I play or not so long as the playing is good?" I agreed with him, but again called his attention to the fact that I was neither audience nor manager and for that reason could do nothing for him in this matter. He then begged me to fetch Mr. Wolfsohn, which I did. On my way back to the stage with him, I informed Mr. Wolfsohn in soft but firm language that should he so much as incline towards consent to the inequitable arrangement, it would be his last managerial act on this earth, (I being the cause of this finality)! The upshot was that Weingartner, panic-stricken, pale and perspiring, played. . . poorly.

My work with Thibaud continued until his return to France, but our friendship ripened and developed over the years. He served with distinction in the first World War, and in the second he was compelled by fate to make a greater sacrifice than his own life: the loss of his older son Roger, who was killed in the first advance of the French Army. His other son, Philippe, was a prisoner of the Germans in a concentration camp for nearly two years. Who would have believed that these boys, whom I knew as babies, would have to go through such tragic times?

My next assignment was of a different nature. So far, I had not played for a singer, and I was elated when I was told to report to the celebrated Emma Eames. Owing to the glamour of her name, I was prepared for extraordinary artistry. What was my surprise but to discover that when she made a mistake of any kind, she was totally unaware of it until I called her attention to it! Musically, she knew nothing. The Lord had endowed her with a fine voice, and the ubiquitous "coach" did the rest. He it was who breathed life, passion, understanding of the musical phrase, atmosphere, etc., into her. Without his suggestions (which were all that were allowed him, she being a prima donna) she would have been a handsome automaton going through all the motions. Frankly, I was dumbfounded! So this was a world-renowned singer, receiving fees averaging a thousand dollars per performance? For what? A parrot endowed with a beautiful voice could have done as well! Was she an exception? No, she was not, as I learned by experience. She was an average, and the exceptions turned out to be quite the reverse. Such a one was Marcella Sembrich, who was a musician first, and incidentally a supreme singing artist. There were a few others but they were rare indeed. This is especially true of American singers. European singers, particularly in France, will not be taught singing unless they, at the same time, take up the study of some instrument, preferably the piano, so as to be able to accompany themselves should there be need. Besides, they must know solfege and sight reading. They may not have the glorious voices of some of the "two-headed wonder birds," but they know what they are doing at all times without the aid of the musical crutch we call "coach"; and, as for me, they give me a thousand times more pleasure by their experienced initiative than all the mechanical bellowing issuing from the golden throat of some musically ignorant Venus.

Madame Eames, was, to say the least, handsome. I could not find her beautiful, for beauty radiates like sunshine from a warm and human personality. No, she was decidedly handsome, coldly and haughtily. She tried hard to be gracious and what we call "democratic." But one could sense the effort. It was, in spite of this effort, a condescending graciousness. Every word she uttered was carefully weighed and balanced. Of spontaneity, there was none. I heard it said that she had a fiendish temper; but I never witnessed any outburst, and perhaps it had been better for her art had the rumor been true. I have come to the conclusion over long years of

The famed soprano Marcella Sembrich gave this autographed photo to Benoist in March, 1907.

À Mademoiselle Benoit en souvenir de

Marcella Sembrich

New York March 1901

observation, that an artist can only give out in his art what he really is in his innermost soul. He may acquire manners; he may study to become benevolent in appearance; he may give a fair imitation of generosity; but when he gives forth with either his voice or his instruments, he stands revealed, his soul stark naked, and he can disguise nothing. And Madame Eames sang what she was: haughty, cold and unapproachable. A glorious instrument, her voice, and that was all. I played several concerts with her, but without interest and was sorely disappointed.

JACQUES THIBAUD
Violin Recital

ANDRÉ BENOIST AT THE PIANO

Under the Auspices of *The* Musical Club
Unity Hall, Monday Evening, December 21st, 1903

PROGRAMME

1 Sonate . . . . *César Franck*
Allegretto ben Moderato—Allegro Recitative—Fantasia—Allegretto
MESSRS. THIBAUD AND BENOIST

2 *a* Prelude
   b Fugue } First Sonate, G Minor . . *Bach*
THIBAUD

3 Piano Solo — Polonaise E Major . . . *Liszt*
ANDRE BENOIST

4 *a* Rondo Cappriccioso . . . . *Saint-Saens*
   b Serenite . . . . . . *Vieuxtemps*
   c Scherzando . . . . . *Marsick*
   d Melodrame . . . . . *Guiraud*
   e Polonaise . . . . . *Wieniawski*
THIBAUD

Steinway Piano used

64

Chapter
V

Quite a different experience awaited me when I had the pleasure of hearing the great Belgian 'cellist, Jean Gerardy. There was an artist! His tone had the impact of a cannon ball. Withal, it was luminous and pure. His finger dexterity was pure witchery. An amazing fellow! Handsome as a Greek god, and, a rara avis (rare bird), totally unaware of this fact! And what a great lover! The ladies could not leave him alone, and he returned the compliment a thousandfold. To tell the story of his love life would require an entire volume which would, at the same time, be full of repetitions. It was a great joy to accompany such a man; his rhythm was so sure and unfaltering that it was no effort to play with him. He loved life, good food, good wine, and I was about to say "good women," which would have been a misstatement. Shall we just say, women?! However, his generosity and loyalty to a friend were unparalleled, and for this, much should be forgiven him. He proved his loyalty to me in one instance which I would like to recount, for it shows better than anything I can think of, what friendship meant to him.

I must preface this by giving an idea of the financial situation under which we were traveling. Our manager, at that time, was a unique being by the name of R. E. Johnston. He was in appearance not unlike a miniature Wallace Beery at his worst. In addition to this, he was minus three and one-half fingers on each hand, and had one artificial leg that made him limp heavily when he walked. He also wore very obviously artificial teeth that rattled when he

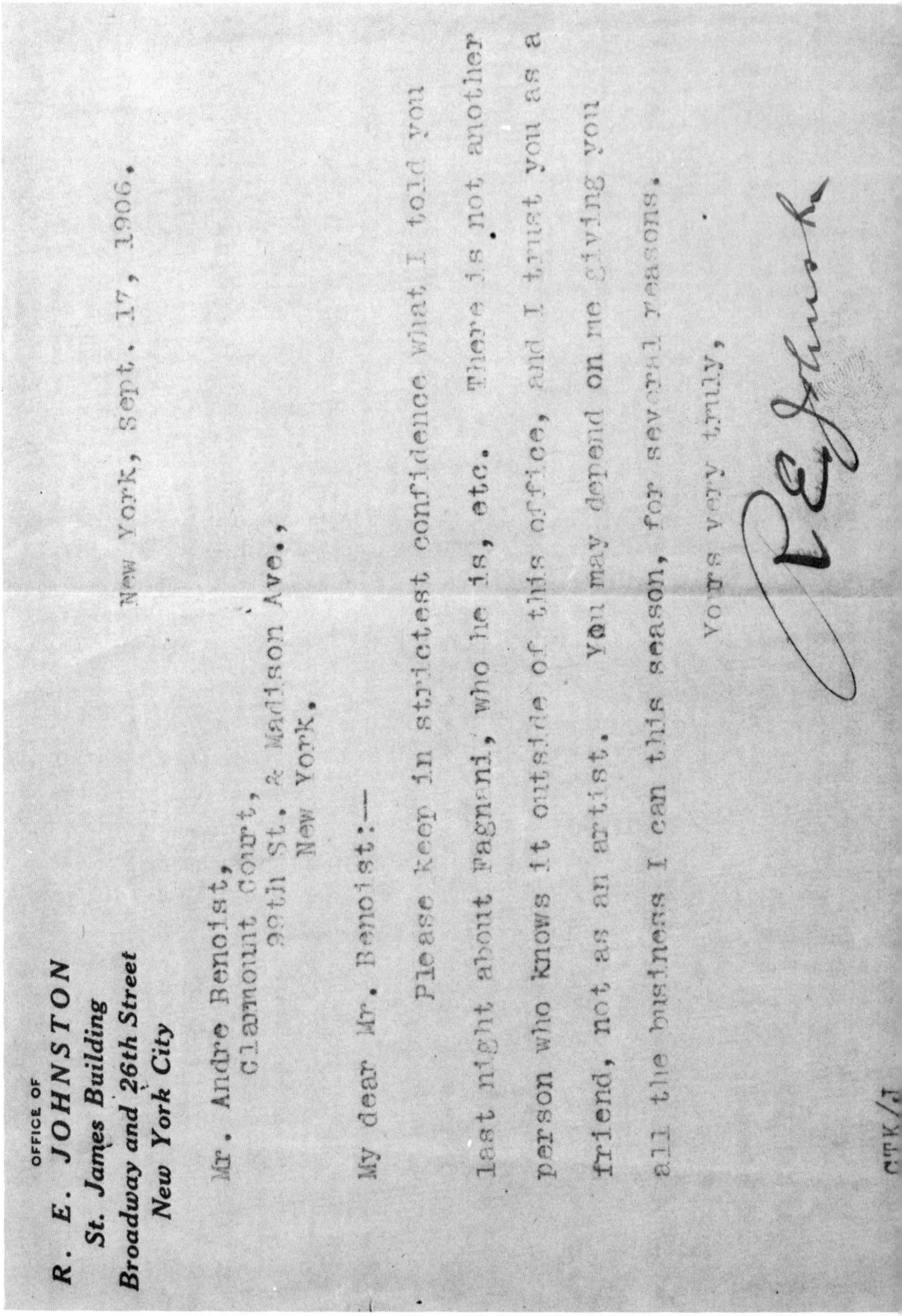

OFFICE OF

R. E. JOHNSTON
St. James Building
Broadway and 26th Street
New York City

New York, Sept. 17, 1906.

Mr. Andre Benoist,
Clermont Court,
99th St. & Madison Ave.,
New York.

My dear Mr. Benoist:—

Please keep in strictest confidence what I told you
last night about Pagnani, who he is, etc. There is not another
person who knows it outside of this office, and I trust you as a
friend, not as an artist. You may depend on me giving you
all the business I can this season, for several reasons.

Yours very truly,

R E Johnston

GTK/J

A mysterious note from R.E. Johnston, Benoist's manager at the time. Dated September 17, 1906.

"To my dear colleague, Benoist. Admiration and affection. Jean Gerardy April 2, 1908." Benoist accompanied Gerardy for quite a long time and they developed a very close friendship.

A mon cher
collègue — Benoist —
Admiration — et
affection ——.

Jean Gerardy
avril (2 — 1908

spoke, and to cap everything, a toupee which had a knack of getting displaced in moments of excitement. From his lips issued a voice of the highest soprano, which in times of stress became even higher. This character had a heart of gold, for he would shed a tear at the slightest knowledge of anyone's misfortune. But in what he was pleased to call "business" he was the most unscrupulous blackguard imaginable. He would have fleeced his own grandmother, if he had been convinced it was "good business."

Under his contract with Gerardy he was pledged to pay the latter a flat fee per engagement. This fee was ample and could take care of even Gerardy's rather extravagant tastes in traveling while leaving him a handsome profit. But Johnston knew that I had been but recently married and was shortly to become a father. He also knew how deeply attached I had become to Gerardy, both as an artist and as a friend. And as he was to pay for the accompanist side of the combination, he set out to explain to me what a great advantage it would be for me to go on this tour at any price. Being very young and inexperienced, I immediately agreed on a ridiculous fee per concert, without taking into account that traveling expenses were high, and moreover there were engagements that Gerardy would play with orchestra accompaniment, and, while I would not be playing at such times, my expenses would continue. All this was beginning to dawn on me after the first few engagements.

One day on a train, Gerardy, seeing me looking rather worried, asked me what was on my mind. Noting my reluctance to answer him he said, "I know; you're in love" (which *would* be the first thing that would come to his mind!). I said, "My dear fellow, I'm married now!" But he overruled that answer by saying, "What has that to do with it? Your wife will always reap the benefit of it!" "No," I said, "that isn't it; you know how beautiful and sweet she is, and that's the only thought in my mind at present!" "AT present, he says" exclaimed Gerardy, "no truer word was ever spoken! Ca passera mon vieux (that will pass, my friend), pay no attention!" Still he was puzzled. He continued, "Well, if that isn't it, then it's a matter of the pocket book!" My face must have shown how near to a bull's eye he had struck for he began to laugh and said, "Then Johnston is at the bottom of the whole thing!" This I could not deny, though I tried to mitigate Johnston's shrewd deal by ascribing the trouble to my own stupidity. But Gerardy would

Andre Benoist's first wife, Barnetta Mueller. Barnetta was an accomplished opera singer. Circa 1901.

have none of that. He insisted that we must, in sheer retaliation, outsmart the profiteer. "But," I said, "how?" And then and there he laid out our plan of campaign, which was as follows: We were on our way to New York for a few days of well-earned rest. From there Gerardy was to start out alone as he had four orchestral engagements on his way to the Pacific Coast, and on those engagements my services were not needed. So it had been arranged by Johnston that I join him at a town called Cheyenne, Wyoming. Those were the original plans. But in the meantime, Gerardy had received a letter from Johnston telling him to continue alone to the Coast where an extensive recital tour had been booked for him; and that there, he could engage a local accompanist at more reasonable rates. As it was Johnston's money which was to pay for this, his penuriousness enraged Gerardy, and this, added to what I had already confessed to him about my treatment, lifted his last scruples. "So," he said, "when I arrive at Cheyenne, I will telegraph that pirate that I refuse to go any further without you being sent on to join me for the Pacific Coast tour. He will then send for you to come and see him, and coax and threaten you with all kinds of boycotts and reprisals if you don't go. On your side, you ask for a fee that will stagger him and make him think you've suddenly gone out of your mind. As he comes up, you come down a little, and you will find that you will meet somewhere in the middle, and that will be about three times the fee you're getting now!" "And," he continued ominously, "if you let me down in this, we're through and I'm not your friend anymore." I was doubtful as to the outcome of all this quibbling, but resolved to follow instructions to the letter.

My days in New York went by slowly and I thought our plans had gone sour. But at the end of two weeks·my telephone rang, and there was Johnston's quivering soprano full of urgency. He wanted me to come to see him immediately. I demurred, saying that I was busy, and asking what was it all about. He said that I was to join Gerardy at once for his tour to the coast. To this I replied that I wasn't interested and could not afford to leave my teaching class for the stipend he usually offered. With this I rang off. In the meantime there must have been a frantic exchange of telegrams between him and Gerardy, who evidently was not budging from his position, for Johnston called me several more times that day.

The last time he telephoned I agreed to come to his apartment the same evening to talk matters over.

Arriving there, I was taken to Johnston's private study where I was introduced to a gentleman he called his "attorney." What an attorney had to do with the matter in hand, I shall never know. Suffice it to say that the seance we had is memorable. The "attorney" began by saying I had double-crossed Johnston. At that time I didn't know the meaning of "double-cross" but it sounded like something villainous. All I could think of replying was "doubtlessly" which I thought was translating the French "J'en doute" (I doubt it)! What I had really translated was "Sans doute" (doubtlessly)! With that they both said, "Ah! so you confess?" "Confess what?" I asked. "That there is a plot," answered the attorney. I told them that I did not know anything about plots, and I would most gladly go on tour with M. Gerardy, but that I could not afford to do so at the fee I was offered; that was all! "Then," said Johnston, "how much do you want"? That was what I had been waiting for, so I mentioned the most absurd fee I could think of while still remaining in the realm of credibility. With that, both men jumped from their chairs and came towards me with fists clenched. I must say they both looked comical for they were middle-aged, bald and fat. I couldn't help laughing when I thought that a good butt in the stomach of one and a good heavy tread on the other's toes, and they would be yelling with pain. But it didn't come to that. When they saw me laugh, they looked at each other rather self-consciously and sat down again. The upshot was that what Gerardy had shrewdly foreseen came to pass. They came up a bit in their offers, I came down a little and after a while we met somewhere in the middle which produced a fee that was completely satisfying, to me at least, for the others said I was an unmitigated scoundrel and a robber. Secretly, I was rather proud of myself!

The tour that followed is one of the happiest memories of my career. Gerardy was one of the finest companions anyone could wish for, though sometimes his vagaries led to trouble, as the following adventure will show. We happened to be in Los Angeles and between concerts, when time was beginning to hang heavy for my friend, who with his restless nature loved excitement, and mostly feminine excitement! What to do?

At that time Los Angeles was not the insane asylum it now is since it has been Hollywoodized. Or as some wag put it, "Six suburbs in quest of a city," to paraphrase the play by Pirandello. No, Los Angeles came near justifying its name! It was dull and provincial, and its best hotel was the Hollenbeck. Ah me! That Hollenbeck, with its high ceilings, high bay windows, drab lace curtains, cavernous rooms with high beds, all decorated in faded greens and yellows! And IT RAINED! Yes! In the "super climate" city of Los Angeles! It had one advantage however: one did not have to travel miles to get to one's destination. It was all cozy and self-contained, but dull.

Consequently I was dispatched by my friend to ferret out the nearest oasis in this desert. From the hotel porter I discovered that there was such an oasis not too far removed to be reached by a comfortable carriage with two horses, which he promised he could provide for us. "But," he added, "it will cost money!" Knowing what Gerardy thought of the latter commodity, I reassured him on that subject and set out to report. The answer was a long and fervent "hurrah," and "When do we start?" I explained to him that the name of the town was San Bernardino or St. Bardoo for short, and that in St. Bardoo the festivities only began after dark, so that I had ordered the carriage for that evening at seven. I reckoned about an hour and one-half for the drive which would give us time for dinner either on the way or upon arrival. But once on the way, my friend would not stop for anything, so anxious was he to arrive at our destination.

At last we found ourselves on the main street of this budding metropolis. It was a typical frontier town such as is often depicted in our modern movies. Our carriage had bogged down in a crowd surrounding a bar room the front of which was non-existent, so that one could see clearly what went on in its well-illuminated interior. We noticed an elderly man dressed in Mexican garb holding a guitar. This man was having quite a pow-wow with a man we took to be the owner of the saloon. He was accompanied by a young girl who could not have been more than seventeen or, at the most, eighteen. She also was dressed in Mexican fashion. Suddenly the pow-wow came to an end, and the elderly man addressed a few words to the young girl whereupon, to our amazement, the latter proceeded to remove her garments one by one, laying them in a neat pile in a corner. On top of the clothes and with the utmost seriousness and absorption she laid her vast sombrero and stood up revealing herself completely naked! Then she began a slow graceful dance, accompanied by the elderly man's guitar. When this was over, the man took up a battered tambourine and passed it through the crowd, collecting what he could in money. Strange to say, there were no cat-calls nor lewd remarks. The young girl, in the meantime, had donned her clothes with the utmost seriousness and stood by, demure as ever. Then everyone went about his business as if nothing strange had happened. That was our first sight of St. Bardoo!

I had noticed however that my friend Jean had been in whispered consultation with our driver, and, as we resumed our way, I asked him where we were bound. "You'll see," he answered. We finally arrived before a rather imposing house from which issued sounds of gaiety. At our ring, the door was opened, and from then on I was not left in doubt as to the sort of place we had come to. I sat down in a quiet corner—probably the only quiet corner in the "reception room." My friend remained for a few minutes in whispered conversation with the flashy blonde, whom all addressed as "Madame," and then disappeared down a corridor, along which I noticed an old-fashioned wall telephone. It surprised me in this type of place, for in those days telephones were not as commonplace as they are today. But I made a mental note of its existence. As no one seemed to bother with me, I sat drinking my beer, and must have dozed off. I woke up with a start and, looking at my watch, saw it was one-thirty in the morning, and the room was deserted. I glanced out of the front window and to my joy, saw our carriage still standing where we had left it, with the driver asleep on the seat. He had been faithful to his promise, the exaction of which had cost me a pledge of double pay for waiting time. And well did my foresight stand me in stead! I tip-toed back to the door through which I had seen my friend disappear and opened it softly. Gerardy was lying on the bed, fully clothed while his girl companion, also fully dressed, was sitting by a light, knitting. It was a picture of real domestic bliss; but to my mind too blissful, and I became suspicious. The girl motioned me not to wake him, but meanwhile I was feeling his pockets and discovered that all he possessed of value had disappeared. His wallet containing his money and papers, his gold watch and a diamond ring, all gone!

After repeated shakings I could not arouse him! I was in a quandary! As I sidled out of the room I spied the telephone on the wall under the stairs, and that gave me my cue, just as the Madame, no doubt awakened by the noise, came into view. She ordered me out of the house and with the most voluble cursing and swearing said that if I did not clear out at once she would have me beaten within an inch of my life. I was standing under that welcome telephone which I unhooked, covering the mouthpiece with one hand, telling the Madame that if she did not immediately have my friend's possessions put back in his pockets and have him carried to our carriage, I would yell police and bloody murder in the telephone, and where would she be then? Secretly, I was bluffing, for how would it look in the headlines next day "Jean Gerardy found in house of ill fame?" And I too! For no matter how innocent I was, how to explain at home? Nevertheless, I stuck to my guns, or rather telephone. The upshot of it was that what I had ordered was done, and with a well-placed kick, the Madame ordered us never to darken her door step again. We did not need the urging!

All the way back to Los Angeles, Jean swore he would never forget how I had saved his life, and I forgave him his foolish exaggeration, as he was just beginning to come out of his stupor, which had been caused solely by the "knockout drops" or, as they are called today, "Mickey Finn" that had been given him in a cocktail, the result of which was only a dull headache for the next couple of days. But the episode had been a salutary lesson, and for a long time thereafter I had no trouble with his restlessness.

Our stay in the "City of Angels" finally came to an end, and it was with a feeling of excitement that I looked forward to our visit to the real metropolis of California which, in those days, was San Francisco. The contrast between the two cities was enormous. Little Los Angeles was still asleep although beginning to feel growing pains. On the other hand, San Francisco was already a full-fledged city; brilliant, enthusiastic, alive. Cosmopolitan above all. There, at the palace of the St. Francis Hotel, one could meet celebrities from all over the world. And the city was not a bit self-conscious about it. There was nothing of the parvenu (upstart) in its attitude. It took homage graciously, as if it were due deservedly.

On our arrival, we learned that the New York Metropolitan

74

Opera Company was playing at the Mission Opera House—a delightful piece of news—for a good many of its members were our friends. Among them was the charming soprano, Marcella Sembrich, who had been so kind to me in my faltering beginnings. Also the beauteous Sybil Sanderson, erstwhile friend of the French composer Massenet. The cast included the French baritone, Gilibert and his friend, the tenor Edmond Clement. This bevy of artists was capped by the tenor of tenors, Enrico Caruso. We renewed acquaintances at each other's hotels with dinner parties and teas, all vowing that they would be present at Gerardy's forthcoming recital the following Sunday afternoon. And they came in force, armed with overflowing enthusiasm which they showed with wise discrimination. For all loved Gerardy. Of course the concert was an overwhelming success.

There was to be one more recital, but this time in the evening. This concert was to take place on a Monday night and owing to the fact that the Opera was to perform that same evening, its members could not be present. So to make up for their absence, our friends arranged a large supper party at the Fiesta Café after their performance Tuesday evening. This we gratefully accepted, as we had arranged to get reservations on a train to Portland, Oregon, for Wednesday at two hours past midnight. But at the last minute the railroad official let us know that the reservations we had called for were unavailable, and that if we wanted to arrive in Portland in time for our concert there, we had better leave San Francisco a day earlier, by the same scheduled train. There being nothing else to be done, we agreed, though bitterly disappointed at what we thought would cause us to miss a delightful party. But our friends of the Metropolitan would have none of postponing the event. They suggested that we send our luggage in advance to the train in Oakland, from which it departed, and stay with the party until one a.m., which would give us an hour to get to Oakland and our train. This was carried out to the letter. The Fiesta Café was situated in the basement of the Flood building at the corner of Powell and Market Streets, and the entrance was down a broad staircase which led to the restaurant proper. As we descended these stairs, the large orchestra intoned "Hail to the Chief" to the tune of which we were ushered to a large table above which a large flowered horseshoe was suspended over the place of honor. This welcome from so

Schumann-Heink · Calvé · Clement · Galli-Curci · Dalmores · Martinelli · Aïda · Hempel · Witherspoon · Whitehill · Bori · Ruffo · De Luca · Journet · Melba

Caruso · Tetrazzini · Homer · Destinn · Gadski · Eames · Sembrich · Gluck · McCormack · Farrar · Scotti

PHOTOS COPY'T MISHKIN DUPONT FOLEY GARO MANUEL BERT FALK VICTOR-GEORG MATZENE

Most of the great singers of the time were friendly with Benoist because of his ability and dedication to being the world's best accompanist. Many of the singers shown here are mentioned elsewhere in this book.

many fellow artists was deeply touching. But thrilling as was the occasion, I had to watch the time. For certainly Gerardy was in no condition to know the time after all the excitement and rather plentiful libations administered to all of us.

Time to leave came at last, and bundling ourselves in our overcoats, (for it was cold), we started for Oakland and just made our train with about three minutes to spare. Needless to say, no sooner aboard than we were in the arms of Morpheus! And sleep we did, until we were rudely awakened by a knock at the door of our drawing room. I sleepily looked at my watch and found to my horror it was only half past seven! Furiously, I called out, "Go away and don't bother us! We want to sleep!" But the growling voice of the conductor came back with "Tickets, please." So there was nothing to do but open the door. I started giving him a piece of my mind about waking people up in the middle of the night but his reply was even more virulent. "Pipe down," said he, "you ought to be glad you're both alive enough to be awakened. Don't you know what's happened?" The expression on my face must have assured him of our ignorance, for he proceeded, "Well, Gents, there ain't no more San Francisco; it was wiped out by an earthquake this morning at 5:13; just got the news at the telegraph office at Salem." Of course we took it for granted that, though grim, this news was the conductor's idea of an early morning's joke. How could it be otherwise? Hadn't we left San Francisco at 2:00 a.m. and left it its brilliant self? What the man said was impossible, and it was not until we reached Portland and saw the headlines in the morning papers that the full impact of the horror we had escaped by three hours, reached us. Had we been able to get the Pullman reservations we had called for, we would have been caught in the catastrophe, and we realized that it was only because these reservations were unavailable for the Wednesday train that we had been compelled to leave one day earlier.

It was not until weeks later that I received a letter from my old friend, Edwin Franko Goldman, apprising me of some of the tragic as well as humorous occurrences that happened during the aftermath of the tragedy. Fortunately he escaped unscathed, except for the loss of his personal belongings during the fire that followed the earthquake. The Metropolitan Opera Company lost all its scenery and costumes, but none of its personnel was injured. One of the funniest scenes must have been when Enrico Caruso was discovered in Market Street, sitting on what was left of the car tracks, on a suitcase, clad in his pajamas, wearing a high silk hat, and moaning, "La mia voce! Povera voce! E andata! Dio Mio!" (My voice! Poor voice! It's gone! My God!) and sobbing his heart out. Useless to dwell further on this painful subject, the details of which have been reported by better scribes than I. But we never forgot by what fortuitous circumstances we were enabled to continue our concert tour, which otherwise would have been blighted.

As it was, the rest of our journey proved uneventful, and Gerardy's series of triumphs continued until it was climaxed and ended with our recital, the last of the season, at Carnegie Hall. We then regretfully parted, he to return to his beloved Belgium, and I to resume the practice of my profession.

The real trouble with Gerardy was that he began his career as an infant prodigy, and through the very precocity of his art was thrown together with older men like Ysaye and Pugno. With the first I had never played in public, but often in private, as when he needed an accompanist he generally had with him his life-long friend, Camille Decreus or the wonderful Aimee Lachaume. With Pugno I had studied quite a bit and we became fast friends. Both were giants on their respective instruments—unforgettable performers—and to hear them play their violin and pianoforte sonatas together was a memorable experience.

But those two were also giants in gastronomic ability and knowledge, and consequently in size. How Pugno was able to cross hands at the piano with his short arms over his huge paunch remains a mystery to this day. It was our habit at that time to have an evening of music at one or the other's quarters, ending with a late supper at the old Café Martin, which was then still situated on University Place, way downtown. Now anyone who knows New York at all well is aware that in the late hours of the night, New York, in that neighborhood and all the way downtown to the Battery, is as quiet as a graveyard, owing to the fact that all the wholesale businesses as well as the financial district just below are closed, and tourists or strangers do not frequent such streets as Broadway at that hour. Consequently, our little crowd, which consisted among others of Pugno, Lachaume, Marteau (the French violinist), Gerardy and myself, all led by the great Eugene Ysaye,

78

An autographed photograph of Camille Decreus, a classmate of Benoist at the Conservatoire. Decreus later became the accompanist of the famous Belgian violinist Eugene Ysaye, and he accompanied him on Ysaye's only recordings made for Columbia in 1912 and 1913. The date of this photograph is 1939.

Eugene Ysaye and Ernest Chausson in the garden at his home on the Rue de Courcelles, Paris in 1895.

at the latter's suggestion, started for a walk as far down as Wall Street, at which point our evening's libations began to take effect. We were all in high spirits, though no one was what one could call intoxicated. Just happy and contented. With that in mind, Ysaye suggested that we all join hands at arm's length so that we reached clear across Broadway from building to building. So in this manner, we started north, singing at the top of our voices, the echo of which in this canyon must have awakened the dead! All went well for about two blocks, when suddenly from the darkness emerged the burly form of a helmeted Irish policeman. "And what the hell do ye think you're doing," he quoth, his r's rolling with wrath; "Ye all shut up or I'll take ye to the clink and teach ye to disturb

Eugene Ysaye and Jacques Thibaud at the time he was to introduce Brussels to the Brahms violin concerto. Ysaye and Thibaud were always a happy pair!

the peace"! With that, Ysaye, being our natural leader, came forward, and drawing himself up to his full and impressive height, said with his choicest French accent, "Do you not know who I am? Why, I am the great violinist, Eugene Ysaye, do you ondairstand?" Came swift as a pistol shot from the Irish representative of law and order: "I don't give a damn who or what ye are! You shut up or you all go to the calaboose. Now scat." With that, we could see Ysaye's height suddenly diminish; his girth even seemed to shrink and he quietly went to the rear beating a safe retreat behind Pugno, who, though he did not understand the entire proceedings, thought it the better part of valor to let the enemy take possession,

A photograph autographed to Benoist from the famous French violinist Henri Marteau.

82

and calmly led us away from the majesty of the law. Yes, Ysaye and Pugno were gargantuan in everything they did, except when they encountered the law!

Another incident which comes to mind from those days was the case concerning Pugno and his hotel proprietor. Since Pugno was inordinately fond of the good things in life (especially those connected with the table) he always stopped at a certain hotel in New York which was far more celebrated for its cooking than for its sumptuous appointments.

This hotel made a specialty of a certain dish of which the great pianist was very fond, and upon finding that the preparation of this dish had somewhat degenerated, he complained bitterly to the indignant proprietor. When finding that the latter had paid no attention to his grievance, Pugno thought the most dignified way of reminding him of his duties was to write him a letter. So he did, and then carefully went out to the corner letter box to mail his missive. This started a rather protracted correspondence, each man in turn using the most forceful invectives and epithets in their choicest native French. The climax came one day when a letter arrived in which the proprietor announced that he would wait upon the "most honored Mr. Pugno" in his apartment that same afternoon. I happened to be present at the time this letter came, as were the accompanist Lachaume and the 'cellist Gerardy, and I can still see the dramatic way that Pugno threw out both arms to heaven saying, "If that base inn-keeper as much as steps into my apartment, I shall extinguish him; nay, annihilate him"! With the terrible thought in mind that bloodshed might ensue, we hid in the adjoining room. There we palpitatingly awaited the fateful hour. The proprietor was a very short and slender man and Pugno with his tremendous avoirdupois would only make a mouthful of him, unless we were on hand to prevent it.

We heard a knock at the door. A low murmur of voices within. Then a dead silence. . . we hardly dared to breathe. Unable to stand the suspense any longer we threw open the portieres and what meets our astonished gaze? The huge Pugno clasping the diminutive hotel proprietor in his arms and each weeping copiously on the other's shoulder and between sobs releasing the most profuse apologies! So ended the feud between a great pianist and a great cook!

An autographed photograph of the pianist Raoul Pugno, whom Benoist remembered not only as a great musician, but also as a huge man. "How Pugno was able to cross hands at the piano with his short arms over his huge paunch remains a mystery to this day." Circa 1900.

Chapter VI

A short time later, I had the pleasure of coming in contact with the first great singing musician I had encountered so far. He was the most magnificent Spanish baritone, Emilio di Gogorza, and I had never heard anything approaching the perfection of his art. It is a revelation in potentialities when a singer combines a voice of the utmost beauty with an instinct for the phrase, perfect breathing, musical feeling, and lucid enunciation. He did! And was kind and generous to a fault. The following happening will bear witness to that fact.

It was at a concert in Troy, New York and Mr. di Gogorza had just learned a recently published song by Richard Strauss. Its name was *Cecily*, and as was usual with Strauss, it was inordinately difficult for both singer and accompanist. We had rehearsed the piece thoroughly and I felt reasonably sure of my part, though a bit in doubt as to its impression on the audience, for idiom was rather strange for that period. I played the introduction, di Gogorza joining me perfectly on cue. At the turn of the first page, to my dismay, no voice was heard and looking up from my music, I saw di Gogorza blankly staring at me. Naturally enough, the audience thought that I had committed some heinous musical offense, for there was a moment of deadly silence. I felt like running off-stage and burying my head under a pillow. But suddenly di Gogorza stopped staring at me, and, turning to the audience, said "Ladies and Gentlemen, I crave your indulgence; the mistake was entirely mine; I had a lapse of memory; we will do the song over again and this time I assure you I shall not forget!" He was cheered to the echo! By this you can measure the man and the artist.

One of the most wonderful examples of coolness under trying conditions I have ever heard of happened while I played for the distinguished American soprano Florence Hinckle. It was a joint recital with the Russian violinist Efrem Zimbalist, and the evening had begun none too auspiciously. The concert took place in Morristown, N.J. Zimbalist thought it would be nice to drive out by motor car from New York, and though we started in ample time, we got lost somehow and didn't reach our destination until nearly nine o'clock. By that time everybody was more or less irritated and nervous, except Madame Hinckle who greeted us smilingly. Her first number was Schubert's *Du bist die Ruhe.* In the middle of it I noticed that the audience was anything but engrossed by the splendid performance; but instead everybody's head was describing a series of semi-circles looking towards the ceiling of the church where we were playing. It suddenly came to me as a shock that what the audience was so interestedly following with their eyes were the lively antics of a huge bat that was circling above our heads, coming nearer and nearer at each turn to the platform. My heart was in my mouth and I was quite ready to leave *Du bist die Ruhe,* its composer, and the audience to the care of the musical bat. But seeing Miss Hinckle's courage, I was ashamed to show the white feather and so I stuck to my seat; although I must admit it took every ounce of will power in my possession to accomplish this feat, especially when once or twice that bat came flopping blindly against my music stand. But the miracle was Miss Hinckle. Everyone knows that the song she was singing requires, even under ordinary circumstances, the utmost calm, self-control and smoothness of production. And there stood our singer, utterly calm, self-possessed, without a quiver in her voice, merely following the antics of the bat with her eyes, and she finished her song amid such an outburst of applause that the roof of the staid old church must have trembled on its supports.

An example of trouble an artist's vanity may lead him into can be shown in the case of Henri Marteau, the French violinist. Owing to the sudden illness of his permanent accompanist, I was engaged at the very last moment to play for this artist at a concert in Bridgeport, Connecticut. In view of this, we tried as far as possible to arrange a program that would need no rehearsing, as there was no time for it. One of the numbers we chose was the middle movement of the Beethoven *Kreutzer Sonata.* Personally, I was opposed to program-

Efrem Zimbalist, one of Professor Leopold Auer's early and most famous students.

ming this piece on the ground that it was rather inartistic to perform part of a typical ensemble number which could only be properly appreciated when played as part of the entirety. But I was quickly shown that, like children, some accompanists should be seen and. . . hardly heard! Consequently I subsided. But when it came to the public appearance and I found that Marteau was to perform his part without notes, I again demurred on the same grounds as the first time. I explained that since I was to use the printed page in performance, and this was strictly an ensemble piece, it was inartistic for one of the performers to play by memory. "Well," he said, "it isn't my fault if I'm sure of my memory and you're not, is it?" I agreed with him and went on. We began the piece and all went fine until the first violin variation started. Then suddenly the violinist began to flounder helplessly, his memory apparently at fault, until I picked up the violin part on the piano, which permitted him to come in properly on the repeat. The next day the press rebuked him severely both for his want of taste in performing by memory, and by doing so, daring to forget. I have often wondered if he ever tried the same thing again!

One morning I was awakened by the ringing of the telephone. At the other end was Henry Wolfsohn who sounded very excited. It seemed that he wanted me to meet a young Viennese violinist who was showing promise of becoming a star of great magnitude. His name was Fritz Kreisler and I had already heard fine things about him. Naturally I was delighted, and Wolfsohn made an appointment for me to meet the artist then and there. Of course I was still a novice and it was with trepidation that I awaited the young man's opinion about my usefulness to him. But Kreisler had such a charming, calm manner that he at once put me at ease. He played with a golden tone and dazzling technique. At first sight, one wondered at his perfection, for his right elbow was raised high most of the time, contrary to the orthodox way most violinists are taught. But with him it was unimportant, for no matter how wrong it looked, it always sounded beautiful. And what more could anyone ask? I have heard very musical people say, sincerely, that they would rather hear Kreisler play out of tune, than other violinists in perfect pitch. This is understandable, because he has the supreme gift of being thoroughly human and thus able to probe the human heart to its innermost depth. Beside which, he is Viennese. What more need I add? So I will

An autographed photograph of Fritz Kreisler, whom Benoist accompanied during his first performances of Kreisler's works including the "Chanson Louis XIII et Pavanne." The photograph is dated December 16, 1940.

not expatiate upon the artist; for he is too well known to need more comment. The man, even in those youthful years, was as his art.

An example of his modesty comes to mind. Some years ago, I happened to be in Chicago with my friend Albert Spalding, on our way to the Pacific Coast. We had arrived in Chicago in the morning and were not due to depart until late the same evening. It being a Sunday, things looked rather dull waiting for train time, when on glancing at a newspaper we noticed the announcement of a violin recital to be given by Fritz Kreisler at the Auditorium. "Let's go," said Spalding. I concurred. Off we went, when on the way we met a mutual friend whose destination was the same. That was when Mr. Kreisler had at last been recognized by public and critics as one of the elect, and the hall was packed to the doors. The audience had shown throughout the recital that it idolized him, and he was recalled over and over again to play his favorite encores. At last it was over and, accompanied by our mutual friend, we went backstage to congratulate the artist over his well-earned success. Our friend, evidently not knowing of my early days with Kreisler, leading me to him, introduced me formally. Spalding's face was sphynx-like. But Kreisler turned to our friend and with a smile said in French: "Celui-la? Mais il m'a connu quand j'etais dans la deche!" (That one? Why he knew me when I was still hard up.) Such is modesty!

But to go back to those early days when it was difficult to obtain engagements for this artist. At this distance it seems hard to understand that such a thing was possible. But nevertheless such was the case, as Mr. Kreisler will bear witness to himself. The idol of the moment was Ysaye, and with the American public, in music at least, one idol at a time is all it will digest. Everyone admitted that here was certainly a fine artist, but when it came to proving it with coin of the Republic, he went to hear Ysaye. And the critics! How they loved to show their erudition by making silly comparisons and spouting beautiful long words, the meaning of which I doubt very much they understood themselves.

Speaking of the gentlemen who sit in daily judgment in our metropolitan press room and give glib and oftimes clever opinions as to what is good or bad in music, I wonder whether they are gifted with a sense of humor, along with the gift of omniscience? If they are so gifted, they must often smile on re-reading some of their "reviews". Also, have they human feelings, carefully hidden behind what they are pleased to call their "professional integrity"?

I am in no position to evaluate what harm or good can be caused by a critic to a writer or a painter, not knowing enough about either profession; but ordinary common sense prompts me to think that the case is different from musical or dramatic criticism. Paintings are exhibited for everyone to see, and can remain so, long after the criticism has been published and read. If the public likes a painting, it will either buy it or visit it in some museum, regardless of what is written about it. The same applies to a book, be it novel, drama or poetry.

But a public performance, be it music or a play, is evanescent. Once the performance is over, who is to prove it was either good or bad? Unless a particular performance is recorded, it is not even a subject for discussion, and still less a subject for a definite opinion. This can be proven by reading the divergence of opinion on a given concert or play in the daily press. The dissenter will reply that, after all, a critic has a right to his own opinion. True! He has! But only as a private citizen. The moment he publishes a review in a newspaper, it ceases to be an opinion and becomes a verdict.

And this verdict is believed, owing to the reputation for accuracy and truthfulness enjoyed by the newspaper publishing the review. This, combined with public gullibility, managerial thirst for publicity and artistic vanity make this state of things static. I doubt there is a remedy, or a need for professional criticism.

Criticism seldom hurts the established musical artist. But in all fairness, let us, as concisely as possible, examine the case of the beginner in the musical profession. He has worked hard for years to make himself technically proficient. He has often bled himself financially to obtain the proper instruction, or someone, be it his own family or a friend, has believed enough in him to help him financially. He must love his art, or he would never have put up with the difficulties surrounding his ambition. He must believe in himself, or he would be unable to convince others of his talents, be they ever so dubious. Then comes the time when his advisors judge him ready to face the general public and start on his professional career.

Real drama hovers over this first appearance. The rental of a hall, managerial fees, advertising, a new gown in the case of a woman, a new dress suit in the case of a man; all this entails a considerable outlay, which must be scraped together by any means available. Is it any wonder that, with all this on his mind, the debutant is not always at his best on such an occasion? But this concert means everything to him; and if his reviews are unfavorable, he will not be accepted by any of the "combine'" managers; and the young artist knows full well that without the latter's help, his career is practically nipped in the bud. And what a frail bud it is!

Do the gentlemen of the press take all this in consideration? Never! Their "professional integrity" forbids it! Why not use the old rule of "the survival of the fittest"? But for heaven's sake, let the infant first attain maturity before you give him the coup de grace! And by the same token, it would not be amiss to think that by being a little more conservative in their judgment, many of their victims would die a natural death artistically, if their shortcomings were too obvious. I wonder what would happen if their tactics were adopted in the mercantile world? It would be pleasant to think that critics realize that their responsibilities are greater than merely pointing out artists' shortcomings.

Mr. Kreisler was a very young man when I had the honor and pleasure to accompany him. He already had the same lovable qualities that have lasted him over the years. He was kind and tolerant, never a fault finder; always a helper and sound advisor. He liked card playing, good beer, and convivial company. That is not to say, however, that there weren't occasions when I felt inclined to be the cause of his untimely demise! I vividly recall one instance when Mr. Wolfsohn rang me up concerning a concert with that artist in Poughkeepsie, New York. He told me to be sure to catch a four o'clock train from Grand Central Station, which Kreisler would also catch, and to meet him at the entrance gate to the train. I arrived at the gate at ten minutes ahead of time and I waited. As I watched the hands of the big clock drawing nearer to the appointed time I was getting more nervous, knowing my man as I did. At one minute of four I bribed the guard to hold the gate one minute after the hour, which he promised to do. Between four o'clock and one minute past, a cloud appeared in the distance. It was composed of two bags, a violin case, coat tails and a hat, in the midst of which panted my friend Kreisler. We made the train, and as Kreisler breathlessly subsided into a seat, I gently reprimanded him for risking missing the concert; but he was at the same time so contrite and delighted, that I dropped the subject, simply inquiring about what had delayed him. His face, which I noticed was badly in need of a razor, was beaming with joy as he answered, "I have just bought something new, something unique, marvelous, sublime! Only in America can such things be found!" I was frankly puzzled, and begged him to show me this astounding object. So he opened first one bag, then the other one, then his violin case, and finally, his face getting darker all the time, started rummaging through his pockets, one by one and with the utmost care. He finally looked at me with utter chagrin and disappointment, and said, "Good Heavens! I must have left it in the cab!" Unable to stand the suspense any longer I said, "For Heaven's sake! What was this wonderful thing that came near making you miss one of our important concerts?" "Well," he replied, almost on the verge of tears, "look at my face! That's the answer!" I looked, but could only observe his great need of a barber. "That's just it" he said, "I have religiously kept this

PROGRAM

OF

Josef Hofmann and Fritz Kreisler

Andre Benoist at the Piano

1. Sonata, Two Movements . . . *Cesar Franck*
   Allegro ben moderato — Allegro —
   MESSRS. HOFMANN AND KREISLER

2. a. Air . . . . . . *Goldmark*
   b. Tambourin . . . *Rameau* (1633-1764)
   c. Menueite . . . . *Porpora* (1636-1767)
   d. Humoresque (by request) . . . *Dvorak*
   FRITZ KREISLER

3. a. Ballade, F-sharp major . . . *Chopin*
   b. Mazourka . . . . . . *Hofmann*
   c. Rhapsodie No. 11. . . . . *Liszt*
   JOSEF HOFMANN

4. Sonata Op. 47, " Kreutzer " . . . *Beethoven*
   Adagio sostenuto, Presto, Andante con Variazioni, Finale Presto
   MESSRS. HOFMANN AND KREISLER

5. a. Dance Slave . . . . . *Dvorak*
   b. Scene de Czarda . . . . . *Hubuy*
   FRITZ KREISLER

6. a. Two songs without words . . . *Mendelsshon*
         1. Duetto A-flat major
            Spinning song
   b. Overture " Tannhaeuser " (by general request) *Wagner-Liszt*
   JOSEF HOFMANN

93

To Mr. André Benoist
Lessford with kind regards
of Josef Hofmann,

288 Fifth Avenue
New York

beautiful growth so as to have the keen pleasure of eliminating it with the greatest invention of the age that has just come on the market! THE GILLETTE SAFETY RAZOR!" And for that he had jeopardized a concert! And still worse, when we arrived at Poughkeepsie, all the barber shops were closed and he had to appear with that beard lightly sprinkled with talcum!

Nevertheless, Kreisler had only one real idiosyncrasy that sometimes caused me no little embarrassment. When he either ran short of encores, or became tired of playing the same pieces too often, sometimes in the parlor car of a train on the way to a concert date, he would suddenly busy himself with pencil and music paper. And when he was finished, he would turn to me with the sweetest smile and say, "Here is a little thing we shall try out tonight; I think you'll like it." "But," I would demur, "this is written in pencil, and when the light shines on it and makes the graphite reflect its rays, it will be almost impossible to make heads or tails of it!" That would not disturb the artist in the least, and with a friendly pat on the back he would say, "Oh, you can do it alright; you'll see that it will go splendidly!" And that would be the end of it, for who could resist that smile and show of confidence? . . . Until concert time, when I would sit at the piano perspiring profusely over the hieroglyphics facing me while Mr. Kreisler, in beatific bliss, would play like an angel. I daresay I was the only person present who did not have the time to enjoy myself! Thus I first heard his bete noir (Literally translated "black beast." In congruence with the term "thorn-in-the-flesh"), the arrangement for violin of the Humoreske by Dvorak, and the Chanson Louis XIII et Pavane, that became so popular in the repertoire of many artists. This friendship that has lasted over forty years is a prized possession!

At the same time that Kreisler was being so sadly underrated by the press, another young man was having none too easy a time, although in his case, public opinion seemed to be divided. Some claimed that he was cold and unimaginative, while others claimed there had never been another pianist like him since the death of his master Anton Rubinstein. But all agreed that his technique was dazzling. The fact is that he was a pianistic giant; and because he had too much innate taste and musicianship to allow himself the eccentricities of rhythm and exaggerations of dynamics then the prevailing fashion, they called him cold. Far from cold was he! But he substituted tenderness

unsern lieben Hütte Benoît zur
Erinnerung an
Gessford Zorn Hofmann
mon bon et cher Benoît souv[...]

288 Fifth Avenu[e]
New York

for cheap sentimentality. He never distorted a phrase to obtain an effect. His power in climaxes was overwhelming, as opposed to the limpid and carrying pianissimo he used in the softer passages. In short, he had every gift a pianist could wish for. But there were two things working against him that old fogies could not forgive: He was young, in his early twenties, and he had been one of the most amazing infant prodigies ever heard. It is enough to say his name was Josef Hofmann. And more amazing still, Henry Wolfsohn had the utmost difficulty in convincing local managements that, young or old, it was an unforgettable experience to hear him play! Finally, in desperation, Wolfsohn thought it would certainly prove to be a genuine drawing card if he could couple two such giants of music as Josef Hofmann and Fritz Kreisler, and thus send them on tour. I went on that tour as Mr. Kreisler's accompanist and all went well financially on guaranteed engagements. But when it came to draw on their own reputations, would you believe there was practically no response?

So it was, at a concert in Infantry Hall in Providence, Rhode Island. In that huge auditorium there was barely a handful of people! So much for the clever judgment of "the masses!" But the artistic success of both artists was colossal. Encore after encore was demanded by the few present, and the artists gave of their best tirelessly. What charming trips we had: Hofmann would be sitting in a corner of the Pullman car, his heels propped up under him and ruminating like a cow chewing her cud. Sometimes Kreisler would twit him on account of his apparent taciturnity, and he would shake his head impatiently saying, "Let me alone! I'm practicing!" And he was! He would go through his entire program mentally, fingering, phrasing and nuances. He always was the great mental worker par excellence. No wonder he was such a musical giant! His kindness was immense. Very often, when not working himself, he would ask me to sit at the piano and play some of my pieces for him, and correct, finger and annotate them for me, never realizing for a moment that some people would have given almost anything to be in my place. It was after one such seance, that Kreisler, who had been shaving in the next room, came rushing in, and exclaimed: "Josef, you are really in marvelous form today!" "Yes," said Hofmann, looking quizzically at me, "it was really not so bad." It was the most sincere compliment anyone could wish for, but Kreisler's powers of discrimination certainly went down several points in our estimation!

To André Benoist —
with compliments and
all good wishes from an old friend.

Edward Johnson

The great Canadian tenor Edward Johnson, who gained great fame in Italy as Edoardo di Giovanni. Note the inscription to Benoist. A joke is told about Johnson which is probably not true. When he first sang in Italy, his first solo was wildly applauded with cheers SING IT AGAIN. . . SING IT AGAIN. He was flattered and complied. He sang it again and the same thing happened. So he sang it again! Finally after four of the same encores, he told the audience that they must proceed and he would sing again later. "No," they shouted. "You must sing it again and again until finally you sing it properly."

Chapter
VII

There was another artist, but this time a singer, and worse, a tenor, who by his charming and modest manner as well as by his genius for singing, endeared himself to all who had the pleasure of meeting and knowing him. To give an idea of his humorous approach to anything, even at his own expense, the following will do: One day at some party, he was introduced to a rather elderly, voluble, and gushing lady, who, on hearing his name immediately exclaimed, "Oh! You are a real tenor, then?" Upon which he quickly replied, "Indeed not, Madam! I am a *man*, but with a high voice, that's all!"

His name was Edward Johnson, and to say his artistic path was strewn with difficulties would be an understatement. From the first note I heard him utter, I was charmed. His voice, while not being of the largest, had a limpid and pure quality seldom heard; his phrasing, breathing, and enunciation were the acme of perfection; and his qualities of heart and soul were such as to enable him to reach your heart at once, while everything he did was apparently effortless. In other words, his art was ideal. Was all this recognized by Press and Public? Indeed, NO! His managers at that time were the Henry Wolfsohn Musical Bureau, and it took all their astuteness and perseverance coupled with their unfaltering belief in their artist, to obtain, even at a very reasonable fee, any engagements at all! It seems incredible that public judgment can so often be at fault, but the press is even worse. For this is not the only case in which I have seen artists almost defeated through the lack of understanding of their work by critics, who a few years later would suddenly "discover" this same artist. And this, often at the decline of his career!

However, friend Johnson was made of sterner stuff, in spite of his bantering ways. And so one day he decided to leave the United States of America behind him and never come back until he had made a name great enough abroad to earn him the recognition to which he logically felt his art was entitled. For who in the dear old U.S.A. could believe that a fellow by the name of Johnson could sing?

It so happened that my wife and I were in Italy in 1913 as guests of the Spalding family, I being accompanist for Albert Spalding at that period. And all Italy was ringing with a name that was magic in the realm of operatic singing. From general gossip we learned that this man "had everything." Mr. Spalding and I had just returned to Florence from one of our tours, and Mr. Spalding's father told us that, at great pain and expense, he had been able to buy enough tickets to enable all of us to hear the famed tenor. Of course we were delighted. The day following our return, my wife and I were strolling along the Tornabuone in quest of a tea shop, when who should heave into our sight, but one whom we affectionately called Eddie Johnson. Our surprise was mutual. I told him how I came to be in Florence and in return I asked him what he was doing there. "Oh," he said with a good-humored chuckle, "I'm working tonight!" I inwardly had visions of poor Eddie carrying a spear in the chorus of the opera, and feeling rather sorry for him, did not pursue the subject any further, but invited him to have a cup of tea at Doney's with us. After a desultory conversation, that touched on this and that, we separated. On the way back to the Palazzo, Spalding, my wife and I could not help feeling that it was too bad that he had come so far to accomplish so little, but we admired him for his bravery.

That evening was the great event, *Don Carlos,* at the Polyteamo Fiorentino with Edouardo Di Giovanni as the star! Everyone was terribly keyed up and excited. In this frame of mind we awaited the anticipated moment when the curtain would rise. Certainly Di Giovanni could not have wished for a more brilliant audience. The entire "Who is Who" of Florence was assembled in the vast gilded auditorium, and that included the Italian nobility, as well as the wealthiest class of England and America. The curtain at last rose and the opera began with the usual nonsensical preliminaries to the rather silly plot. And then with majestic steps entered the great

An early autographed photograph of Albert Spalding.

star, quite magnificent in his stage finery. He began to sing, and it suddenly dawned on me that here was no Italian tenor bellowing at the top of his voice. Everything that came from his throat flowed smoothly and unforced, in golden tones. I quickly borrowed a pair of opera glasses to see at closer range who this phoenix was and what he really looked like. What amazement was mine when I recognized the well-known features of my friend, Eddie Johnson! I passed on the information to the rest of our party and we were all frantic with surprised delight! Edouardo Di Giovanni indeed! Why of course, how stupid of me! It is an exact translation of Edward Johnson! And "I'm working tonight!" But then, how should I have guessed the truth?

His return to America was a genuine triumph, and this he enjoyed under his own name just as he had planned, and fully deserved. Today he was the Director of the same institution that formerly would have none of him. Poetic justice if ever there was any!

Thus the days of probation in the profession I had, by then, definitely chosen, flitted by, with very busy winters and restful summers, the latter usually spent between study and pleasure. I had met Madame Schumann-Heink several times at various concerts when I was playing for other less well-known luminaries of the concert and operatic world. But I had never played for her. So I was surprised and pleased at the start of the summer of 1910, to receive a note from her asking whether I would care to come to her country place at Singac, near Caldwell, New Jersey, a few times a week to coach her in her repertoire for the forthcoming winter season. Not only was I surprised, but deeply flattered. For, to quote Madame Nordica, "the greatest compliment that can be paid you is when someone is willing to sacrifice a prized possession such as money for the privilege of obtaining your services, regardless of what they consist. Remember that compliments in themselves are cheap and easy to give!"

My reply to Madame brought an answer setting a day and hour for arrival at Singac and the following week I was on my way. I was met by a nondescript sort of hack and taken to Madame's place. It was a rather large rambling house, of the type still called a "Jersey farm," but this one was comfortable in the extreme and contained all the modern conveniences known at the time. Madame received

102

The great German opera star Ernestine Schumann-Heink, whom Benoist accompanied and whose huge girth generated a strong body odor. One hot day Benoist blew out his breath sharply as a sign of the heat, but Madame Schumann-Heink misinterpreted the breath as a reaction to her body odor and appologized. "Yes, I always have this odor in the summertime." This photograph was inscribed to her colleague Benoist at Newark, N.J. in 1902.

103

me clad in a light cotton dress fitted very loosely over her ample form. Her art is too well remembered today to need comment. Besides we have phonograph records that testify to its unparalleled beauty. On seeing me she exclaimed, "Ach! Du kleine, bist schon hier?" (Ah, you little one, you're already here?) She had touched a sore point; at least it was sore then, for I *was* short, and still am; but I have arrived at a time in life when I can reason that what can't be cured must be endured. And cheerfully! She never changed her appellation of "Du kleine" until one day I rebelled, and told her in the most diplomatic way I could muster that height meant nothing; that Andrew Carnegie, E. H. Harriman and Napoleon were all short men, and that this did not interfere with their careers. Cocking her head sideways and looking at me quizzically she said, "You are right! From now on I shall call you Nap, after your great compatriot!" And she never did call me anything else to the time of her unfortunate demise!

One broiling August day, Madame was sitting next to me, at the piano. At the end of one number, feeling the heat intensely, I suddenly blew out my breath between half closed lips, as one usually does when feeling unusually hot. Madame must have completely misunderstood my signal for she turned to me and said ruefully: "Ja, Ich reiche immer so im Sommer!" (Yes, I always have this odor in summer.) I turned purple and had great difficulty convincing her that that was not what my sign had meant.

Another amusing episode happened one day, when she had asked me to bring some music she needed to the Metropolitan Opera House, where she was rehearsing her part in *Rheingold*. The scene happened to be the one where the Rhein Maidens are supposed to be swimming down deep in the great river. It has to be rehearsed very carefully as the position of the singers is very awkward. They lie on their stomachs in iron cradles suspended by steel wires from the flies and run back and forth and up and down on pulleys. When Madame caught sight of me down on the stage, she exclaimed, "Fine position to be in for the mother of six children, what?"

Chapter VIII

One morning I was called to the telephone where I was greeted by the screechy soprano voice of R. E. Johnston, who without preamble said, "Do you want to play for Lillian Nordica?" I said, "Of course I would like to, but how come?" "Don't ask so many questions," he retorted, "but take an early train tomorrow morning for Irvington-on-the-Hudson, and ask any cabby for Madame Nordica's house. He'll take you there. She wants to meet you!" And so the following morning I arrived at the prima donna's country home. It was rather large, but unpretentious. It had the homey look that the French so aptly describe as "un desordre savant" (an intelligent disarray). After waiting quite a while, a vision loomed into the range of my sight! It must have been a man. Of that there could be no doubt from his carriage. He was huge and had snowy white hair and the ruddy complexion of the outdoor type. But he was attired in a white silk Japanese kimono embroidered with roses; around his throat hung a triple stranded rope of pearls and on his white locks rested a string of daisies! I was dumbfounded and gulped before I could find my voice. "I am the accompanist Madame is expecting," I explained, upon which the vision nodded and said, "Yes, I know, Madame sent me down to tell you she will be with you in a few moments; by the way, how do you like my attire? Madame dressed me, one of her whimsies, you know. . .", and his voice trailed off rather ruefully.

And then entered the Queen of Song, as she was known. Truly, she was a queen, in every motion of her body and every inflection of her voice. She possessed the "grand manner" in everything she did or said. She carried herself in the simple house gown she was wearing as if she were about to offer a curtsey at court. In short, she played the role of Lillian Nordica with supreme perfection. She graciously introduced me to the "vision" and named him in turn, George Washington Young. I later learned that he was the equivalent of what today is called "the boyfriend." She later married him, but that venture was no more successful than her first marriage to the singer, Zoltan Dohme. The only similarity being that this husband succeeded in cleaning her coffers dry by investing her money "cleverly." Poor lady, in spite of her regality, her taste in music was better than in husbands! But as an artist in presenting a song, she had no peer! As Isolde, who could forget her? But strange to say this great artist did practically everything by sheer instinct. Of course she had been taught to sing perfectly. But of music technicality as such, she had no idea. Everything she learned had to be drummed into her at the piano. She herself could effect playing a little at the piano with one finger, and in common with many people who hardly know the instrument at all, mostly in the key of G flat, which also means, mostly on the black keys. Why this should be a general practice with those not familiar with the keyboard will always remain a deep, dark mystery to me and to many others I suppose. I have, however, often met with this sort of thing, and among those that came to my notice as a glaring example is the "great American composer," Irving Berlin, who wrote me over his own signature that "As you know, I can't read a note of music, so I shall have the composition you sent me played by someone who knows how!" He, also, only played on the black keys.

But to go back to Madame Nordica. I knew some of her early history. How as a young girl, she had already shown the promise of a luscious voice, but having expressed a hankering for the operatic stage, she was disowned by her New England family, and left her native town of Farmington, Maine, in disgrace. It was then that she went to Boston where she studied with the singing master O'Neill, who at the completion of her studies with him, advised her to go abroad for further advice and experience. He also advised her to abandon the name Lilly Norton, and to adopt the one under which she became world famous. So she arrived in Paris, where she met the celebrated tenor Jean de Reszke, to whom, she often told me, she owed the chiseled polish and refinement of her art. He

In 1908 the great singer Lillian Nordica autographed this photograph to Andre Benoist. She was known during her career as *The Queen of Song*.

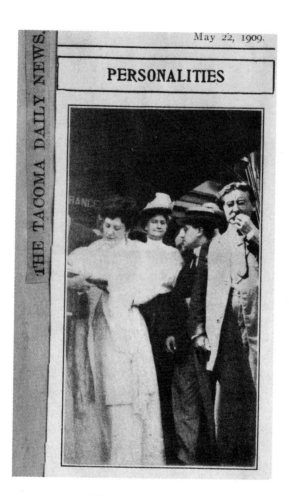

THE TACOMA DAILY NEWS.

May 22, 1909.

PERSONALITIES

Lillian Nordica autographing programs in May, 1909 in Tacoma, Washington. This is one of the penalties of fame as a musical celebrity. The side view of the man with the straw hat is Andre Benoist; the gentleman on the right is President Theodore Roosevelt.

scolded and coached, coached and scolded, until he considered her ready for a debut. This she made with the utmost success, and from then on her career was a series of artistic triumphs. I say - *artistic*, for financially her reward was as usual, slow in coming.

In fact, an episode which happened when she first went to Russia will serve to illustrate the difficulties that faced a young artist even in the eighties of the last century. It was told to me first hand by another world-renowned prima donna of former days, and will bear telling a little later. Suffice it to say that when I met Madame, she had just turned fifty, and was still a glorious looking creature, in full possession of those gifts that endeared her to everyone. But, as all human beings, she also had some idiosyncrasies that, I must confess, surprised me in one so habitually gracious.

How often she asked me to be at her house "sharp at 8:30 a.m. and ready for hard work," and never came down from her room until lunch time, when, instead of the stern prima donna, she would be the most genial hostess imaginable, full of witty quips and interesting anecdotes! She would sing a few songs after lunch, and then suddenly take it into her head to go for a drive. After that, being weary, she would postpone work till the next day. Enlightened by my previous experience, I would turn up an hour or so later than the appointed time, only to find that she had been at work a long while and was rebuking me severely for my tardiness. This mood would pass off immediately, and we would then plunge into hard work. Madame Nordica was the most indefatigable worker I have ever met, once she started. Lunchtime would come and go without her even thinking of it, and many a time I have prayed to Heaven that the blessed butler would come to announce that longed-for meal, a thing he was always loath to do when Madame was in the midst of her work. Overcoming his fears he would finally timidly make his announcement, and he would then adjourn only to find that the chops and potatoes were almost burned to a crisp. To which Madame would ruefully say, "Yes, you can't do good work and eat good meals at the same time!"

Our tour began uneventfully in a routine manner. Madame traveled in a private car. And if anyone should be under the illusion that this is either fun or the acme of comfort, let me hastily dispel this idea. In the first place, private cars were always attached to the slowest trains, because the fast limited trains would have

Lillian Nordica in her costume. Circa 1909.

already taken on their full complement of cars, and an extra one would slow them down. Also, being always at the tail end of a train, one got the full benefit of the swing around curves! When standing still, the car was sent to the railroad yards overnight, where the shunting of cars and locomotives back and forth would form an unwelcome accompaniment to our dreams! The car had the advantage of containing a piano, which was good for practice, but when the time came for this, one usually got carsick from the constant swaying, and so went to lie down instead! Madame was accompanied on tour, as usual, by a solo pianist and a baritone who "filled-in" while she rested between numbers, so the cabins were crowded and we were constantly getting in each other's way. Therefore, it was decided that we would petition Madame to permit us to travel by regular Pullman. This, though surprised, she graciously allowed, although it augmented her expenses considerably.

Her one bete noir ("black beast") was the fear of finding that the piano we were to use at the concerts would be tuned to the pitch of 440 to A, which was concert pitch and fine for violinists, as it made their instrument more brilliant. But she was used to 435 to A, and it was one of my chores to go to the hall in time to verify the correctness of the pitch. In one of the towns where we were to perform, we arrived late, so that I barely had time to run to the hall on my usual errand. Once there, I found to my dismay that the piano was tuned to the higher pitch. What to do? I tried to reach the tuner by telephone, but to no avail. To make it worse, the Madame, who never came to the hall before concert time, suddenly appeared on the scene, having suddenly developed a whimsical desire for a walk, which she usually detested. With a sweet smile, she inquired as to the state of the piano. I had to admit it was slightly above pitch, upon which her eyes suddenly turned green with rage. "And what do you propose to do about it?" I told her of my ill luck in trying to reach the tuner, and that it seemed impossible to do anything more. Whereupon I was the recipient of one of the most resounding and best-placed slaps in the face anyone could well wish for! "Don't you ever tell me a thing is impossible," she exclaimed. "That word is not in my dictionary! Do you think I've slaved a lifetime to place my voice at the right pitch to have it tampered with by the stupidity of some small town tuner?"

111

A concert of Nordica (front, center stage), with Bend
leading the orchestra, so to speak, so they co

seated directly to her right. He played the piano,
follow the singer's varying tempi.

Madame Nordica

ASSISTED BY

Mr. André Benoist

Pianist

THE COLISEUM

MONDAY EVENING, APRIL 19, 1909

Plat opens at the Salesrooms of
The Starr Piano Company,
Thursday, April 15, at 8 a. m.

NICHOLSON PRESS, RICHMOND, IND.

A typical program of Madame Nordica and Benoist.

PROGRAM

❧

1 Polonaise No. 2 - - - - *Liszt*
          MR. BENOIST

2 Aria "dich Theure Halle" - - - *Wagner*
          From "Tannhauser"
          MME. NORDICA

3 English Songs:
    a Now Sleeps the Crimson Petal - - *Quilter*
    b Angels Over Bright and Fair - - *Handel*
    c The Year's at the Spring - - *Mrs. Beach*
          MME. NORDICA

4 March Militaire - - - *Schubert-Tausig*
          MR. BENOIST

5 French and Italian Songs:
    a Vielle Chanson - - - - *Bizet*
    b Nell - - - - - *Faure*
    c Mia Picirella - - - - *Gomes*
    d Mattinata - - - - *Leoncavallo*
          MME. NORDICA

6 German Songs:
    a Die Lotus Blume - - - *Schumann*
    b Der Astra - - - - *Rubinstein*
    c Waldesgesprach - - - - *Schumann*
          MME. NORDICA

❧

THE STARR CONCERT GRAND WILL BE USED

However, no sooner had the volcano erupted than it subsided, and when Madame realized what she had done in a fit of temper, she was as contrite as a little girl caught with her fingers in the jam pot. And she suggested that since there was nothing else to do, she would leave out some of her high notes, and do the best she could under the circumstances.

The next day, being Christmas, we tried our best to be cheerful, though it was uphill work. Towards midday, arrived upon the scene a specimen that needs a little description. His official title was "Personal Representative for Madame Nordica." At least that's what it read on his superbly engraved visiting cards. He was tall and willowy, his features handsome, and his motions, grace personified. His clothes would have been immaculate and well-tailored had he been stranded on a desert island, and his haberdashery would also have matched. He wore an embroidered silk handkerchief protruding from his sleeve cuff. He was wont to proclaim himself a pure-blooded Virginian and his name was William Fenton Chauncey. He looked it! Once in a while when in especially good humor, this creature would condescend to address us as though we were human, but that was only on rare occasions. This Christmas Day, he appeared before us looking as official as he could, and in the gruffest manner he could summon, he said, "Immediately after the matinee concert, you are to come to the car, as Madame has something important to say to you three!" With that he departed, leaving us to cogitate on the meaning of the word "important." We suddenly saw the writing on the wall! Madame had had enough of traveling and this was the end! And there we were in Pullman, Washington, having to travel some three thousand miles to get back home, without an engagement in midseason! What a life! Who wants to be an artist? And so on, ad infinitum.

But the show must go on! And it did, in spite of the gloom that had settled upon the company. Not a word from Madame to any of us. Once in a while, I thought I could detect a little malicious smile lurking on her features. But even that I ascribed to the pleasure she might have in getting rid of us. The concert finally came to a close, with the familiar applause and calls for encores, and we gloomily repaired to the hotel to get rid of our formal stage attire. Then, forlorn and depressed, we started the pilgrimage to the car through heavy snow. There, the porter asked us to wait a few moments on

RECITAL BY MME.

NORDICA

ASSISTED BY

FREDERICK HASTINGS, Baritone

ANDRE BENOIST, Accompanist

ORCHESTRA HALL
Wednesday Evening
February Third
1909
R. E. JOHNSON, Manager

Lillian Nordica shown in the costume she wore for Isolde. Circa 1909.

the outer platform. It was bitterly cold and we didn't like it one bit. After a few minutes, the door was opened, and with the utmost ceremony, we were ushered into the dining compartment, which, to our amazement, had been completely transformed. It was a veritable bower of flowers, illuminated by all kinds of colored lights. On the table glittering with beautiful silverware, was a miniature Christmas tree, and at the head, stood Madame Nordica attired in her most attractive gown, on her head a diamond tiara, and smiling her irresistible smile! "Children," she said, "let me welcome you all to what is probably your first Christmas dinner in this forlorn part of our great country; let us all forget our little dissensions; eat, drink and be merry!" And turning to me, in an aside, she murmured, "Will this earn your forgiveness for my little love tap of the other day?" What can one say under such circumstances? I was speechless, and could barely stutter my appreciation. Thus, Madame Nordica!

Some days later, we were rehearsing in the car, when the porter came in to announce that a young man was at the door craving a few moments of Madame's time. I was for telling him that Madame was busy and would see him some other time. But she inquired as to what he wanted and the porter said that he had told him he was a composer, who had walked several miles to come here, and that he looked dishevelled and under-nourished. Eventually the young man came in, and I must admit that he did look the worse for wear. He showed us several of his compositions which demonstrated a sound talent for melody without too much originality. One little song Madame kept looking at over and over, and finally gave him her word that this she would launch. I have never known this lady to break her word, and this case was no exception. She launched the song, which soon became one of her greatest popular successes. It was called *From the Land of the Sky Blue Waters*, and the young man who had brought it to her under such pitiful circumstances was destined to become one of our most successful composers. His name was Charles Wakefield Cadman. I wonder whether he remembers the circumstance of his discovery?

Humorous incidents sometimes happened to highlight our more serious moments. Among them I recall one that sent Madame into peals of laughter when I related it to her. On one of our more tedious runs, we found ourselves confronted by a Pullman conductor who, being as bored as we were, was, accordingly, very garrulous. He had a long, cadaverous face under his gold braided cap, chewed tobacco, and was gifted with a Western twang you could cut with a knife. This came from the side of his mouth via his nostrils. He paused for a moment, cocked his head to one side, not unlike a curious bird, and singling me out, said, "Say, this yere woman in the private car; what'd she do?" In a spirit of pure mischief, thereupon I decided to pull the elderly fellow's leg and see what would happen. So with a side-glance of warning and a nudge meaning "don't interfere" to my companions Hastings and Showers, I answered, "Why, my dear man, I'm surprised at your ignorance! That's Madame Nordica, the famous tight-rope walker, didn't you know?" "No," said he, "Ain't never heard tell of her. How the heck can she afford a private car at fifty dollars a day and expenses with that kind of business?" "Why," I retorted, "this woman is wealthy and can well afford to travel as she does; only she loves to walk the tight rope and she likes to have people see her do it. Of course she charges high prices for the admission tickets and then it's hard to get any." "Gee," came his reply, "I wish I could see that performance!"

"Alright," I said, "I'll tell you what I'll do; I'll see that two tickets are left at the box office in your name tonight, and as long as you say that you'll be in town over night, all you'll have to do is to claim them and so you'll see the whole show." Arrived in town, I arranged with the "Great Poo-Bah," William Fenton Chauncey (who for once agreed to enter into the fun with the lowly), to leave two tickets for seats well down in front for our friend, so that I could keep an eye on him from the stage; and so the concert began. It was hard to keep serious under the circumstances, and at intermission Madame inquired what was the cause of my giggles. I begged her to wait until later for the answer, as laughing was none too good for her throat in the middle of a concert. That made her all the more curious, but I was adamant and refused any further information. Besides, I wanted to wait for the end of the concert to see the old fellow's reaction. At last this came, and seeing him hover near the stage door, I rushed over to him and asked him how he had liked the "show." One single word summed up his entire appreciation of our efforts: "ROTTEN!", after which he disappeared into the crowd, and we never saw hide nor hair of him

"To Mr. Benoist, souvenir of many hours of interesting music.—
Lillian Nordica."

121

again. When later on I recounted this to Madame, she greeted the story with peals of laughter and said, "I am surely glad you did not tell me all this at the concert, for not only couldn't I have gone on, but I'm afraid I would have burst a blood vessel in trying to keep serious!"

Another rather amusing incident took place when we arrived in Los Angeles. There existed at that time a very exclusive artists' and professional men's club called *The Calumet* , of which I had been an honorary member for some years. But this fact was unknown to our friend Chauncey. Now this club, when an outstanding celebrity came to Los Angeles, was wont to arrange a gala reception and dinner in his or her honor, as the case would be. One day, Chauncey came to us and recited the following: "The Calumet Club of Los Angeles has been pleased to honor Madame with a large reception and dinner, and if you should care to be present, I shall try to arrange it so that you too should be invited." This, in his most pompous manner. Mischief again bubbled up within me. My two companions, of course, knew of my long membership and again I cautioned them with a glance to keep quiet, and I said, "But my dear Chauncey, how wonderful that would be. Do you think you really could wangle an invitation for mere assisting artists?" "Well," said he doubtfully, "I can try anyway." That ended our conversation for the time being. I immediately rang up the President of the club and told him the whole story. Upon which he asked me to come at once to see him and that he would have several members of the board with him; then we could decide what would be best to teach this grotesque individual a sound lesson. When we were gathered, this is what was arranged: I was to be head of the reception committee, and was given carte blanche (full control) as to the proceedings, such as precedence, admission, table placing, etc.; and so arrived the fateful evening. Being head of the reception committee, it was my duty to go to the entrance as soon as the doorman announced that Madame's carriage had arrived. And there I was, flanked on either side by two other members, all very ceremonious. I ushered Madame inside, to her intense astonishment, introduced her to the President, who then took charge of her, and went back to the entrance where I had asked Chauncey to wait until I had ascertained his status and his right to be in a musician's club. Did he play an instrument? "No." Did he sing? "No."

To dear Benoist
from Lillian Nordica

191

The first Mrs. Andre Benoist.

Did he do any performing on the stage at all? "No." He was "only" Madame's personal representative. "My dear fellow," I said, "you'll just have to sit down here and wait until I consult with some members of the board as to what we can do about you, and, if they decide to let you in, where to place you. So just arm yourself with patience and as soon as we come to a decision, I'll let you know." I found it in my heart to feel sorry for the poor chap, for I never in my life have seen such an example of acute deflation. But we all felt he needed a sound lesson, and so we went through with the performance. At the suggestion of some members, we set up a small table at the side of the large banquet hall, and there we placed Chauncey together with Hastings and Miss Showers, who were delighted with the whole thing. I was placed at Madame's left, while our President naturally took the right. Between courses I gave Madame a little idea of what was going on and why, and with a little chuckle she said, "Serves him jolly well right, the foolish boy!"

Madame's ready wit could at times be most amusing, as an incident that happened in Knoxville, Tennessee will prove. The local theatre in which we were originally scheduled to play proved too small, as foreshadowed by the advance sale of admission tickets, so the management decided at the last moment to have Nordica appear in a large skating rink. The only drawback to this idea was that the rink had no stage. However, a regiment of carpenters was drafted and set to work erecting what they were pleased to call a stage. It was just a plain pine platform, and we hoped and prayed it was strong enough to hold the weight of the Steinway concert grand and ourselves at the same time. Moreover, it was so bare that the management thought it would be a good idea to borrow a bit of scenery from the theatre. Of course there was no time to view this until concert time, for when I came to look at the piano in the afternoon, it had not yet been put into place. Consequently, when Madame walked onto the stage in the evening, with her inimitable queenly grace, I noticed her look back at the scenery and give a quiet chuckle in which the audience partly joined. Then I gave one look myself and noticed that the back piece was full of small nude angels in flight. But owing to the absence of height, it had been found necessary to cut the back piece in two, so that some of the little angels were only half there. In a whispered aside to Madame I

CARNEGIE HALL
Tuesday Afternoon, March 23, 1909
at 3 o'clock

SONG RECITAL

BY

Madam
Lillian Nordica

Assisted By

MR. ALBERT SPALDING
Violinist

ANDRE BENOIST
At the Piano

Management, R. E. JOHNSTON

Program

Mein Freund ist mein (From "Songs of Solomon")
    Peter Cornelius
Stille Sicherheit (N. Lenau)   .   *Robert Franz*
Im Kahne (Vilhelm Krag)   .   .   *Edvard Grieg*

Madame Nordica

Program continued on second page following.

A typical recital wherein Madame Lillian Nordica used guest artists to keep the crowd warm while she was taking a rest.

Introduction and Rondo Cappriccioso   *Saint-Saens*
Mr. Spalding

Mein Liebe ist Grün (L. S.)   .   *Johannes Brahms*
Seligkeit (Otto Roquette) *Frank Van Der Stucken*
Im Mitten des Balles (Count Leo Tolstoi)
Peter Tschaikowsky
Zueignung (Hermann von Gilm)   *Richard Strauss*
Madame Nordica

Der Nussbaum (Julius Mosen)   *Robert Schumann*
Ich Grolle nicht (Heine)   . .   "   "
Waldesgespräch (Eichendorff)   "   "
Madame Nordica

Vieille Chanson,   .   .   *Georges Bizet*
Nell (Leconte de Liske)   .   *Gabriel Faure*
Mattinata,   .   .   *Ruggiero Leoncavallo*
Care Selve (From Opera "Atalanta")   *Handel*
Madame Nordica

Berceuse   .   .   .   *Gabriel Faure*
Polonaise in A   .   .   .   *Wieniawski*
Mr. Spalding.

Twilight (Mary Baldwin)   .   *Walter Rummel*
There was an Ancient King (Heinrich Heine)
Georg Henschel
Damon (Goethe)   .   .   .   *Max Stange*
Madame Nordica

An die Musik (Schober)   *Franz Schubert*
Der Erlkonig (Goethe)   "   "
Madame Nordica

Everett Piano Used

For special announcements see second page following

Andre Benoist with his two daughters. Circa 1908.

said it was indeed too bad that they had to treat the poor little angels in such a cruel way. And smiling sweetly, she whispered in reply, "Yes, but they were thoughtful enough to leave the better half." I found it difficult to go on playing without exploding in laughter.

This tour really ended my connection with the great lady, for her next trip was to be in a new field: the Far East, including Japan and China. And I was loath to leave my home surroundings to go so far afield.

Madame Nordica never returned from that ill-fated voyage. On the way home across the Pacific, she became so ill that the steamer had to make a special stop at Thursday Island to let her enter the hospital. There she died shortly after landing.

Well it was, too, that I decided to stay home, for it was at that time that tragedy overtook me. My beautiful and gifted young wife caught a bad cold which in a short time developed into pneumonia, and within a very few days she died, leaving me a widower with two babies, two and three years old. It seemed more than anyone could bear, and even after this long span of years it seems dreadful that one so young, so beautiful, and so gifted should have met so untimely an end. She was barely twenty-six, and I a year older. My age, and the resultant lack in strength of character, is my only excuse for taking the weak man's remedy. I embarked on a career of drinking which left me most of the time in a completely befogged condition but which at the same time rather dulled the aching void inside me. Through the mental fog, however, I faintly remembered having promised my very dear friend Edwin Franko Goldman I would play the Grieg Concerto at a concert which he was to conduct. But in my mental condition I found it impossible to settle down to work, and kept putting off practicing from day to day. I did not even want to listen to music of any kind. So I drifted along until one day Mr. Goldman, or rather Eddie, as we affectionately called him, reminded me of the engagement.

Now, to break a promise to Eddie was unthinkable. He was the first true friend I had known, almost from the time of my arrival in America. He was, in those days, a cornet virtuoso of incomparable tone and technique; in fact the most brilliant pupil of the great Jules Levy, who in his day had been a sort of Paganini of the cornet. So when Eddie reminded me of my promise, I was appalled.

The concert was only ten days off and I hadn't touched a piano in weeks. But I saw at once that this was no trifling matter, and that to continue on my usual course was to invite disaster. The imminence of this concert was like an icy shower which brought me back to my senses. That night I went to bed sober and the next day I was hard at work once more, though Heaven knows what a struggle it was to keep my mind from drifting back to my grief. The fateful day of the performance came at last, and that day can only be described as a wakeful nightmare. Torn between the struggle to refrain from drink and the worry lest my memory would fail me, I arrived at the hall in a state of mind next to frenzy. But my good friend immediately relieved my mind by suggesting that I use the score on the piano, as, so he said, he had known some of the finest artists had done when playing with an orchestra. This I did, and I had only a faint recollection after the concert, of noisy hand-clapping, repeated bowing, and then blessed sleep to relieve frayed nerves. To have played that night, for the first time, without the encouraging presence of my departed love was indeed a bitter cup. But I never went back to drink after that.

One of Benoist's best friends was Edwin Goldman, the famous cornet player and bandleader. Benoist credits their friendship with saving him from the problem of alcoholism after the death of his first wife.

To my "old chum" Andre with my best wishes.

anuary 2nd 1923.

Edwin Franko Goldman

OVIDE MUSIN

BELGIAN VIOLINIST AND PEDAGOGUE

with over fifty years' experience as a virtuoso and FORMER HEAD
OF VIOLIN DEPARTMENT at the ROYAL CONSERVATORY of
LIEGE, BELGIUM, offers

Exceptional Opportunity to Violinists:

OVIDE MUSIN is holding classes at his studio, 769 Carroll Street, Brooklyn. Special attention is given to artistic phases of violin technique, and the interpretation of classics. Master Classes Weekly.

From Arthur M. Abell's Review in Musical Courier in April 29, 1920

I RECALL the furore Ovide Musin created as a virtuoso in the eighties, and in Liege, when at the zenith of his powers. He played with a great deal of warmth and élan, with a brilliant technic and a beautiful tone. His interpretations were noble spontaneous and individual. One thing he had in a degree which I have never heard from any other violinist, — his staccato. I have heard him play a rapid long run staccato, down bow, as fast as the best of violinists could play it. Then he would repeat it with two staccato strokes to each note, and then again with three strokes, keeping up meanwhile the same tempo. I have never known any other artist that could do it. Musin had a staccato of incredible speed and clearness. He always claimed—I have often talked with him about it—that any one could acquire it, but I think it was a special gift with him."

OVIDE MUSIN

For information address:

Belgian Conservatory of Music

769 Carroll Street   **Brooklyn, N. Y.**

An advertisement Musin took out in *The Violinist* magazine (now defunct). Musin also wrote an autobiography which he published himself after being unable to find an independent publisher.

Chapter IX

Earlier in these reminiscences I gave a slight topographical idea of the man R. E. Johnston. But I think he is entitled to a little more enlarging upon his background, and how he happened to become interested in the managing of artists. From the many conversations I had with him, the following is a summary: He was originally a traveling salesman, or as he put it, a "drummer" for a firm manufacturing silk ribbons. One day, on a train, he fell in with a gentleman who made a profound impression on him. This was easy, for it must be admitted that the one thing in life which Johnston was sincerely fond of was music, and more especially violin music. The man Johnston had met was the renowned violinist Ovide Musin, who had come from Belgium for a concert tour. The latter was bitterly complaining about the dishonesty of his present manager, and said that he was just about to give up his tour and go back to his home country. Of course Johnston had heard him play, for he never missed a violin concert if he could possibly help it. On the spur of the moment an idea flashed through his mind, upon which a long conversation ensued, the upshot being that he, Johnston, would take over the management of the Musin tour on a percentage basis. It, Johnston continued convincingly, would be easy, as he had had a good deal of experience with musical artists. This was partly true as he had shaken hands with a good many! Thereupon, he telegraphed his firm, severing his connection with them, and found himself suddenly launched on the career of Impresario. From ribbons to music would be a good name for his odyssey! However, the Musin tour finished, he found himself at loose ends, having no other artist to promote.

But in the back of his mind there lurked the memory of some rumors he had heard of another immensely gifted Belgian violinist who resided in Brussels. Nothing loath, he took the first available steamer and went over to Brussels. He found the correct address and arrived there, walked up five flights of stairs, knocked at a door, and on being bidden to enter by a sleepy voice, found the great artist in bed. He was a little taken aback, for after all, had he not made an appointment? Did this not savor a bit of rudeness? But no, explained the artist, it was only that he did not have his trousers on. "Well," quoth Johnston, "why not put them on so we can converse like human beings!" "That," replied the artist, "is where the difficulty lies. It is a matter of only twenty five francs which that confounded pawnbroker insists on collecting before he will give them up, and if you will step over to his shop and pay him, I shall be in a better position to receive you in the conventional way. Also, would you mind bringing back with the trousers, a roll and coffee?" Even Johnston, hardened as he was in the ways of the world, was a little staggered. However, he did as he was asked, but inwardly noted the penury in which he had found the artist, and secretly vowed he would profit thereby. At last he returned with the trousers, accompanied by a waiter from a nearby cafe, bearing coffee and rolls. Having consumed these and made himself somewhat more presentable, the young man proved to be a cadaverous looking individual, with a mane of hair that almost reached his shoulders. He looked undernourished, quite pale, and very interesting, thought Johnston. Upon being asked to play something, the young man started on the *Chaconne* by Bach, which happened to be a composition Johnston adored and by which he generally judged a violinist's capacities. In which he was right, for, while being atrociously difficult, it is undoubtedly one of the greatest tests of an artist's imaginative powers, as well as being a technical test. Johnston was literally bowled over by the artist's conception of this great work and without further ado, proposed to bring him over to America for a trans-continental tour. At this, the young artist demurred. "But," exclaimed Johnston, "you evidently have very little money and I am in a position to have you earn plenty!" "Yes, of that I'm sure," came the answer, "but it is so nice here with all my friends; I have a good job in a fine cafe that pays me well enough, and why should I leave these home

Three young violinists from Liege, Belgium when they played in a small recital hall in Ostende in 1876. They are, from left to right: Ovide Musin, Eugene Ysaye and Arthur Gide.

Eugene Ysaye, the great Belgian violinist and friend of Benoist.

surroundings to go all over creation among alien people? I think I would be miserable." These discussions went on endlessly until Johnston finally persuaded the young man that after all, the tour once ended, he could always come back to his home port. That decided it. And so came the day of arrival in America. Johnston had photographs produced that made the artist look like a caricature of Paganini at his worst. He had these labelled in large red letters *AN INSPIRED GENIUS* and sent broadcast. Owing to this sensational publicity, Carnegie Hall was crowded. But this time against all expectations, the publicity, strong as it was, had even underrated the artist. His name was EUGENE YSAYE. Need I say more? His sensational success placed both these men in the front rank of their respective professions, and Ysaye became a legend. As a matter of fact, when he played, he was like a lion let loose. But it is profitless to expatiate upon qualities that have remained standards by which most violinists are judged even today.

Ysaye was also a faithful and loyal friend of mine. I have never played with him in public, but often privately. This was always a great pleasure; for, freed from the necessity of showmanship, with which he was plentifully endowed, he would sail into the music like a huge cruiser intent on arriving in port in a spectacular manner. "Grand manner" really best describes everything he touched in music. By the time I became acquainted with Ysaye, he had completely lost his undernourished appearance, and had grown to enormous proportions both in height (which he always had), and in girth. He looked Falstaffian, and was a gargantuan eater and drinker. He often would reminisce of the days when a meal was but a problematic dream to be solved only by shrewd political maneuvering. One of his stories made a deep impression on me. It seems that at the time of his first marriage, he was desperately poor. He had a friend in Paris who was just as unacquainted with "the source of all evil." Now this friend wrote him a letter which came with a carefully wrapped package, explaining that, not having the wherewithal to purchase a suitable wedding present, he had written the accompanying composition for Ysaye and his bride, and he hoped they would like his modest gift. The composition was the immortal Sonata in A Major and the donor was Cesar Franck. Modest indeed!

I have digressed considerably, but only to give an idea of the man

To André Benoit — Affectionate Souvenir
of Mozart Sonatas —

Albert Spalding

July 1908

Johnston, who rang me up one Spring morning and excitedly said, "Benoist, I have gotten myself in a pickle and I want you to come down to my office as soon as you can possibly do so!" Johnston in a pickle? thought I; that must be interesting. Arriving at the office, I was taken to the "inner sanctum" and there sat Johnston simmering and almost at the boiling point. What was the matter, I queried. "Well," said Johnston, "here's the story: you've no doubt heard of the young fiddler, Albert Spalding?" I allowed that I had. In fact I had heard a great deal too much. The usual press drivel; that he had gotten lost somewhere in the Alps, that he had eloped with some Russian Countess, etc. etc. "No," said Johnston, "that isn't the one; you mean the other young American, MacMillan." "Alright," I said, "in my mind they're birds of a feather. Now, what?" "Well," he replied, "this one is really a great fiddler. I heard him play and I can judge. But that's beside the point. I had heard of this boy, and also that his family was endowed with plenty of worldly goods. So I thought it a great idea to go to Europe where they reside in the winter, to see if they would like the boy to come over for his first American tour under my management. Of course, they would be expected to pay all the expenses of advertising, promotion, advance work, traveling, etc." "Well," I said, "you were going true to form!" "Wait a moment," came the reply, "that isn't all of it; I talked with Mr. Spalding, Sr. for hours, and when I was through, I had signed a contract guaranteeing a tour of thirty concerts at a fixed fee! In other words, *they* had hooked *me*, R. E. Johnston!" I could not help saying, "Let that be a lesson to you. Never underrate your opponent!" "That's all very well," said Johnston, "but I have not heard that boy play for quite a while now, and I wish you'd go over and hear him for yourself and give me a report as to what you think of his chances over here. Will you do that for me?"

While I did not relish the idea too much, having had some sad experiences in that way, I consented, and Johnston made an appointment for me to meet the young man the next day. I arrived at the time designated at a mansion on Riverside Drive, which, it appeared, belonged to a friend of the Spalding family. There I was met by a very young man, shy and extremely reserved. We talked for a few minutes of this and that. The young man spoke fluent French and Italian, (besides his native tongue), had traveled exten-

Great violinists of the turn of the Century: 1. Henri Marteau. 2. Martin Marsick. 3. Jules Massart. 4. Joan Manen. 5. Francis Macmillan. 6. Ovide Musin. 7. Mischa Mischakoff. 8. David Mannes.

A rare 1908 portrait of Albert Spalding.

sively and knew everybody who was worth knowing. I thought, "If he plays half as well as he talks, it will be interesting indeed." He played finally, and I was immediately entranced.

Whether it was Bach, Beethoven, Mozart, Brahms or even Debussy, it was right. This boy had everything. But he had one major fault, which was on the verge of a crime: He was an American, not by adoption, but his people had come to America as early as the Seventeenth Century. How could a real American be a great musician? That would be the general consensus and I was to be proven right. However, I had come to meet this boy at two o'clock, after lunch, expecting to remain for about half an hour, but I remained until close to dinner time, and even then literally had to tear myself away. Little did I know then what a lifetime friendship and collaboration this meeting portended. I duly reported to Johnston, who thought I had gone out of my mind when I told him what I thought of his new artist. Shortly thereafter, young Spalding sailed back to Europe where he had already been appreciated, and where several engagements were awaiting him. On my side, a tour was starting for which I was quite keyed up and full of curiosity. It was to be with the great Italian diva, Luisa Tetrazzini, and came out thusly. . .

Chapter X

I was awakened one morning by the ringing of the doorbell, and a telegram was handed me that contained a rather laconic message from one William H. Leahy, asking whether I would be interested in going on tour with the famous coloratura soprano Luisa Tetrazzini, at quite a high fee. That name, of course, I knew well, for it had become involved in a protracted law suit, and the newspapers were forever full of it. But Leahy. . . who in thunder was Leahy? I racked my brain for nearly a half hour, and then the whole story came back to me. When I first went to California in 1901, Leahy, or rather "Doc" Leahy as everybody called him, had been the general manager of the old Tivoli Opera House, where for the top price of 75 cents one could see and hear *La Traviata, Aida, La Boheme* or what have you in the operatic repertoire, all done very adequately by a fair company. Among other singers, there was one in particular who created quite a sensation. Her name was Tetrazzini and I suddenly remembered "Doc" telling me how he had been able to secure her services. It seems that when he first heard of her she was singing in Argentina or Brazil. The reports were so laudatory that in his impulsive way he thought he would make her an offer. Of course, he knew that any reasonable offer in American dollars would prove an almost irresistible bait for an artist used to the small fees paid an unknown in that part of the world. On receipt of Leahy's message, Tetrazzini, although she had an ironclad contract with her present management, decided to accept it. She shrewdly figured that, although a rear entrance, here was an open door to the United States and fame and fortune. But how to get out of the present country, where penalties for breach of contract were very heavy, going so far, in some cases, as a jail sentence?? And for this, young Luisa had no relish! Consequently this is the way she set about to circumvent the law:

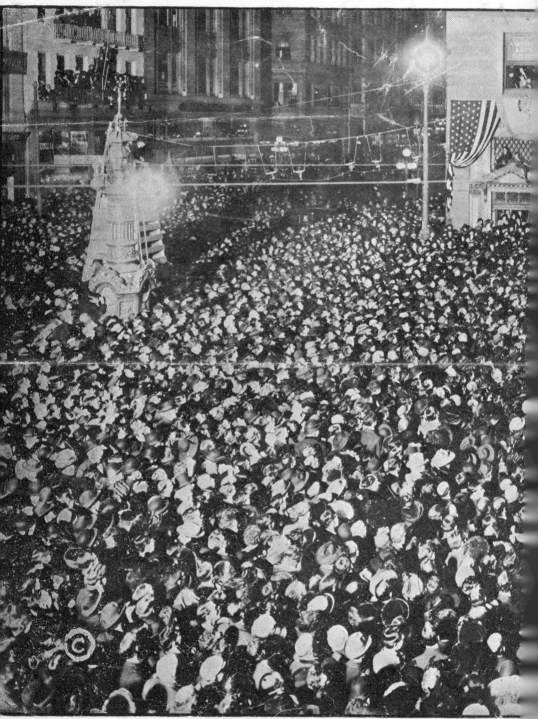

TETRAZZINI'S CHRISTMAS GIFT TO THE PE

SAN FRANCISCO (250,000 People in Attendance)

An autographed photograph of the great soprano Luisa Tetrazzini, with whom Benoist toured, shortly before joining forces with Albert Spalding. Dated December 16, 1910.

Being quite slim and petite, she dressed herself in a young man's clothes, bought a boyish wig, and pasted on her upper lip a downy mustache. Thus she boarded the steamer unrecognized. But to her horror, once in her cabin she heard a commotion on deck, and on inquiring from the steward, was informed that the police were looking for a lady who was escaping from the law. Thereupon, not knowing what better to do, she ran to the men's lavatory and stood herself alongside other men in the position nature ordained for the stronger sex. So that when the police came to investigate that supposedly private part of the ship, her back being to the door, all the dogs of the law saw were the backs of six males, all very much occupied. With deep apologies they withdrew, and our diva's worries were over.

In due time she arrived in San Francisco, and there made her debut at the Tivoli. Although that Opera House was not recognized as first class, she managed to create a sensation and for a while was the talk of the town. However, as suddenly as she had appeared on the musical horizon, she disappeared. She had had an offer to sing in London, and frankly told Leahy of her good fortune. And goodhearted as he was, he did not care to stand in her way to further conquests. The only stipulation he made in releasing her from her obligations was that, should she ever come to America again to sing, it would be exclusively under his management. She cheerfully agreed.

I will not dwell on her success in England, for that is history today. Suffice it to say that on the strength of that success, one of our great impresarios of that time, Oscar Hammerstein, went over to London and made her such a dazzling offer that Luisa, blinded by it, completely forgot her promise to "Doc" Leahy and signed some sort of preliminary agreement with Hammerstein. Arrived back in America, and having heard of the new arrangement, Leahy immediately started an injunction suit against Hammerstein, claiming that his agreement with the prima donna predated the one with Hammerstein. With that began a series of suits and countersuits that kept her name on the front page of the newspapers daily. All good and free reclame.

The upshot was that Leahy won the final round, for the time being at least, and hence his telegram to me. Naturally I wired back accepting the offer and awaited further instructions. These came finally, asking me to meet the Signora at the old Manhattan Hotel. On the day appointed I went there, and was received by none other than my old friend Leahy. After much reminiscing, Leahy suddenly yelled "Hey! Luisa! Come in here a moment" and from an inner chamber waddled the queerest figure of a lady my eyes had beheld in a long time. She was practically as broad as she was high, and on her head was a reddish wig which had apparently been donned in a hurry. This was Luisa Tetrazzini! The Signora did not speak; she twittered. I was introduced and all she found to say in acknowledgment was, "Ma! e carino il piccino" ("My, the boy is very cute"). Of music, not a word. Cautiously I inquired whether the Signora would perhaps like to try singing something with me at the piano, but she demurred. However, after much coaxing, she consented to try a few bars of "Una voce poco fa" and at the fifth or sixth she stopped, saying "Basta cosi, va bene?" ("That's enough, OK?").

With that, she twittered some more in voluble Italian, much of which I did not understand. She was addressing a short, fat Italian, the possessor of the blackest, shiniest hair and the pastiest complexion imaginable. I inquired later from Leahy who he was and what was his official position. "I don't exactly know," answered the latter, "but it seems he is a former Italian or Roumanian tenor who had fallen on evil days when the Madame picked him up somewhere, and he is constantly complaining of being tired, though he eats like a horse. There doesn't seem to be any sentimental attachment between the two, for, as you will learn in time, Madame has no use for the male of the species, except at rare times when something in her nature appears to reverse itself, and then there's the devil to pay. But wait, and you'll find out!" Thus Leahy.

I must confess that never had I such an attack of stage fright than at the American debut of this peculiar prima donna. To this there were several contributing causes. In the first place, I never did rehearse with her. All she did, was on the day before the concert, warble in half voice the different cadenzas she interpolated here and there in her several arias. Of the song literature, she was almost totally ignorant, with the exception of two or three old Italian ones. Moreover, at three o'clock on the afternoon of the concert, Leahy rang me up frantically saying, "What shall I do?

A newspaper clipping taken during the tour with Tetrazzini. From left to right: Frederick Hastings, the baritone who toured with them; Andre Benoist; Guy Golterman; Mrs. William Leahy, wife of the manager; Mme. Tetrazzini; Tetrazzini's husband; Mr. Bauman of the Anheuser-Busch Company; Walter Oesterreicher; and William "Doc" Leahy, manager of the tour.

Andre Benoist's business card for the 1911-1912 season.

What shall I do?" I suspected catastrope and mentally prepared to pack my luggage, thinking we would all soon be on our way homeward bound. So I gingerly murmured into the receiver, "Why, what's happened?" Leahy's voice was shaking when he replied, "The Madame is ill; she is doubled up with cramps, and Dreamland Skating Rink is sold out at five dollars a seat! 6,500 seats! I'm ruined!" Upon which I inquired, "What does Madame say?" "Oh," said Leahy, "she says she will sing no matter what!" "Well," I said, "What are you worrying about then? If she says she will sing, she will sing." "Yes, but how?" came the reply. "Well," I said, "that's something to worry about, but only after the concert, so let's forget it for the present; I have enough to think about now." And with that I hung up the receiver.

At the appointed time I arrived at the rink. The huge auditorium was crowded to capacity. I knocked at the door of Madame's dressing room and was bidden to enter by a weak voice. There was our diva, seated on a chair, her knees up, and her heels dug in the rim of the seat. She was green under her makeup and perspiring profusely. In the most optimistic voice I could muster, I inquired how she felt, to which she replied in her own English, "I no fella good but Ah singa, Ah allaways singa!" "My!," I thought, "this is a

150

night to remember!" Then Leahy entered and in a tremulous voice announced: "Luisa, it is time." Her heels came to the floor, and with a visible effort she raised herself from the chair and straightened herself. A slow smile sketched itself on her face and she started for the stage. I, in her wake, felt like an assistant executioner following the condemned to the guillotine. An ovation greeted her appearance. Thunders of applause, cries of "Welcome Luisa" welled up from the frantic audience. In response she had the unbelievable fortitude to drop a low curtsey. I stood by, ready to help her up if need be. But it was unnecessary. She slowly straightened up, a look of agony under the fixed smile. At last she began to sing. It was the "Cara Nome" from *Rigoletto*, and never have I seen such a fantastic exhibition of beauty of tone, skill of singing, and true heroism. Her roulades and trills came forth perfectly, and she ended with the high E which she attacked pianissimo, started for the exit door, and as she approached it, swelled the E until it sounded like a clarion. She held it as she bowed low and disappeared. I followed her as pandemonium broke loose in the hall, and slowly she went back to her dressing room, resumed her seat, raised her heels once more, and said, "Ah no fella good, bot Ah singa, Ah allaways singa!

Heroism is not only found on the field of battle. In this manner, she finished the program, with long rests between numbers. Her success is still a legend in old San Francisco. In fact, as a proof of her gratitude to the city that had first recognized her talents, she offered to sing on Christmas Eve on the street in front of the San Francisco Chronicle. This offer was quickly accepted, and the City erected a stand in front of the Chronicle Building on which was placed a grand piano. A crowd of over 100,000 people filled the street in reverent silence as Madame began to sing, and when it was over, San Francisco had proved to its coming rival, Los Angeles, that its climate was good enough for a world-acclaimed diva to risk her voice and well-being by singing in the public streets! They named the place where she had sung Tetrazzini Square.

But, great artist and courageous as she was, this woman had her very childish side. She neither studied nor rehearsed. She was even too lazy to have her hair dressed. This hair, which was really lovely, she would arrange in close pigtails around her head and over this she would don a reddish wig. So that on any occasion she would be ready to go forth in the world with the hairdo she desired at the moment.

She had three diversions that were paramount in her life on tour: First came eating large platters of spaghetti; second came the movies; and last but not least, playing dominoes. Her superstitions were innumerable, but one stands out in my mind. She would only sing on Mondays and Thursdays, which she considered her "lucky days." No matter what fees were offered her to sing on any other days, she would flatly refuse, and no argument could budge her from her decision. All this would complicate bookings tremendously, and poor "Doc" Leahy was constantly in hot water over it. Once in six or seven weeks, the impresario would be at his wit's end. The first time this happened, he rang up frantically saying, "She says 'Ah no singa tonight' and when I asked her why, she said, 'Ah wanta a man!' Now Ben, what shall I do?" There, indeed, was a problem! For generally after discovering a male sufficiently devoted to the cause of music to be willing to comfort the lady, one look at her waddling figure caused him to shake his head with discouragement, implying the phrase: "I pass; no bid." But sometimes by adding a bit of pecuniary reward to diplomatic persuasion, the matter was concluded to everyone's satisfaction. The result was high good humor and a superb performance by the prima donna. The tour went on for some weeks in a routine manner, and at last the constant playing of the same accompaniments for the same arias began to pall on me. To vary the monotony, I thought it might help to elaborate a little on some of the piano parts which, as often is the case with Donizetti, Bellini, and Rossini, are rather thin and stupid. I thought the Madame too, would be pleased by the enhancing of her musical background. What was my surprise then, when one morning I was sent for preemptorily, and on arriving at Madame's sitting room, found her, surrounded by Leahy and the oleaginous former tenor Bazzelli, all in a thunderous mood. What it was all about I could not fathom. I racked my brains to think what I could have done to produce this effect, when "Doc" Leahy suddenly yelled: "Luisa claims that you are a spy sent out by Hammerstein to spoil her effects on the stage!" Naturally, I immediately thought that this was a practical joke; but no, it could not be. The grim faces before me were not in a joking mood. I tried to look as innocent as possible under the circumstances, and mildly inquired what all the fuss was about. "Well," translated Leahy, "Madame says that you are continually changing her accompaniments, and that you have been paid by the Hammerstein clique to do this so as to upset her and thus spoil her singing." I couldn't believe my ears. Such utter nonsense! Could anyone be stupid enough to believe such a thing? But there it was, and I was face to face with it! It took me hours to convince all concerned that what I had done was only with the in-' tention of adding beauty to the performance; and when realization finally dawned on Tetrazzini, she melted into tears, kissed me on both cheeks and asked that I just play what was written in the score. There followed a general spree of back-patting from Bazzelli and Leahy and a copious lunch which ended a most embarrassing situation. And in proof that the whole episode was a thing of the past, at the end of the tour Madame was pleased to give me, as a princely present, a gold Jurgenson Chromometre repeater watch, which I still treasure to this day. But only as a museum piece, for I soon noticed that when wearing it, its weight made me limp on one side!

One of the most amusing incidents I can recall during the Tetrazzini tour occurred in St. Louis. It so happened that we had a few days to rest in that city, and, having an evening free, Madame suggested that we go in a party to a variety show which had been highly recommended to her by friends. The star of the show was that wonderful comedienne, Marie Dressler, and Madame was so taken with her performance that she insisted on going backstage to meet her. This was done, and through some rather able translation in addition to fervid gesticulation, it was given to understand that Miss Dressler had been invited to have dinner with Madame Tetrazzini the following evening at the Hotel Jefferson. It must be realized that Miss Dressler spoke no Italian, and our diva hardly any English. Consequently, I was placed between the two so as to do any translation necessary. Bazzelli, Luisa's "husband" was placed on her left, where, as she quaintly put it, "she could keep an eye on him," as he might imbibe a wee bit too much. And it must be admitted that Bazzelli already was beginning to show symptoms of having partaken of a few comforting cocktails.

Then came Miss Dressler, flanked by a stalwart red-headed

Irishman, whom she introduced as her husband. He also seemed to be in a flowering condition and swayed a bit as he carefully lowered himself in his seat. He was placed on his wife's right. This, for the same reason, Miss Dressler asked me to explain to our prima donna, that the latter had given for wishing to have *her* husband near her. Up to that moment, both ladies had been their most dignified selves, but when the third course had been served accompanied by many toasts drunk in delicious champagne, the ladies had reached the lachrymose and confidential stage themselves, and I was beginning to experience considerable difficulty in continuing the translation of all the hardships each had been through in trying to maintain their individual husbands at the right temperature! The last I remember of them was their leaning across me, in each other's arms and weeping copiously over their mutual sorrows. Marie Dressler came to our concert the following day, and her verdict was that Luisa would be a great "hit" in vaudeville. Little did she realize how true was her prophesy.

This last tour ended and Madame Tetrazzini went back to Europe, where another series of triumphs awaited her. But these were of short duration, for an unfortunate marriage to a boy of twenty-three, and sundry careless investments, began to downgrade her career. Added to this, her growing obesity aided by her overindulgence in the gastronomic pleasures coupled with a lack of exercise, combined in bringing on a shortness of breath which proved fatal in her art. The last time I saw her was in a variety show in Boston. She had become so stout that, being unable to walk on the stage gracefully, she had been placed on a small platform around which her long skirts had been draped, and upon this scene the curtains parted. It was rather a pitiful sight and performance. Once more the depressing thought came to me: Why, oh why do artists not know when to end their careers in time? Anyway, for Luisa death came suddenly to bring an end to further humiliations.

Chapter
XI

Springtime was upon us, and it was with intense surprise that I received, one bright morning, a message from Albert Spalding, asking whether I would be interested in coming a few times a week to his home in Monmouth Beach, New Jersey, to help him prepare his repertoire for the following season. I gathered from what he said that his European accompanist, Alfredo Oswald, the son of the distinguished Brazilian composer, would not arrive in America until the autumn, and this would be a pleasant opportunity to renew our acquaintance as well as to play some interesting music. Of course, besides the pleasure, there was to be remuneration. The combination proved to be an irresistible lure, and I accepted with enthusiasm.

Those summer months are unforgettable to this late day. The atmosphere of the Spalding home had this happy balance that lies between the most free and most lavish hospitality, coupled with gentle but strict discipline when it came to art and the study thereof. But when the day's work was over, and all gathered around the festive board, the interest of all concerned in everything that mattered in the universe was so intense that it was the most exhilarating experience imaginable to be present. And let me add that the Spalding hospitality was extended to anyone they deemed interesting, so that these gatherings would assume at times the most heterogeneous aspects. It was true democracy in operation! As for young Spalding's playing, I can only say that even in those early days, everything he did was guided by an unerring instinct for beauty and perfection. His tone, while being more silk than velvet in texture, was penetrating and true. In short, it was a summer of musical delight, which alas came to a close too soon. In

This was the Spalding summer mansion in Monmouth Beach, New Jersey. Over the years all of the mansions in the area gradually succumbed to the times and all that remains of this magnificence are the gates, overgrown with weeds.

spite of the stress of a forthcoming tour, I tried to follow the career of this young man from a distance, and could not help marveling once more at the imbecility of the musical critics. They not only contradicted each other, but oft times would contradict themselves. One especially, the late H. E. Krehbiel, wrote such scurrilous articles that in themselves they became a source of propaganda, thus acting as boomerangs! Endless feuds took place in the press rooms, until the matter became almost comical. This Krehbiel I knew well, having traveled with him when he was giving learned lectures on the English version of Wagner's *Parsifal.* I had to do the illustrating of the spoken word at the piano. And in my conversations with him, I found that he gathered most of his information from different reference works and encyclopedias, which anyone of us could have done equally well, given the time to devote to this sort of research.

His judgment, I found, was tinged on all things by what he either read or heard. And this was one of the high Gods that sat in judgment of an artist's value to the world! However, I was too occupied at the time to go into the matter thoroughly. And I was none too happy about my forthcoming assignment.

But, before proceeding, I must return for a moment to those happy first days of summer in Monmouth Beach. For among the numerous characters I had the pleasure of meeting at the Spalding home, one stands out. His name was Juan Buitrago, and he had been one of young Albert's first violin teachers. At the time I met him, he was advanced in years. His face, deeply lined, was as though it had been carved out of granite, but with this difference: instead of carrying a harsh or forbidding expression, it radiated benevolence and kindness. This old gentleman's manner was courtly in the extreme and every gesture or motion savored of the Old World. He would sit quietly by the hour listening to our rehearsing, nodding his head in time with the music, and when it was all over he would, with a courtly bow, express his delight in what he had heard. I did not at first understand the relationship that existed between Mr. Buitrago and the Spalding family and it was not until quite later that it was explained to me by one of Mr. Spalding's grandmothers, Mrs. Boardman.

It seems that Mr. Buitrago was a native of Colombia, in South America, and having had an unfortunate love affair with a great ar-

Mischa Elman autographed this photograph to Benoist in 1908. Elman was the most popular of violinists until Heifetz came upon the American scene.

tist, (rumor named the great pianist Teresa Carreño), he had remained a bachelor. Not having any living relatives he had become a close friend of the composer MacDowell's family, with whom he from then on had made his home. When the famous composer came to an untimely end, Mr. Buitrago was quite forlorn, for he had not lived alone for so long a time that the prospect of so lonely a life appalled him. Besides, as was natural for one of his type, he was not blessed with worldly goods, though that did not seem to worry him. When reference was ever made to finances, he would shake his shoulder length gray mane and murmur, "Oh, one needs so little!" Then came the following Christmas and young Spalding was asked as usual what would give him the greatest pleasure to receive on that occasion. He was, of course, given several choices, none of which seemed to satisfy him. At their wits' end, the family asked him what it was he really wanted. And the embarrassed reply that came in halting words gives an idea of the boy's generosity and selflessness that later developed into the great human being he became: "Well," quoth he, "I would like to have Mr. Buitrago make his permanent home with us until his end comes." This was granted at once and so it was done. After many happy years with his adopted family, the old gentleman died in Florence, Italy and was buried in the Spalding family plot.

I must now retrace my steps a bit to return to the period of the Spalding debut. At that time appeared on the American musical horizon a violinistic comet that left a long tail of debutants behind him. The heralding and glamor that prophesied his coming had been unequaled since the days of Kubelik. He was sponsored by a combination of managers that wielded unprecedented power and prestige. These were Daniel Frohman, Oscar Hammerstein and Henry Wolfsohn. He was presented to the American public in ten Sunday night appearances at Hammerstein's Manhattan Opera House. Such a launching could not fail to spell success, provided the subject of all this colossal propaganda had the gifts to justify it. And this young artist had those gifts and in plentiful quantity. His name was Mischa Elman and he made history overnight. He came fresh from triumphs in London and Berlin, and backed by these, his assurance on the stage was overpowering. He astonished everyone by his dazzling technique and gorgeous tone.

He was at times rather erratic as to rhythm, but, in his case, that

A brief note from Josef Bonime, Mischa Elman's accompanist at the time. Mischa Elman seems to have straightened out the true meaning of the note by writing the word LIAR and signing his name.

was ascribed to youthful exuberance. Such allowances were never made for American artists. They were immediately damned, then ignored, as many learned to their sorrow. But to return to young Mischa. It would be trite to speak of his career, for everyone is aware of his worth. Many stories have been told about him, as a man, and many have either caricatured or maligned him. For my part, I only played with him once in public and enjoyed it thoroughly. I found that through the years, he was a loyal and generous friend. We often have visited each other and played together at each other's homes, which at that time were in the same neighborhood on the New Jersey coast. I would like to quote an example of his quick wit. We were playing a piece that ended in a flamboyant flourish. As Mischa struck the last chord, a passing train emitted a long drawn-out whistle, completely drowning out the violin and piano sound. Quick as a flash, he turned to me and slyly said, "Succes d'estime" (indifferent success), essaying a multilingual pun.

160

Mischa Mischakoff at a concert he gave at the Bohemians in New York in 1976. He was assisted at the piano by Edmund Battersby while Dr. Herbert R. Axelrod was the page turner.

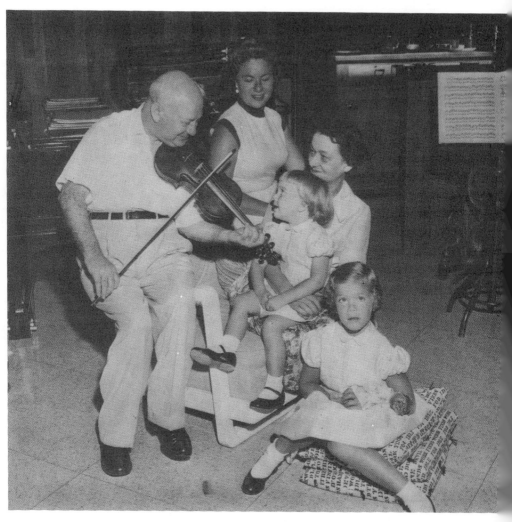

Mischa Elman with his family in his later years.

Another story that comes to me shows his kind heart and generosity toward a fellow artist. At a gathering of musicians in Chicago, at the home of Mischa Mischakoff, another noted violinist, during an interlude in the ensemble playing, Elman inadvertently laid one of his priceless bows on a chair. Evidently, Mischakoff must have failed to notice the bow, and sat down on the chair that held it. Result: broken bow for Elman and broken heart for Mischakoff! The poor fellow could not be consoled for his awful deed. Of course, everyone present expected fireworks from the temperamental Elman. But to the general surprise, the latter took Mischakoff by the arm and endeavored to calm him. After partially succeeding in this, Elman proposed that all hands repair to the nearest coffee shop and there refresh themselves, as his guests, and forget about the whole thing. I have mentioned this little story to help dissipate a current belief that all artists are notoriously "temperamental." As a matter of fact, the so-called business man, who so smugly looks upon artists as something queer in the scheme of creation, is the one who sins most grievously in that direction. What is this mysterious kink that is popularly known as "temperament"? Of course, it is a misnomer. True temperament is a natural impulsiveness that warms the heart; it should be at the root of all artistic endeavor, provided it is controlled by a logical and well-balanced mind.

But what is really the general conception of the word "temperament" is "bad manners under stress." That is not true of the really great artist. It most often appears in the mediocre one, who finds it necessary to put on this "act" to cover deficiencies in his or her work, and thereby often succeeds in blinding the injudicious. No! The truly "temperamental" one is the business man. For when anything goes awry in his office, see him tramp up and down, curse and swear everybody around him into a blue funk, and blame all that happens on his underlings. . . only to go home at night and weep on his wife's shoulder over the hardships he has to endure from his stupid employees! Besides, what is paramount in this man's world? First, the desire to accumulate more and more money, which usually goes partly to his government and partly to his heirs. Secondly, golf, football, baseball, card playing, a round of night clubs, and entertaining. The latter comprises so many boring things that it seems useless to elucidate.

Thelma Given, a child prodigy of Prof. Auer. She passed away in December, 1977.

Now contrast this with the wide range of interests that confronts the real artist-musician. He also must be a "business man," for must he not estimate his worth at its true value? Must he not sell his services, if only to a management? Must he not know a great deal about psychology, philosophy, humanities, etc.? Have read innumerable books on all sorts of subjects? Be amiable, considerate, and try never to offend anyone? Yes indeed! Or he would not be able to convey to the listener all the contents of the great music he interprets.

But to return to the boy, Elman. He undoubtedly blazed a trail which was followed by a great many aspirants for public favor in his same field. There were Max Rosen, Thelma Given, Toscha Seidel and numerous others; but none succeeded in displacing or even approaching him in public favor. It was not until 1917 that his throne began to rock slightly, and that was under the impact of another comet of the same kind and source. But that is another story!

165

Efrem Zimbalist is a famous introvert. He still lives in virtual seclusion in the midwest. His son, Efrem Zimbalist, Jr., is a famous television personality.

Chapter
XII

In the meantime the enjoyable summer of 1910 came to an end, which meant for me an approaching season of free-lancing. Among the artists I had the pleasure of accompanying was a newcomer, Efrem Zimbalist. He, like Elman, came from Russia. He had studied under the same masters, and came from the same people. But there the resemblance ended. I met Zimbalist, together with my newly wedded wife, at the home of friends of his where he was staying, and I must admit that to our intense surprise I had rarely come in contact with so negative a personality. He was so shy that conversation became at once difficult. He also was modest and retiring to a fault. However, we carried on as well as we could, and upon inquiring as to whether he was looking forward to his playing in America, picture our astonishment when he replied, "Well, yes, but I don't like to play the violin! I wish it were the piano instead, which I really love!"

One incident comes to my mind which happened in Baltimore, Maryland. We were there to play a recital at the Peabody Conservatory of Music, and it was about an hour or so before we had to start for the hall. We were in Zimbalist's sitting room at the Stafford Hotel, which is just across the Square from the Peabody Institute. He was practicing a few passages from the program we were to perform, when I felt myself suddenly so ill that I was unable to stand up. Nausea and cold perspiration assailed me. "Ah!," thought I, "something you ate in that infernal dining car on the way out." Zimbalist in turning towards me, must have noticed something wrong, for he asked me what was the matter. I told him. "Good God," he exclaimed, "is that the way my playing affects you?" I tried as best I could to assuage his fears, which was

Benoist's first rented home in Monmouth Beach, New Jersey.

difficult in my rather weak condition, whereupon he had me plied with remedies which proved beneficial enough to enable me to go through the performance as scheduled.

The season was busier than I had anticipated, but finally it came to an end, and with this ending came visions of another happy summer of music with the Spalding household as a background. But this time, instead of coming to Monmouth Beach as a commuter, I would be installed as a neighbor. We had discovered, with the aid of the Spalding family, a little cottage which fulfilled all the dreams contained in old English story books. We rented it for the summer, and never having had time for a honeymoon since my remarriage, my wife and I decided that this would be an ideal time to remedy the unavoidable delay caused by the pressure of professional engagements.

168

Monmouth Beach proved to be a perfect setting for study as well as recreation. I had heard a great deal about its former glories, when in the gay eighties it was one of the exclusive resorts of the wealthy or famous or both. There were still "des restante de splendeurs" (remnants of splendor), especially along the ocean front. Places that housed such people as Diamond Jim Brady, Lillian Russell, the George Bakers, the Lewis Nixons, etc. The natives of this quaint village were mostly fishermen and sundry workers with their families. But now, with the disappearance of horse racing from the neighborhood, gone were the ancient glories of beautiful equipages drawn by teams of blooded horses; gone were the beautiful highly corseted ladies, holding a parasol in one hand and a lorgnette in the other. Alas! The automobile was beginning to rear its ugly head; there were even rumors afloat that some had witnessed mad speeds of twenty-five miles an hour, and that something ought to be done about it! This could not go on! It was becoming a public menace!

The family from whom we rented our little cottage was rather remarkable. The matriarchal system was in full force in their home. Their name was Mr. and Mrs. Oliver Dodd Byron and they both had spent their life in the theatre. Mr. Byron was an old Shakespearean actor, and everything he did or said savored of the great Bard. His every gesture and expression were grandiloquent. He would lift a refuse container with amplitude of motion, and in stentorian tones would explain the reason for his carrying it. His wife Kate was born Kate Krehan and had been all her life a comedienne, somewhat on the order of the more recent Marie Dressler. She was a sister of the great tragedienne Ada Rehan, who, upon entering the more legitimate side of the theatre, decided to omit the K in her name so as to avoid confusion between the two actresses. Kate Byron was unique and inimitable. You could have cut her Irish brogue with a knife and her fund of anecdotes about her sister, the Barrymores, the Russells and the Drews, to all of whom she was allied either by blood or marriage, was limitless. She must have been deep in her seventies when we first met her, but her energy, wit, and repartee kept us in roars of laughter every moment.

On the other hand, Oliver's humor was sly and subtle, as became a true Shakespearean. They had both retired professionally, while their son Arthur was on the road to become, in his turn, a famous actor. Mr. Byron had, with the aid of his son, built most of the cottages from which they derived their income through rentals, with his own hands. That was his hobby and his joy. And it was in one of these that we were to spend one of the happiest summers we had known. The season was enhanced by the presence of the Thibaud family, who had taken a house in our vicinity. Musical evenings after daytime practicing, wonderful dinner parties, tennis playing and beach swimming, all contributed to making the season pass like a dream.

As I said before, Mr. and Mrs. Spalding were princely in their hospitality. But their sweet simplicity of approach together with undisguised pleasure in seeing others enjoy themselves, surpassed even this hospitality. Both my wife and I learned to love and admire them for qualities too numerous to enumerate.

One morning, while sitting on the veranda quietly smoking, Mr. Spalding, Sr. turned to me and casually remarked, "You seem to get along very well with Albert." I agreed, adding that I could not think of an easier person to get along with, both musically or personally. His one eye (for he had lost one in a dreadful accident) beamed at me. I could read delight in his every feature. "That being the case," he went on, "how would you like to accompany him on a permanent basis?" I must confess to my astonishment, but I replied that nothing would give me more pleasure, though I added, "I have certain commitments for the autumn that cannot be cancelled." I explained to him however, that this commitment was only for a fall tour which would end in early December. "Why that's fine," he exclaimed, "Albert isn't starting his European tour until after Christmas, and when you are finished with your forthcoming tour, you can join us in Florence, where the European tour will start!" Thereupon financial arrangements were discussed for a few minutes, after which we shook hands, and I went back to the piano.

An autographed photograph of J.W. Spalding, Albert's father. The Spalding family made their fortune in the sporting goods field.

Yours truly
E. W. Spalding
Aug 22. 1915

That is the only contract I ever had with Albert Spalding, and in fact the only contract I ever had with any artist I was associated with. I have never found it necessary to go through any form of legal arrangements with any one of them, and have never had any reason for regretting it. Unlike a great many "business men," I always found that the artist's word was his bond, and that whatever he or she promised was almost always honored. Of course, they may, as a rule, be a little less business-like, but also they are less liable to quibble as to certain small details that can always be arranged amicably without loss to either of the parties concerned. Their minds are more elastic and resilient, for which reason they are more apt to see the other fellow's point of view.

As all good things come to an end, this lovely summer too had ended and we turned our steps city-ward. Also came the time to start rehearsing with Frances Alda for her forthcoming fall tour. I had heard a great deal about this prima donna that made her almost a legend. For example, her reputation of having a repertoire of curses that would easily rival that of a stevedore or longshoreman. In private life, she was Madame Gatti-Casazza, a lady of questionable repute, and rumor had it that the Director of the Metropolitan Opera House, to preserve her professional reputation, had found it expedient for decorum's sake to legalize their union. Be that as it may, these were only rumors and there was no way of either proving or disproving them.

I arrived at her apartment at the Alwyn Court one fine October morning, and was, to my surprise, ushered into a charming bedroom. At the foot of the bed stood a small upright piano, and in the bed Madame was reclining comfortably, attired in a filmy nightgown. She informed me that she generally rehearsed that way as it gave her greater opportunity to rest. During this explanation, the filmy gown had a way of slipping out of place, thus sometimes revealing charms that would have proved more attractive in being divined than revealed. For Madame was very buxom. Her features were hard and stern, except when she smiled, when her rather lovely brown eyes would light up with a sweet expression. Her type might have been Spanish, Italian or Semitic, but in reality, she was Australian, as her rather cockneyish accent unmistakably showed.

At last we started rehearsing, and I immediately sensed that here

172

The famous prima donna Madame Gatti-Casazza and her husband.

was a fine artist indeed. Madame Alda did not have a large voice, but it was rich and velvety in texture, very expressive, and she never forced its volume beyond its natural limits. She was extremely musical and learned with great ease. She also was an exacting and strict taskmistress as well as completely ruthless in anything that concerned her "rights." This I was to learn by actual experience. I had arranged to accompany her for her entire autumn tour, which was to end in early December. These arrangements had been made before I had agreed to accompany Spalding on his European tour; but, as this did not require me to sail until the 15th, I felt that I had allowed plenty of time between the sailing date and the end of the tour. What I had not counted on, however, was that the European tour was to include Russia, and that this was the only country on the continent that required a passport from its visitors. Having already obtained my first citizenship papers, this did not worry me. But I soon learned upon due inquiry that this was not sufficient, and that to obtain a passport one had to be a full-fledged citizen. Whereupon I started wheels in motion through friends who were interested, to have a judge sit especially on my case, and thus give me my full citizenship. This was done, but unfortunately I was called to appear on a day when I was due to play for Mme. Alda in a small midwest town. On thinking the matter over, I thought the best thing to do was to tell her the exact truth and throw myself on her sense of fair play. I offered her the choice of any accompanist in the land she cared to select to substitute for me, regardless of expense, which I told her I would be only too glad to pay. But in spite of my pleading and trying to show her that it was well-nigh impossible to get another judge to sit especially for my case, she was obdurate. All arguments I advanced she would counter with "You've made an arrangement with me and you'll damn well stick to it." The upshot of it was that by frantic telegraphing back and forth, my friends were finally able to obtain another sitting which took place just one week before my sailing date.

Thus, on December 3rd, 1912, I became a proud American citizen, and had barely time to make the proper arrangements for my Russian passport, without which my whole European venture might have fallen to pieces. But that seemingly did not concern the prima donna, and when I left her at the conclusion of our tour, I

An autographed photograph of Albert Morris Bagby, the manager of
the concerts of Gatti-Casazza and Benoist. Bagby began his career
as a pianist. He studied with Franz Liszt.

To
André Benoist
in remembrance
many years of frien
Albert Morris Bag
1939

An autographed photograph of the great Polish pianist Ignaz Jan Paderewski. Paderewski appeared in joint recital with Gatti-Casazza, Albert Spalding and Andre. Circa 1915.

could not help remarking to her that I was glad that female Shy-locks were a rarity still in our world. To which she rejoined, "What the hell do you think I care for your little affairs! I look out for mine, you look out for yours!"

But with all her faults, this lady could be impish too, as the following happening will show. As anyone who follows music at all knows, there was an enterprise called the Bagby Morning Musi-cales, taking place every Monday morning at the Walfdorf-Astoria. These concerts were managed by a character who would deserve pages of description, but is too well-known to need them. He was Albert Morris Bagby. He was pure American, but looked half French and half English. He usually had three artists on his pro-gram and they were all stars in their own rights. Bagby himself had been a pianist of sorts in his early youth. As a matter of fact he had studied with Franz Liszt. But his first efforts had not been success-ful, upon which he had had the ingenious idea of organizing these morning musicales. Through his connections in the "beau monde" (High Society) of New York, they were an immediate success and at the time I speak of had been running for years. I mention this to show the temerity of my old friend R. E. Johnston, who, wishing to set up some sort of competition to this bonanza, thought it would be a good idea to organize a counter attraction. This he set out to do at the Biltmore Hotel. And, desiring to open the new series with great eclat, he engaged Frances Alda, Albert Spalding and Ignaz Jan Paderewski for the opening performance. This combination proved to be a great attraction, for the subscriptions poured in. However, Johnston did not realize what he had under-taken when he had engaged Paderewski to appear on a program with other artists.

The great pianist had a rooted aversion to such a procedure, and when he discovered what he was in for, he had his secretary write Johnston a letter to the effect that he would appear at this par-ticular concert only on condition that the other two artists would share the entire first part of the program, after which he would play a short recital of his own, thus ending the program alone.

I must admit that when we heard this news, we thought it pretty high-handed procedure, for it did not sound as coming from a "good trouper." The person who resented it more than anyone of us was Alda. Now I saw at once that the reputation she had gained for high voltage vocabulary was thoroughly justified. This went on and on, until a humorous gleam came into her eyes, and she suddenly said in a calmer tone, "All right! Let the old so and so have the whole second part of the program! You watch! It's going to prove to be a boomerang! For my part I'm going to sing encores at the slightest provocation! And you, Spalding, you do the same! Now we've each got two groups in the first part and I assure you we're going to make the most of them! You just watch!" Came the great day, and the ballroom was filled, mostly with ladies that looked like either mummies or resurrected mementoes of other days. "However," said Johnston, "they paid for their subscription." Alda's prophesy came true. By the time Alda and Spalding had finished their part of the program, it was verging on one o'clock, and the ladies in the audience were getting restless. The poor dears were getting hungry! It was nearing lunch time. But the maestro was not quite ready yet. His own piano had to be wheeled in place, the lights had to be adjusted, etc., etc. By the time the pianist walked onto the stage, a general exodus had begun in the auditorium, all bent on reaching the dining room. The maestro gloomily scanned the hall and noticing a few ladies still tip-toeing down the middle aisle, hoarsely exclaimed, "If no one here cares to hear me play, I might as well retire!" And the few remaining ladies were so crushed that, having forgotten their hunger, they thought it the better part of valor to remain!

Chapter
XIII

The rest of the Alda tour went on rather uneventfully, to come to an end in due time. The tenth day of December, 1912 found me embarked on my first European venture since I had landed on these hospitable shores as a boy in 1894. It was with a feeling of strange excitement that I boarded the Hamburg-American steamer *Cincinnati* which was to take me to the continent which I had left as a raw recruit and was now to re-enter as a full fledged professional. What was in store for me amid what now had become strange surroundings? Here, all my friends were prejudiced in my favor. But in the old sophisticated countries of Europe, what would be the reaction?

I tried to forget about these matters in the pleasure I anticipated both in the trip itself and in meeting again with the Spalding family. There were to be two ports of call before our final arrival at Genoa. The first was Funchal, in the Madeira Islands, and the second, Naples. As we were to remain there about twelve or fourteen hours, I thought it best to alight with some luggage and go to a hotel, for a change and rest. As I walked down the gangplank, I noticed a typical Italian "lazzarone" (lazybones) leaning against the dock parapet and smoking a cigarette, a beatific smile lighting his swarthy features. I walked over to him, and with the few words of Italian I could then muster, I told him that if he would be pleased to carry my bags to the nearest cab, I would be prepared to pay him for this service. He looked up at me quizzically, and with the same happy expression muttered, "Non ho bisogno, Signore, ho gia mangato oggi" and turned away. Literally translated in English, this answer, "It's not necessary, sir, I've already eaten

Two views of Florence, Italy where the Spaldings had their villa. The top view is the Arno River; below is Ponte Vecchio.

today" would describe the Italian character of that day. After some search, however, I discovered one chap who evidently had not yet eaten that day and he consented to carry my luggage for the munificent reward of . . . four cents, American value!

Twenty-four hours later I was suddenly plunged into the midst of the Italian Renaissance! Florence! Who, having undergone its spell, has not at once succumbed to it? It cannot adequately be described. It is a city. But a city that should be put in the glass case of a museum. It so reeks of the traditions for which it has become famous, that the very modern-minded people who inhabit it seem rather incongruous in their modern attire. The background of its old Palazzos, its stone-paved streets, together with some remnants of crude and primitive customs, baffle one in estimating this "shrine-city." Useless to repeat all that has been said about the streets frequented by Dante and Beatrice, and all the trite things that have been spoken and written about this jewel among cities. I only wish to give the impression it had on me.

From the smoky station I was conveyed to the Casa Spalding. This fine old house had been built by one of the Princes of Talleyrand, and from what I understood had been bought by the Spalding family when the princely coffers were depleted enough to require liquidating their estates. It was generally referred to as the Palazzo. But then, in Italy, any private house of any pretension is called a Palazzo. In the same way that in Russia anyone possessing some acres of ground and at least 50,000 rubles becomes a prince. The Spalding house, while being old, had been reinforced with good American plumbing, innumerable bathrooms and central heating, which all made for most comfortable living. But what made it the most sought after and delightful place imaginable was the charm and graciousness of its hosts.

Mr. and Mrs. J. W. Spalding had a way of offering their hospitality that made you feel you were conferring a favor upon them by accepting it. Of course, music, music and more music! And why not! They were ideally equipped for it. The two story music room, where Liszt had played in the old days, the two Steinway concert grands, and the perfect acoustics; all invited both the best in performance, as well as the keenest attention in the listening. I arrived just before Christmas, and that holiday at the Casa Spalding was a genuine fiesta. I never had time to feel homesick,

The inside of the Spalding Villa in Florence. The stairs lead up to a study, a long, narrow room with paintings showing a panorama of Florence.

The main entrance stairs of the Talleyrand Palace featured deep red carpet, marble and gold leaf. After entering a small courtyard and being inspected by the concierge, one was allowed to ascend these stairs to the main floors.

for something was going on all the time. But rehearsing and study hours were never neglected. And there was plenty to rehearse to prepare for the forthcoming tour, which was now fast approaching. It was an unalloyed pleasure to work with this young man. A great deal of this was done away from the instruments. Each one having studied the technical difficulties of a piece, we would talk matters over, such as tempi, dynamics, accentuations and a thousand matters that go to make up a complete performance of any composition. I have seldom met an artist who had a clearer or more logical conception of the meanings of a given composer. Whether it was Bach, Mozart, Beethoven or some of the modern composers, his understanding of their style was always suited to the writer. I ascribe this to his omnivorous reading and his unfailing memory for anything and anyone who had made an impression on him. He knew the song literature as well as he knew that of the piano-forte, and had studied acting with Joliet of the Comedie Francaise in Paris. Consequently his knowledge of literature embraced the French and Italian as well as the English. In addition, he had concertized with Pugno and Saint-Saens, and all of these things tended to broaden his musical intellect limitlessly. He had the gift of making his friends devoted to him. His enemies could find nothing better to say than, being a child of people in comfortable circumstances, he could not possibly be a great artist. Which seems to me the acme of stupidity! For greatness in anything does not choose the background from which it comes.

I do not believe that poverty is a help nor wealth a drawback to any endeavor whatsoever. Mozart was born poor, Mendelssohn wealthy; which did not prevent each one from composing beautifully each in his own field and style. And no artist was ever launched without some financial help. What the jaundiced mind seemingly cannot bear to think of is that an artist's own people have enough trust in his ability to make a career; that they be willing to do their own launching instead of depending upon the good will of some strange angel; and the strangest thing of all is that these same dissenters will condone a family financing any other career, such as law and medicine, for one of its own members. But MUSIC; No! There seems to be some peculiar stigma attached to the procedure! An aspiring artist must first of all have his soul torn to shreds by dire want and poverty before he can understand the

184

To my dear Alice and André, with much love from Marie B. Spalding
mary 6th 1930

Mrs. Marie B. Spalding, Albert Spalding's mother, autographed this
photo to Benoist in 1930.

The music room at the Spalding villa in Florence, Italy.

message of the masters! What balderdash! Artists are born, and sometimes, by hard work and perseverance, added to a sufficient quantity of ego (but not too much), they emerge from the general run. To all this must also be added that mysterious imponderable: LUCK! For without it, no amount of talent will see him through.

It is the same with composing. Many people have the effrontery to have printed with their name the caption "composer-pianist." How do they know they are composers? These, as well as poets, are born. One can learn how to compose, or how to write poetry. But unless there is a gushing font of invention within the individual that prompts him to express something within him that will not be denied, he remains a clever artisan and not an artist.

That may well be the reason that our so-called modern music is, for the most part, immensely clever, but seldom touches the heart strings. As a matter of fact, the last thing the composer of today would wish to do would be to touch heart strings. That would be a sign of weakness. No indeed, one must be "tough" and hard in this age of realities. Heaven forbid that one should pander to sentiment. That emotion is only for the weak!

The truth is that all this nonsense is expressed simply to cover up the sterility of the average composer. For had he the real ability, he would walk in the footsteps of his great forefathers. To walk in their footsteps does not mean to imitate them; but to express something truly moving in a fresh way, in the same way their spiritual forebears expressed something new in their generation. If harping on dissonance is something new, I must confess amazement. For since the art of music began, it was always possible to write in two unrelated keys. The only trouble was that most people did not like it. It is said that in old China people liked century-old eggs; they also ate bird's nests. They were thought good. But that does not mean that *we* must enjoy them.

Besides, what is this stigma attached to the fact that one school of composing is the descendant of another school? Do we not, all of us, descend from someone? As a matter of fact, parents are often proud of their children's resemblance to them. And vice versa. Why not? Brahms certainly descended from Beethoven. Did that take away one iota of his originality and genius? No, it only added to his greatness. Once in a generation there arises a creative genius like Debussy, but the followers then study his "formula," and see-

Benoist and Spalding at the time of their collaboration in Florence.

ing his success, start to imitate him, instead of attempting to create an idiom of their own. Again, sterility! However, enough of this profitless cogitation, and let us return to the magic of Florence. Its friendliness, its lovely narrow streets and its shadowy doorways from which issued sounds of artisans singing or whistling at their work. The image of the superb Duomo and the stately Palazzo

Vecchio; the graceful bridges across the Arno, the Ponte Vecchio especially, through whose upper gallery the Medicis used to walk from one place to the other in fear of their lives, and numberless other landmarks are indelibly engraved in my memory.

The Italian people, though extremely sensitive, were generous and appreciative to a fault. One instance comes to mind on my first attempt to buy something worthwhile. It was a hat, but what a hat! There is in Florence a public market called "Mercato Nuovo" or New Market. This is to distinguish it from an earlier one which existed seven hundred years ago. It is held in the open air and specializes in certain items on different days of the week. On the day I was strolling through with my wife, it appeared to be the day for the sale of hats. Men's hats exclusively. There were all kinds: soft felts, hard felts, straws; in short, everything a man could dream of in that line. I came to attention before a stall showing Panamas. One in particular drew my gaze. It was of a texture such as one reads about in books. More like woven silk than straw. I stood in a fascinated trance, and the merchant whose property it was evidently must have become aware of my admiration for the hat, resulting in the following:

Merchant: "I see that you admire this fine Panama."

Client: "Yes indeed, I've never seen a finer one!"

Merchant: "You show good taste! It is indeed very beautiful. Why don't you buy it?"

Client: "Why my dear sir! That kind of hat is only for rich people, and I am far from being wealthy enough to afford such a jewel!"

Merchant: "But the hat costs only seven hundred lire. Surely that is not much for an American gentleman!"

Client: "As to the first, you are right. Seven hundred lire is not too much for so magnificent a headgear; and if I had the means, I would be willing to pay even more than you ask for this gorgeous hat, for it is worth it. But unfortunately, though I am American, I am not

In the wintergarden of the Palace in Florence: Andre and Alice Benoist; Albert with several Baronesses.

191

one of the wealthy class. I am a musical artist by profession and you know full well that that is not conducive to wealth! I would gladly have offered you all I have in my pocket were I not ashamed to make so puny an offer for so superb an object, so I will have to forego this joy with tearful regret."

Merchant: (With tears in his voice) "How much has the signor in his pocket?"

Client: (Shamefacedly) "Alas! Only three hundred lire!"

Merchant: "Well, it shall not be said that one so artistic and so appreciative of true beauty shall go without it! You must have this beautiful Panama, as no one else would be fit to wear it. Please, with my compliments, I will accept the three hundred lire and feel well repaid!"

Of course, I had been warned as to the love of bartering and haggling the Italian merchant has, provided it be conducted on strictly diplomatic lines. For if you would try a frontal attack on an Italian merchant, you would find yourself against a stone wall. But with kindness and diplomacy, almost anything could be accomplished in that blessed country.

At last came the time when our peregrinations would start, and I left dear Florence, with deep regret.

Chapter
XIV

One of the first countries we visited was enchanting Holland. There, Spalding was already known, having played with the great Dutch accompanist Coenraad Bos, who really was instrumental in introducing him to his compatriots. So that when he appeared in Holland he was greeted like a prodigal son. They simply adored him. But for my part, I was worried lest I make a fiasco, coming after so renowned a colleague as Coenraad Bos. The latter was not only an outstanding accompanist, but a very distinguished pianist in his own right. His ensemble playing was a treat to hear and his touch in anything he played was velvety. He had first come to America as a partner to Dr. Ludwig Wullner, the celebrated German lieder singer, and with him had scored an immediate success. This was a rare occurrence, for in those days accompanists were hardly noticed by the press, and much less by the public.

But as I said, Bos was outstanding. And to play in his home city of the Hague was an ordeal. Although Spalding's success was a foregone conclusion, I had heard that Dutch audiences were peculiar, and so they proved to be. Their loyalty to an artist they have taken to heart, is proverbial, but this loyalty is contingent on the artist's continuing his artistic integrity. For once he strays in the wrong direction, his Dutch audience leaves him until he is known to have recovered his skill. However, I was not prepared for the lukewarm applause that greeted our appearance. "That," Spalding explained to me later, "is Dutch skepticism in evidence." This was the audience's attitude all through the recital. At the end, they applauded enough to warrant the playing of a few encores, and when they saw that no more were forthcoming, I noticed to my surprise that, while the applause did not augment in any percepti-

193

Coenraad V. Bos, the greatest of the Dutch pianists in his day.

ble manner, all present arose in a body, and stood at their seats, bowing to the stage! "That," whispered Spalding, "is what is called in Holland, an ovation." "Good Lord," I replied, "that's the politest ovation I ever saw!" To my surprised gratification, the press seemed to be pleased with my work. As for Spalding, his press was unanimous in singing his praises and though one of the most modest artists imaginable, he could not help but react happily to the warm welcome extended to him in so musical a country.

It must be borne in mind that in Holland, music is the national pastime. What baseball is to America, music is to Holland. You will for instance, find that the local baker plays viola, and thereupon goes in search of another tradesman who might play a bit of violoncello. Then the two will make inquiries as to a fair violinist or two and forthwith form a quartet that will meet at one or the other's home once or twice a week. This is average procedure. A rather touching incident bears witness as to the state of mind of the typical Hollander. After one of the recitals at the "Diligentia" Hall in the Hague, we found in the dressing room a magnificent cluster of fresh roses. The card attached only carried the following: "From an admirer." We puzzled over this for a while, when Spalding, tired but happy over his success, said, "Enough of this guessing; it's probably from the Queen, and she's too shy to admit it!"

So we turned our steps towards our temporary residence, the Hotel des Indes, a few steps from the hall. As usual, we were greeted at the entrance by the elderly but still magnificent "portier" (glorified doorman), very brave in his superb goldbraided uniform. Now it must be borne in mind that in a hotel like the "des Indes," the portier is not what we call a porter. No indeed! He is a functionary, a major-domo, a general poo-bah, and Keeper of the Keys. It is part of his duties to greet every one in the manner he is entitled to, either by his wealth, position in life or his renown.

It is he who escorts you to your room, bearing your key, if he feels you are entitled to such an honor. It is he who advises you where and when to eat, what costume to wear on such an occasion, and whom you might meet at such and such a place. He is full of information of every kind, but is the soul of discretion . . . provided the temptation is not too great; and he is prompt to remember that the financial rate of exchange is thus and so. In other words, he is a cross between a diplomat and a financier. As I said, this great being

195

greeted us gravely and ceremoniously, as is proper between the lofty of the earth. Then, as we were leaving him, he leaned forward murmuring, "I hope Mr. Spalding enjoyed the flowers as much as I enjoyed his music. You are a great master, Mr. Spalding. Good day, Mr. Spalding."

On several occasions, we had heard people expatiate on the musical prowess of a pianist about whom, up to then, we had heard very little. Neither had we ever heard him play. Nor had we had occasion to meet him. His name was José Iturbi. There were all kinds of rumors afloat about him. How he had been "discovered" in a Lausanne cafe by Monsieur Gaveau, the French piano-forte manufacturer, how he had been a success overnight, and what an irresistible "Don Juan" he was. As our tour of Holland came to an end, we began to forget about the whole matter, and it was not until the following year that we were suddenly reminded of it during our second journey to the Netherlands.

One morning, while we were rehearsing in Mr. Spalding's sitting room, a knock came at the door. We heard the invitation, "Come in," the door opened, and there stood a stocky, rather swarthy young man, about twenty-eight or thirty years old, very erect and soldierly-looking. He announced, "My name is Iturbi. I've heard you play. Superb. I want to know you." Both artists shook hands and I sat quietly in a corner, watching the show. Greater disparity of manner could be imagined only with difficulty. The stocky little Spaniard, speaking in staccato phrases, contrasted oddly with the grand, suave manner of the rather tall Spalding. A bantam rooster contrasted with a sleek greyhound!

But they got along famously from the first. Their musical ideas seemed to coincide perfectly.

Then Iturbi suggested that they play something together. "Ha, ha," thought I, "that's where the great soloist comes to grief." But no! Iturbi was as much a wizard at ensemble playing as he was a soloist. A twinge of jealousy! No, when art is on that level, there is only room for unqualified admiration, and one bows thankfully. They played and played, when Iturbi, in his staccato way, suddenly turned around, and pointing to me said, "And who is he?" Spalding explained that I played his accompaniments. "Yes," said Iturbi, "That I gathered, but you have not introduced me!" Spalding performed the rite, apologizing for its tardiness,

196

The main hall of the Hotel des Indes in the Hague, where Spalding and Benoist stayed during their tour of Holland.

whereupon Iturbi in his peremptory manner said, "Play something." No sooner said than done. Our old favorite, the A Major Sonata by Cesar Franck. It is a composition in which one easily loses contact with one's surroundings. One gets so immersed in, and saturated with its passionate measures that it is easy to forget what seemed obvious the moment before. And that was what happened to me by the time the piece was ended. I was awakened from my trance by Iturbi's words. Putting his arm around my shoulder, he said, "You belong; we'll be friends." And so it was. This friendship has lasted over thirty years so far.

Our next meeting was to take place under tragic circumstances. In the meantime, we had several delightful parties at Iturbi's apartment in Paris, where we also had our headquarters; my wife, little son and myself. His little girl and our little boy used to play together in the Parc Monceaux, while we two would play endless two-piano duets.

The winter months flew by, and we decided that after a trip to England we would spend the rest of the summer at the great seacoast resort of Scheveningen in northern Holland on the North

Sea. It is a charming place and its proximity to the Hague makes for a combination of country and city diversions. It is also blessed with the concerts given at the Kuurhaus by the Amsterdam Concertgebouw Orchestra with which appear some of the greatest soloists in the world. What was our surprise and delight when we saw a poster announcing that Iturbi was to appear soon to play his great "war horse," the Tchaikowsky B Flat Minor Concerto. What a musical treat we had in store! In addition, we anticipated the pleasure of a reunion with a charming friend.

But alas, the reunion was to be anything but happy. A few days before he was to arrive, we learned from the orchestra management that Mr. Iturbi refused to come, owing to the sudden demise of his wife, and that he was too broken-hearted to attempt to play this concert. It was a terrible shock to us, for the Señora and my wife had become very much attached to each other, and we both had looked forward so much to entertaining the couple. All sorts of rumors were afloat, the most reliable of which was as follows: It seems that the Señora was playing the orchestral accompaniment on a second piano while Iturbi was rehearsing the solo part of the Tchaikowsky Concerto. During one of the pauses between movements the Señora excused herself as it was time to take a cough mixture for a cold she had contracted. In the bathroom, she must have mistaken one bottle for another, containing poison, for when she returned and attempted to continue playing, she suddenly collapsed and expired before the horrified Iturbi was able to summon help. No wonder he could not bring himself to perform so shortly after such a tragedy.

However, such organizations as the orchestra in question are notoriously hard-hearted and they held him strictly to his contract which included a heavy pecuniary penalty in case of disappointment. And Iturbi at that time was in no position to forfeit it. Consequently, after much telegraphing back and forth, he finally agreed to play, but in no case the Tchaikowsky. For it, he would substitute the Beethoven G Major.

We met him on arrival, and a more broken human being I have seldom beheld. We did not speak much, for what can one say in such a circumstance! We watched him closely throughout his performance and could clearly see his tears rolling on the keyboard. But he played like a hero; one of the most unforgettable perfor-

An autographed photograph of the great pianist Jose Iturbi. 1935.

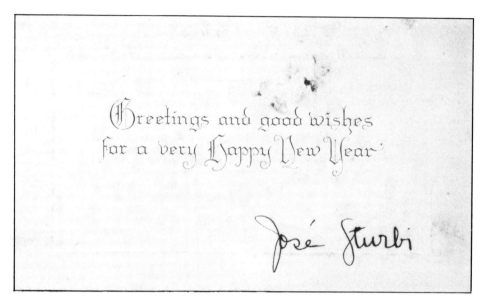

Iturbi's 1935 Christmas greeting.

mances I have ever heard. Afterwards, we sat up with him most of the night, trying as well as we could to console him. However, time appears to heal most wounds and I daresay, his were no exception. I too, had had my tragedy early in life and I could see that life would in time claim him again. But little did we dream one day Iturbi would turn out to be a cinema actor-star. How unpredictable are the ways of providence!

Chapter XV

This memorable summer came to an end too soon and we all drifted back to Paris for a few days of home life. Our autumn tour was to embrace Norway, Sweden, Denmark, Finland and Russia, and it was with keen anticipation that I prepared for the long journey ahead. Useless to dwell on Spalding's success in each and every country we visited, for he was hailed everywhere as a king in his chosen profession. The Scandinavian people had this in common with their Dutch neighbors: they adored music. That did not mean that they did not have their moments of intense levity, for jazz and swing were already rampant among them. But like a thoroughly civilized people, they could take or leave it at will. It did not constitute their world, as it practically does ours, but only a part of it, and it was welcome in its time and place.

Legitimate musicians have often been blamed for their narrow-mindedness regarding the lighter forms of so-called modern dance music. This is a wrong indictment. I believe that what the average musician really objects to is the utter monotony of "jazz." It is always written in four-quarter time, and it all sounds alike. But that is not all. It is, in certain quarters, continuous. I have often wondered what would be the reaction of a guest who, invited to an eight a.m. breakfast, would be served caviar, hors d'oeuvres and champagne, instead of coffee with eggs and cereal? He would probably be shocked out of his wits and admit that he liked it all very much, but only at eleven p.m. at a lively party.

Benoist's group on their Scandinavian tour.

The same is true for jazz and swing. Fine in their time and place. But as a steady diet, they are merely drugs. Enough to watch the average youths on the dance floor to realize this. They do not look happy; they do not smile; they look self-conscious and try to look bored; their faces bear an imbecilic expression that is reminiscent of the self-absorbed look on the face of a dervish in a trance.

On the other hand, watch the Viennese at their dances. See their shining eyes and their graceful carefree motions. This reflects the real joie de vivre (joy of life) which the jazz addict will never know. Moreover, the so-called dances concocted on this music are ungraceful in the extreme. They resemble more the jumping jack antics of a gathering of cannibals around some jungle festivities and intoxicated from imbibing some poisonous extract of noxious roots or leaves. And all this utterly lacks grace, courtliness, or even self-respect. When questioned in any manner regarding these dances, the usual answer is: "Good gracious! Can't young people have a good time and enjoy themselves without the interference of old fogies like you?"

202

Harold de Bildt and his Siamese cats. Stockholm, 1914.

Personally, I think it is just as possible to have a good time with a modicum of decorum and manners, as it is when acting in a way that would put stevedores on a spree to shame. It seems a long and useless discussion, but it is pleasant to open the "steam valves" once in a while.

However, there is another side to the question. It is undeniable that the form of music that is called "jazz" (which in reality is nothing more than a use of syncopation in the tune or the accompaniment or in both, to the accompaniment of persistent drum beats), can be used as a basis for a new form of art. This has been proved by such gifted composers as the late lamented George Gershwin. But most of our modern composers feel that they *must* compose in a modern vein. They merely *wish* to compose, whereas they should *have* to compose. Unfortunately, they are sterile, and to make up for the lack of the fountain of genius, they choose to produce strange cacaphonic concoctions they call music.

If you dare to disapprove, you are called a reactionary and are told that you are attempting to retard progress! As if anyone were able to retard true progress! As if progress could be retarded! Progress can no more be retarded, than Niagara Falls can be dammed by a heap of straw. To progress, something new and vital must be created, something whose urge is so strong that nothing can stand in its way. Not so with the anemic wanderings of our "poor misunderstood geniuses." It is their appalling sterility that drives the assassins from "tin-pan alley" to the great masters of the past when they need a really fine melody. Like the prostitutes they really are, they disguise these masterpieces with their faked cosmetics and serve them to a public who would not take them in their original cleanly washed state.

As to the serious modern composer, who sometimes invents a simple and sweet melody, and then, suddenly becoming ashamed of its simplicity, immediately seasons it with the paprika of continuous dissonances; he is very much like the hen in the story, who becoming tired of laying oval eggs like all her competitors, one morning decided that this must change, in the name of real progress. So she picked up a hatchet and started squaring off her eggs. Then looking at them with pride, she exclaimed, "At last! Now I am truly modern!"

Let us leave this to breathe the clean Scandinavian air! This tour

George Gershwin, a famous composer, also painted.

proved to be enchanting. It may have been the novelty of the long nights and short days, the latter having only two or three hours of actual daylight, and those rather dark, but the fact remains that, in Norway, or Norge as the natives call it, the hospitality is so intense that it is sometimes overwhelming. The food was beyond description, and the lavish use of butter and cream, staggering. Also there was the profuse use of "spirits," which the average Norwegian carries with ease and . . . pride! Among the many dinners to which we had been invited, one stands out as coming near to laying us low. It was given at the home of a Dr. Maartens, who was reputed to have two passions: music and food. His convivial table was proof of the latter! This particular meal began with two kinds of soups, one of meat and one of fish. Then came oysters on the half shell. This was followed by baked fish, a roast of beef, roast venison, broiled squabs, stewed hare, ices, and innumerable deserts. Not to mention that with each dish came all sorts of vegetables as well as diverse wines, and at the end, with the coffee, brandy flowed like water.

Another dinner I remember with a chuckle was one given us in Copenhagen by the American minister then incumbent, Maurice Francis Egan, one of the rarest souls it has been my lot to meet. He was gracious, kindly, benevolent and witty. Among the guests invited were a certain Comte and Comtesse de Beaucaire, the French minister and his wife. The latter was undoubtedly nearly eighty years old, and only too obviously made up to look thirty. She resembled an embalmed corpse recently disinterred, and she had a decided talent for being coy. After being introduced to her, I found it difficult to hide myself from her pursuit; "But," thought I, "we'll soon be at the table and then I'll be rid of the old girl for a while at least." To my dismay, Mr. Egan, having formed the mistaken idea that my conversation might be diverting, and that moreover I spoke French, placed me next to the lady.

At close range and under the cruel dazzling light of a crystal chandelier, the countess' appearance was not noticeably improved. Her face had been so heavily enameled that it gave the impression of being an old stuccoed wall that would crack at the first impact. Consequently, while she twittered and figuratively wagged her tail contentedly, her face remained strictly rigid in a set smile under what must have been a very expensive wig. Moreover, she wore a dress so outrageously decolleté that even my rather sophisticated gaze sought rest away from the dubious charms so blatantly exhibited.

On my left sat another lady, who seemed much more interesting, but whose every effort at conversation with me had been thwarted by the continuous twaddle of the elderly partner on my right. So anxious was I to be rid of her for even a few moments that I racked my brains for some method of doing this in the most inoffensive manner possible, but to no avail. Then I suddenly had a daring thought.

Perhaps some ribald and footless remark might cause the lady to realize I was no gentleman and therefore leave me alone. So in my choicest French I exclaimed that which in the nearest translation would read about as follows: "Madame la Comtesse, you are possessed with a bosom of the utmost magnificence; it is like twin planets soaring in a sky of silvery clouds and completely dazzling withal!" I hoped at the very least for a severe tongue lashing or a slap in the face, but not at all! From then on, and throughout the evening, I was never let alone one moment until the merciful moment when we could take our leave decently and according to protocol.

For one could not leave until the guest of honor, the Crown Prince, had signified that the evening was over. He stood at the head of the stairs in his fine regalia, bidding each departing guest goodbye, until the poor man must have been exhausted! When the last hand had been shaken, he turned to me and in a whisper said, "Fine job for a grownup man, what? Oh, for a nice American baseball game!" He had been to America incognito and enjoyed them. This we learned later, and having lived in America for a while, we could understand his reaction.

Our next destination was to be Helsingfors or Helsinki as it is now called, the capital of Finland. The journey is made by train to Stockholm and thence by night boat to the little port of Abo across the Baltic. The boat trip was a nightmare realized. The cabins were very small and close, owing to the fact that the portholes could not be opened, as the ice which the boat had to crunch its way through would then be spattered in the cabin along with some of the Baltic salt water. In the center of the outer wall stood a wash basin surmounted by a contraption filled with lukewarm water, under which a species of faucet was attached to let the water into the basin. This water was utterly unfit for drinking and barely for washing. This "fountain" was flanked on each side by a berth, under each of which was located a large steam heat radiator which could not be turned off. Before retiring, we had partaken of a highly seasoned dinner, and between the unbearable heat of the cabin and our parched tongues and throats, life became unbearable. In addition to this, on lying down in our berths, we found ourselves slowly being roasted alive owing to the steam radiators underneath.

In desperation, I arose from my bed of agony, dressed, and went out in search of liquid relief. At long last, I ran into a steward who from some mysterious corner produced what he was pleased to call bottled mineral water. Anyway, thought I, it was cold and it was wet! With this in mind, I returned to our cabin where Spalding greeted me with shouts of joy. After much pulling and tugging, we succeeded in uncorking one of the bottles, poured out two glasses and started to imbibe with avidity. Alas and alack! The remedy was worse than the bite! This water, whose name we found to be "Salus," was well named! It was a medicinal water with a very salty flavor, and made us feel ill at once. However, after untold hours of agonizing thirst we finally slept, from sheer exhaustion. Awakening with daylight, cold water and breakfast in the offing, things began to assume a rosier hue.

The arrival in Helsingfors, to my mind, meant one thing. A step nearer to meeting the great Jan Sibelius. The city itself was charming and typically Nordic in every aspect. Somehow, in those northern climates, one seems to mind ice and snow less than in milder zones. So it was in Finland, where there is an ample supply of both in winter! Perhaps it is on that account that people seem more rugged and serious than in southern countries. And one is never cold indoors. The great porcelain stoves are kept going continuously, and their glow gives a feeling of intimate coziness.

Two matters stand out as I recollect my first visit to Helsingfors. The first is meeting the great Finnish composer, Jan Sibelius. I had heard a great many stories concerning this half-legendary figure of our musical world; that he was unapproachable, boorish, rude, and isolated in his greatness as well as in his remote home; that he was never quite sober and had been known to throw visitors

Jan Sibelius, the famous Finnish composer.

Famous violin personalities: 1. Kathleen Parlow. 2. Maud Powell. 3. Nicolo Paganini. 4. Louis Persinger. 5. Maximilian Pilzer. 6. Gaetano Pugnani. 7. Henri Petri. 8. Alexander Petschnikoff

210

out at the slightest provocation. Of course, I had taken much of this gossip with a grain of salt, knowing full well that anyone as renowned as Sibelius would have all sorts of nonsense attributed to him. Ironically, we soon learned that he was not living in his home retreat, but right next door to our temporary quarters, the Societet-shuset, at the Hotel Finlandia, where he could keep warmer than in the country. Also, our local manager, on trying to make an appointment for us, found that we would be most welcome at tea time that same afternoon. On learning this, Spalding and I looked at each other, intending to convey "this is too easy; there must be a catch somewhere."

But there was not. That afternoon, on sending our names up to the master, we were told to come up at once. The man who greeted us with grave courtesy was extremely tall. He was quite bald, and his face was stern, with features that might have been carved out of granite. His eyes looked tired, but the harshness of his features was relieved by the sweet and benevolent expression of his mouth. He spoke good but slow English. He said he had heard fine things of Mr. Spalding's playing and that he would surely attend his concerts. He inquired as to the musical situation in America, saying that he had been asked several times to come to our country, but the length of the trip was a strong deterrent.

Of course we got on the subject of his magnificent violin concerto. "I understand," he said, "that it was first played in your country by a lady?" I agreed with this, explaining that I had had the honor of accompanying that "lady," whose name was Maud Powell, on that occasion, and I had had a hard time learning the piano part. "Yes," he admitted, "it is a bad piano part. Too dark. I have heard conflicting reports as to how this Miss Powell played it. What is your opinion?" I felt, like George Washington, that I could not tell a lie. So all I could think of as an answer was, "Horrendous, scratchy." His reply was typical, a long drawn-out "So . . . ;" then a silence followed by, "This seems to agree with trustworthy opinions I have heard before." Then tea was brought, flanked by some good brandy, both of which we partook of appreciatively, in view of the climate. And after a little more desultory exchanges of views and information, we took our departure, thrilled and charmed by the interview.

The second surprise was meeting our local impresario. The

Maud Powell, who introduced the Sibelius
Violin Concerto in the United States.

THE OUTLOOK CLUB

OF MONTCLAIR, NEW JERSEY

....

Piano

Song and

Violin

Recital

....

MISS MAUD POWELL - - VIOLINISTE

MR. HERBERT WITHERSPOON - BASSO

MR. ANDRE BENOIST - - - PIANIST

MAY 27, 1904

The program played by Benoist, Powell and Witherspoon at the Outlook Club of Montclair, New Jersey on May 27, 1904.

213

Programme

....

1 POLONAISE E MAJOR . . . . . . LISZT

MR. ANDRE BENOIST

2 A. HEIMLICHKEIT . . . . . DR. KARL LOEWE

   B. DER CONTRABANDISTE . . . . SCHUMANN

   C. ICH DENKE OFT AN'S BLAUE MEER . . WEINGARTNER

   D. HEIMLICHE AUFFORDERUNG . . RICHARD STRAUSS

MR. HERBERT WITHERSPOON

3 SONATE . . . . LECLAIR

   INTRODUCTION, ALLEGRO   SARABANDE, TAMBOURIN

MISS MAUD POWELL

4 A DECLARATION . . . . . LOUIS AUBERT

   B. LA PAIX (MONOTONE) . . . REYNOLDS HAHN

   C. MADRIGAL . . . . . . GASTON LEMAIRE

MR. HERBERT WITHERSPOON

214

Programme

5 A. MAZUREK . . . . DVORAK

   B. L'ABEILLE . . . . . . FRANCOIS SCHUBERT

   C. LENTO . . . . VIEUXTEMPS

   D. ZEPHIRE . . . . HUBAY

MISS MAUD POWELL

6 A. MOTHER O' MINE . . . . . FRANK TOURS

   B. FOREVER AND A DAY . . . . . ALBERT MACK

   C. BY THE SHORT CUT TO THE ROSSES . . . OLD IRISH

   D. BAD LUCK TO THEIR MARCHING . . ALICIA NEEDHAM

MR. HERBERT WITHERSPOON

7 FANTASIE DE FAUST . . . . . WIENIAWSKI

MISS MAUD POWELL

average example of this species is a rather boastful, self-confident party, who usually recites all the efforts he has put forth to make you a success. Without him, he implies, you would not exist. He, it is, who will spread your fame to the four corners of the earth, and you had better appreciate that fact and never forget it. But this was not the type that met our eyes, when he was ushered into our hotel suite. George Fazer (pronounced Fatser) was a mousy little man whose prototype in our country would be Casper Milquetoast. He was soft-spoken and timid. All his replies to our questions were monosyllabic. Only once did he depart from this. When asked what sort of publicity he had used to promote the concerts, he said, "For the first recital, I put an advertisement in the newspapers. If people like you, the second concert will be crowded." And that was all we could elicit from this reticent little man.

But what he had prognosticated came to pass. The handful of people who came to our first concert was replaced by a full house at the second. And the same at the third. Fazer's enthusiasm reached the bursting point, when on the eve of our departure for Russia, he said, "I think you better come back again; you will have a good house." Of all the understatements I have ever heard, that was the strongest. But that is another story. . .

Chapter
XVI

The journey from Helsingfors to St. Petersburg, or Leningrad as it is now called, started in the little toy railroad cars used in Finland which go up to the Russian frontier, where a change is made for the palatial cars of the Russian railroads. The Russian rail gauge is a foot wider than any other road, and the width and height of the cars correspond accordingly, which gives a feeling of spaciousness to the interiors which is difficult to describe. In addition, during the years 1912-1913, the service was truly "with a smile." (I was about to say, with a guffaw!)

Much has been said about the misery of the "lower" classes under the Tzar's rule. It is even probable that there was misery in many quarters of Russia under the Imperial rule. It is also probable that many abuses existed. But the ruthlessness was exercised mostly against people who dabbled in politics. And this sort of thing, which is abhorrent to any of us who have tasted the sweets of democracy, has been going on for time immemorial in any absolute monarchy. In this, Russia was no exception, and it seemed to suit a great majority of its people.

It is true I have never visited the mines of Siberia. But neither have I visited the stone piles of Georgia in the United States. I can only say that my first impression was gained from an isvostchik, or "cabby" in English. The isvostchiks of that period prided themselves on their obesity, and to arrive at the utmost in stoutness, they would wrap themselves in innumerable blankets, which made them look like huge bales surmounted by small human heads. These peculiar bundles of humanity were either singing or whistling some tune all the time. And when they had to make change for payment, they would pull out of their pockets a handful of gold rubles. They would hardly bother to look for kopecks! You could tell that they were accustomed to being tipped royally. They certainly did not look unhappy or downtrodden to me! The same applied to waiters or other menial workers. The wealthy classes spent lavishly, which kept their money in constant circulation.

It is also true that eighty-five per cent of the population were supposed to be illiterate, which did not prevent some of the greatest geniuses, musical or otherwise, from being Russian. It was also rumored that under the Tzars no Jew could ever amount to anything. But what about Elman, Zimbalist, Seidel, Heifetz and countless others? What about the great Professor Leopold Auer, head of the violin department at the Imperial Conservatory? And for illiteracy, what about our southern hillbillies? I can only say that nowhere in my travels had I found a more civilized, courteous and cultured atmosphere than in Tzarist Russia. I know nothing of the modern Soviet Republic, but from the little that is transmitted from within its gates, I only hope it has not deteriorated.

Spalding had been in Russia once before, so that to him it was not, strictly speaking, a new adventure. For me, it was one of the most thrilling moments of my life. In my boyhood, I had read a good many adventure books of Russia, and that country meant to me: Siberia full of tortured prisoners, muzhiks whipped to work, the knout, nihilists with bombs in their hands, and noble princes kicking hapless waiters into the gutter. From the moment I stepped into a sumptuous Russian sleeping car, my mind began to change. Was the delicious and plentiful food served in the dining car a sign of disintegration? Was this the land of savage Muscovites I had read about?

Then the arrival at St. Petersburg, with courteous porters and interpreters at hand to guide you to a charming, old-fashioned, little, open, horse-drawn carriage, driven by a smiling and voluble (in Russian) isvostchik. The arrival at the sumptuous Hotel de L'Europe after a delightful drive down the Nevsky Prospect. The finding that the magnificent room assigned to us connected with a bathroom fit for a Roman consul and was equipped with the most modern open plumbing. Yes, the room was superb, but its very size lent it an air of doom. The ceiling was so high as to disappear into gloom; the dark red chenille curtains that shaded the windows prevented any light from reaching that high. In one corner stood a

An autographed photograph of the greatest of violin teachers, Prof. Leopold Auer. This is a very rare photograph showing Auer holding a violin. Unfortunately no pictures are available showing the young Auer who concertized so successfully before he became a teacher and produced Zimbalist, Elman, Heifetz and so many other super-stars of the violin.

MAILLARD KESSLERE B P

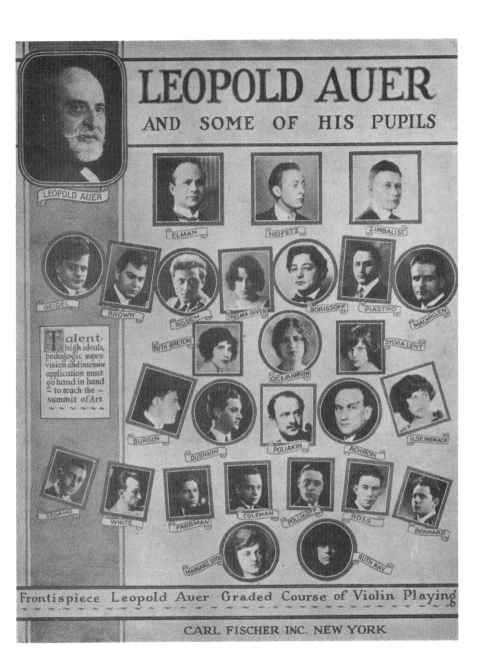

Leopold Auer (facing page) and the frontispiece from his book on violin playing. He also wrote an autobiography. One of his truly great pupils was Poliakin, but he disappeared and returned to Russia when Benno Rabinoff beat him in a competition. Rabinoff was one of Auer's American students.

221

Sergei Rachmaninoff inscribed this photo to Benoist in 1936.

huge desk, behind which one would have expected to find a governor-general of Siberia, ordering a batch of political prisoners to be sent to the torture chamber. This impression was so strong that the first night I slept in that room I had a most horrible nightmare, dreaming that the governor-general was actually seated at this confounded desk, and questioning me. Only his features were those of Sergei Rachmaninoff, who certainly looked the part to perfection!

But leaving these details aside, the hotel was a delight, and its service could be envied with good cause by our own Waldorf-Astoria. As for the Russian people we came in contact with, I am sure the men's clothes must have come from London, and the women's from Paris. I remember one gala evening given by the Tzar in commemoration of the tercentenary of the accession to the throne by the Romanoff family, at which had been invited, as guest of honor, the Khan of Tartary with all his wives. Such toilettes, uniforms, jewelry, pomp and circumstance could not have been seen anywhere else in the world. The performance also was unforgettable. It was the ballet *Don Quixote*, played by the entire Imperial Corps of five hundred dancers, the stars of which were Feodorovna, Michaelovna, Lopukova, Fokine, Bolm, and Nijinski, all headed by the incomparable Pavlowa. Such splendor left one in a daze, and in this frame of mind we adjourned to the famous restaurant, Europe, where to our surprise we found a number of our Russian friends awaiting us, eager to ascertain our reactions. For, by that time, Spalding had become one of their idols. He had some well-merited triumphs at the Dvoriansky Sobrany, or Hall of the Nobility, where all important concerts were given.

At all our concerts we began to notice the presence of an elderly, distinguished-looking gentleman, generally surrounded by youths of both sexes. We could not quite make out who he was, until after our last recital the gentleman came backstage with his entire little brood. He was short, with eyes that shone like live coals, a short beard, and incessant, furious gesticulations. He walked truculently up to Mr. Spalding, and at first I was afraid he meant him harm. But not at all. It was his way of being enthusiastic. He exclaimed, "I am Leopold Auer. This is my class. I bring them here for all your concerts. It is a better lesson than I can give them." With that, he introduced a few: Thelma Given, Alexander Bloch,

223

When Benoist visited Auer in St. Petersburg in 1913, he was given this photograph, suitably autographed, as a souvenir. It was during this visit that he and Spalding first heard Jascha Heifetz.

224

Toscha Seidel, Jascha Heifetz, etc. Then he asked whether we would be interested in coming to the Imperial Conservatory the next day to hear some of his more promising pupils. Would we like to? Needless to say, we accepted the invitation with "alacrity and dispatch." The next day we arrived in due time at the frowning old building that housed the world-famed institution and were ushered to the sanctum of the great master. There we found the professor pacing up and down restlessly with the reverent faces of his ' students looking on. As Spalding entered the room, they rose in a body, bowing respectfully. "Just like home," thought I, "but in reverse!"

The two pupils that stood out in our minds were Seidel and Heifetz. They were about twelve or thirteen years old. Toscha played with fervor and warmth and had the Elman habit of walking while he played, like a caged young lion. His tone was large and luminous. He was exciting. Then came young Jascha. His appearance made the contrast between the two boys startling. Whereas young Toscha, swarthy, fiery, energetic and self-confident, acted like a young bantam rooster, Jascha was fair and blue-eyed, with a mop of blonde, wavy hair that would have been the envy of a Hollywood glamour girl; besides, it owed nothing to the art of the beauty emporiums. His features were of the utmost beauty, in fact, the shape of his mouth would have better suited the aforementioned Hollywood princess. In short, he looked like one of the angels descended from a painting by Raphael. This exquisite youth attacked the outrageous difficulties of the Ernst *F Sharp Minor Concerto* with such sureness that it left one stunned. Technical problems virtually did not exist for him. He just tossed off runs in thirds, sixths or tenths while counting flies on the ceiling. All this he did with an air of boredom and listlessness that sometimes became annoying. His facial expression never changed. Whether his violin sang like a thrush, or his fingers galloped through well-nigh insuperable difficulties, he remained "poker-faced." All he had done was incredibly beautiful, but the ease and indifference with which it had been done left one with a sense of futility. After it was over, we congratulated the lad, to which he replied with a grave little bow and went back to his seat in the class.

All the while, Professor Auer had been pacing up and down like one possessed. Now he came over to us and bluntly asked: "Now you've heard them. Which of these two would you advise me to send to America?" Here was a dilemma! What to advise the great man? Spalding and I looked at each other, and I could see by the twinkle in his eyes that he disagreed with the thought I had in mind. Of course, with the fiery restlessness of Mischa Elman having been such an overwhelming success, there was no doubt that his legitimate follower should be the little bantam Toscha, and I so expressed our opinion. The maestro shrugged his shoulders and in a half whisper said, "Well, we shall see!"

The future did, in fact, tell.

Shortly thereafter, we took our departure from this wonderful country, where Spalding's art had met with such enthusiastic recognition. While reluctant to leave, I for one did not feel too depressed. My heart was singing, for had I not received a cablegram from America, announcing that my young wife was embarking to meet me at Genoa, Italy? And this was to be our honeymoon after four years of marriage; the first opportunity my professional duties had allowed me for this happy time. It was in this frame of mind that we embarked for southern climes. The trip was uneventful up to the German frontier. But there we were suddenly confronted with stark reality.

After the customary luggage examination, during which you ask yourself "Where in thunder did I put those Russian cigarettes; and did I take that bottle of vodka after all?", the inspector suddenly turned to me and pointing an accusing finger at a brown paper parcel I was carrying under my arm, said, "And what is this?" Heaven help me! I had completely forgotten about "this"! It all came back to me, but would the stern guardian of the customs believe me? While in St. Petersburg, we ate liberally of a delicacy called "smoked siguy." It is a fish caught in the Volga and very highly regarded by the connoisseurs. We became very fond of it, and on the strength of that our manager, Charles Kohler, had purchased a whole one for us to take back so that the Spalding family could partake of it on our return to Florence. Not being able to

A photograph of the young Heifetz, autographed in Russian.

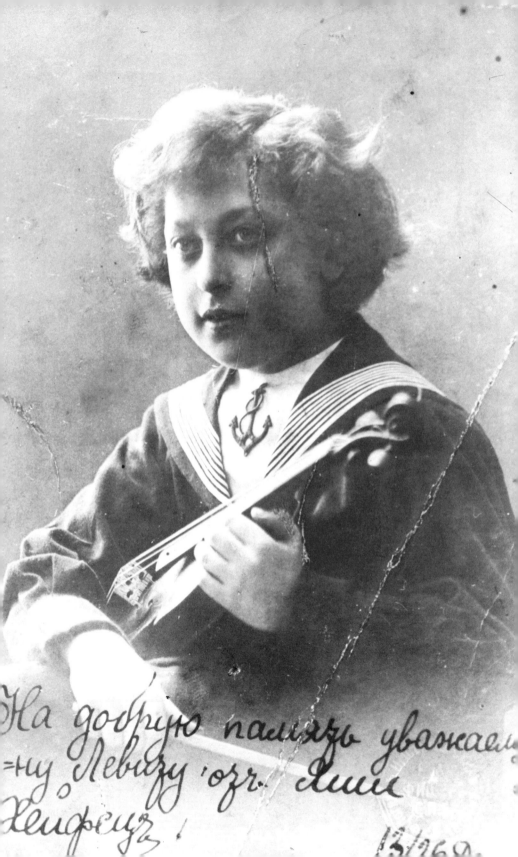

На добрую память уважаем=
=ну Левицу отъ Яши
Хейфецъ!

13/269.

pack it with my belongings owing to its spreading aroma, I carried it under my arm all the way, wrapped in heavy brown paper. The guard having asked his question, the following conversation ensued:

The Guard: "You say, this is a fish?"

I: "Yes sir."

The Guard: "Why do you travel with a fish?"

I: "I don't know. I like this fish."

The Guard: "Is the fish alive?"

I: "No sir, it is smoked."

The Guard: "Why is it smoked?"

I: "It tastes better that way."

The Guard: "Will you eat it on the way?"

I: "We probably will, if we're hungry."

The Guard: "Then it is not an article of importation for profit?"

I: "Oh! No sir! Not for profit! Only for edification."

The Guard: "Very well then; you may take the fish with you, but you will have to pay duty on it. Come with me to the office."

We arrived at the office, where another forbidding individual in uniform was sitting behind some wire meshing. After a short, whispered consultation with our guard, the official behind the wire enclosure brusquely called out, "Achtzig!" "Good Heavens," thought I, "Eighty marks? Why that's about twenty dollars!" And I whispered to Spalding, "We better leave the cursed fish for them to eat!" So in the best German I could muster, I explained that we found the duty much too high. A guffaw greeted my statement. "Surely the gentlemen are joking," said the official, "eighty pfennigs too high? And for so fine a fish? Come now. . . " "Ah, pfennigs! That's a different question," I thought. "About twenty cents; O.K." And thus ended a combination of "Comedy of Errors" and "Much Ado About Nothing."

Heifetz, in one of his many sailor suit outfits, poses with his two sisters, Pauline on the left and Elsa on the right. Throughout his life Heifetz has maintained the unaffected stage presence which Benoist commented on when hearing him in St. Petersburg.

Benoist during his tour of Russia with Spalding in 1914.

With this behind us, we returned to the train that was to take us as far as Milan, where another change was necessary to reach our destination: Florence. Lunch time came, and we started on our way to the dining car, when on glancing into a second-class compartment, I spied a face that seemed familiar. I called to Mr. Spalding and asked, "Look sharp! Isn't that Fritz and Harriet Kreisler over there?" His answer was a sudden rush to the compartment in question; there was mutual recognition, and all marveled at the coincidence of finding ourselves on the same train, etc., etc., etc. We both noticed that Mr. Kreisler's usually sunny smile was absent and he looked rather dejected. Wondering at this, Spalding inquired whether business was satisfactory. "Oh yes," replied Kreisler, "not bad at all." This, of course we knew, for in Russia at least, his concerts were sold out long in advance. That was at a time when, in America, he had to be satisfied with half a house! "No," he continued, "that isn't what makes me so glum. I have decided to leave my fiddle in its box and never take it out again!" "In heaven's name, why?" we inquired. "Well," Kreisler went on, "a few weeks ago I heard a young lad play the violin in such a manner as to make it useless for me to attempt to approach its magnificence. And what's the use of all this slaving, practicing and working, when a mere child seems to accomplish all we have been trying to do for years, as easily as he plays marbles!"

I looked at Spalding and he looked at me, both wondering whom Kreisler had in mind. We inquired as to where he had heard this seven-day wonder, to which he replied, "Why in St. Petersburg a couple of months ago!" Then we knew to whom he was referring. So Spalding put the question direct: "You mean young Heifetz, of course?" An affirmative answer being given, Spalding continued, "In one way you are right; the boy undoubtedly has mastered the technical problems of the violin as I have never witnessed before in one so young, or for that matter, in one much older. He does make his instrument sing in angelic fashion. But is that all there is to it? Has not every artist an individual way of expressing himself? Does not every composition speak in a different way in different hands? This boy, marvelous as he is, has not lived as yet and with his individual character not having had time to develop itself, he still expresses only childish emotions, beautiful as those are. So let us wait until he is a man, with a man's experience, heartbreaks and joys in-

Fritz Kreisler's season's greetings. Circa 1940.

With All Good Wishes

for

Christmas and the New Year

☆

Harriet and Fritz Kreisler

cluded, (that is, if he is able to experience those); and then we shall see what comes out of it all. As to you putting your violin away, even temporarily, nonsense. Why that would mean locking up your life and soul, and you could not live without either! As for me, I shall keep on playing to the best of my ability, not because I like to play better than anyone else, but because I love to play, that's all!'' Upon which we all adjourned to the dining car, where a good meal, accompanied by some delicious wine, put us all in good humor. Time came for sleep and after mutual expressions of satisfaction on this pleasant and unexpected meeting, we went back to our own compartments, on our way to our respective destinations. . .

Chapter
XVII

The rest of the journey passed uneventfully and our return to Florence was the usual return of the prodigals; we were feted, wined and dined to repletion, saw good opera at the Politeamo Fiorentino and had the busman's holiday: music, music and more music! As for me, this time, though more than pleasant, passed only too slowly, as a few days later I was to be off to Genoa to meet the steamer *Princess Irene,* which was carrying my wife from America. She had never been to Europe, and I knew what a thrill was in store for her. Besides, I had a surprise for her of which she had no inkling, as I had only just learned of it myself. During our absence in the northern countries, our Italian impresario Alfredo Carlotti had booked a tour of southern Italy, including Rome, Naples, Palermo, Marsala, Trapani and other cities, and as a climax, we were to sail from Brindisi for Egypt.

Our meeting was romantic in the extreme! I had been away from home about five months and my impatience at seeing Alice was understandable. I arrived in Genoa the evening before the steamer was due. The weather was abominable. Fog, drizzle, more fog and then a downpour. The little Hotel Aquila, which was the nearest habitable place to the docks, was managed by a jolly, rotund little man, who showed me to a tiny single room devoid of the most elementary conveniences. I explained to him that this would not do at all, as I was expecting my wife from America the next morning; that we would, of course, need a larger room with bath, if possible. My very primitive Italian must have misled him, for he suddenly beamed and said in an English that matched my poor Italian, "Si, si, signor! Bridal chamber!" Upon which he led me to a room which seemed to be about the size of Carnegie Hall! This room adjoined a bathroom slightly smaller, in which I thought one would be rather abashed to bathe. The bed must have been specially constructed for giants, so huge it was. And when I returned from dinner, I found every nook and corner of the room filled with flowers! I couldn't believe my eyes. Was this Italian hospitality? I cautiously inquired from the jolly little man what it all meant, but all he did was to continue beaming and, closing one eye, uttered, "The signor's lady come from America for marry, must make nice!" There was no use arguing, so I made the best of all this splendor. Strangely though, the man could not understand how I dared to open the window on retiring. "Bad for eyes," he said, "make you blind!" Whether he was right or wrong, I don't know. But the fact remains that, probably owing to the exciting day I had spent, and the expectation of things to come, I hardly slept a wink. I awakened a little after five, exhausted and bedraggled, to find a clear sky and the dawning sun beginning to show its first rays.

This in itself appeared a good omen, and aided by a good soaking in the huge bathtub, things began to look even brighter. A good breakfast, topped by a choice cigar, and I was ready to face the world. But it was only seven o'clock, and the steamer was not due to dock until nine! By now, the sun was full up, and I thought I might as well stroll out and see something of the great fort. As my steps took me automatically towards the docks, an insane notion began to form in my mind. "Wouldn't it be a marvelous surprise for my little wife, if, standing on the deck ready to disembark, she would turn around and suddenly be confronted by her loving husband!?" Of course I knew that the customs officials usually went out in a small rowboat to board the steamers prior to their dockings, and with this in mind I approached a man wearing a heavily gold-braided cap. I explained to him what was in my mind. He stared at me, horrified, as if I had suddenly gone mad. Said he, "But signor, what you propose is a crime! No official would assume the responsibility of smuggling you on board an incoming ship! He would be put in prison! He would be a criminal! Never, never, say such a thing again!"

Nevertheless, he did not move away. Thought I, "You can't be killed for trying, so here goes." I pulled out a beautiful, shiny,

236

Alice Benoist, circa 1905.

twenty lire gold piece and began playing with it. I could see the gold-braided personage's eyes begin to glisten, and little by little his face lost its forbidding expression. "Of course," I whispered, "any trouble a friend would go to for me, I would be very willing to compensate with a little gift for his wife or children." The man turned to leave, saying over his shoulder, "Wait here;" and went to another official-looking person. After a few moments of whispered conversation, my man came back and handing me a cap similar to his own, said: "Wear this in place of your hat and follow me." I was a bit puzzled, but followed orders, not knowing what would develop next.

What did develop was not too promising. I was ushered to a small rowboat that looked none too reassuring to me, who had never rowed a stroke. I must have looked rather funny, wearing my gold-braided cap and a frightened expression on my face but by that time my customs official was in possession of that lovely twenty lire gold piece, and was in a mood mellow enough to condone any idiosyncrasies I might show. Consequently, he calmed my forebodings by declaring that I would not have to row at all. I was just to sit still in the stern of the little boat and allow myself to be rocked by the soft waves. The latter were not to my taste, for the little, light craft was beginning to dance disagreeably. Fortunately in spite of everything, my breakfast remained static and soon we arrived alongside a cliff of seemingly limitless height, which turned out to be the North German Lloyd ship *Princess Irene*. My companions maneuvered their little craft until it stood flush with a rope ladder, the top of which was lost in limitless space. "Here we are," said one of them, "and up you go. We'll follow you, so in case you slip, we can catch you."

Ah me, what had a romantic notion led me into? What? Me climb this perilously loose rope thing that looked more like a spider web than something designed to support even my relatively light weight? No! I couldn't do it! The two men with me saw my dilemma, and gave me the "choice" of remaining in the boat to be tossed about waiting for them, or rowing back to the dock by myself. There being no real choice, I started up, while the remaining man in the boat held the bottom of the ladder as steadily as was possible under the circumstances. After a period lasting approximately two hundred and thirty-five years, I arrived at an opening about

238

Albert Spalding and Andre Benoist had, perhaps, the closest and warmest friendship of any musician and his accompanist. These two pictures show them jovially clowning at Spalding Villa in Florence. Circa 1920.

halfway up to the main deck and entered, rather embarrassed, to find myself saluted ceremoniously by other people in gold-braided caps. However, my companion soon joined me, and led me up to the top deck where innumerable passengers were assembled, ready to disembark. During a few dazed moments, my companion took the opportunity to hand me my hat while removing the cap that now was no longer necessary, I began to recover my wits somewhat and started looking among all these people for the little speck of humanity that was my wife. Suddenly I spied a small group of people, two of whom seemed familiar. I walked up to them, and to my amazement recognized two of my best friends from the States. "And what are you two doing on this ship!" I exclaimed. "Why, escorting your wife, you idiot, and seeing that she arrives safe and sound to your receptive arms!"

After mutual explanations, it transpired that by pure coincidence they had booked passage on the same ship, and having seen my wife's name on the passenger list, had renewed acquaintances and together enjoyed a delightful crossing. So while I was worrying about her lonely crossing, there she was with two "cavalier servants" at her beck and call, and having a grand time! Evidently, she was still enjoying herself, for when my two friends pointed to her, she was talking a mile a minute to a bevy of people I had never seen before, but with whom she seemed to be on the best of terms. So engrossed was she in the conversation that she never noticed me tip-toeing behind her, and when I got close up, I suddenly let out a tremendous "B o o!" She turned white as a sheet and almost fainted in my arms. What an idiot I had been!! I was beginning to bitterly regret my foolish prank, when I noticed by the unmistakable expression on Alice's face that there was no real cause for remorse!

After lengthy and voluble explanations from both sides, and expressions of happiness at our reunion, the ship at last docked, and we all repaired to the Aquila where a fine lunch awaited us. I draw a discreet curtain over the rest of the day, and the next morning we were off for radiant Florence, where the incomparable "Spalding hospitality" awaited us.

It was not until then that the news of the trip to Egypt dawned on my little lady's consciousness, and at first it was not received with the degree of joy I had anticipated. Quite the contrary, it was

240

Alice Benoist, "Nannie," and Marie Spalding, Albert's mother, in Florence. Circa March, 1914.

with a glum look that she murmured, "I've no sooner arrived than we are to be separated again." "But no," I informed her. "Don't you realize that you're going along?" Then, with a squeal of delight, she began to talk about packing, what to take along to wear, what the customs and habits were, etc. She talked far, far into the night. In fact, when the party, which besides Spalding consisted of myself and my wife, Mrs. Spalding Sr. and her black maid Nannie, we were quite a caravan. Nannie was a great center of attraction among the Italian population, for the latter knew mostly princes and princesses of the African race, those being sent by the potentates of their African possessions, as diplomats or envoys plenipotentiary. Consequently, wherever Nannie went she was greeted by a respectful murmur, the gist of which I made out to sound like "la donna oscura," meaning "the dusky lady."

Italian audiences are different from any audiences I have ever seen. They are far from being reticent. They are free and outspoken. They either love you or hate you, but they are never indifferent. And they never leave you in doubt as to their feelings. One of my first experiences with them was on the occasion of Spalding's debut at the great Teatro alla Scala, in Milan. Now, it must be understood that the Scala is hardly ever used for concerts. It is strictly devoted to opera, and when that rule is broken, it is a gala occasion, for it is an honor paid to the artist who obtains permission to perform there. Only five violinists prior to Spalding have been granted that honor. The first one was Paganini; the second, Sivori; the third, Eugene Ysaye; the fourth, Franz von Vecszey; and the fifth, Fritz Kreisler. So it can be understood with what trepidation we awaited the news that permission had been granted for our concert to take place behind the sacred portals! It came at last, and excitement was rife.

As the date for the concert approached, I noticed that our usually pleasant manager, Alfredo Carlotti, was becoming exceedingly short and nervous in his conversation. I delicately inquired of him as to what was so upsetting, upon which he became volubly full of information. "Don't you realize what this means," he said in an awed voice! "The Scala! Why, if you are successful here, it means that you have the whole of Italy at your feet! If you fail, you might as well go home, never to appear again! And the worst of it is that you will know this from the first phrase you play. Spalding does

Albert Spalding with his Italian manager, Alfredo Carlotti and Alice Benoist on the road to Rome during their 1914 Italian tour. Benoist took this photo himself.

not know all this as yet, and you must not tell him anything about it. It might affect his playing. And you know," he added confidentially, "they may talk to him throughout his playing, either approvingly or disparagingly, but he must not stop; he must go on as though lost in his music! Ah me, oh my, what a life is an artist's and his manager's!"

I was deeply impressed, but secretly I thought the man was grossly exaggerating, perhaps with an idea of making himself very important (although this seemed quite out of character in so charming and modest a person). He was huge: six-feet-two in height and built in proportion. My own height is a mere five-feet-five, and I remember when first he met us at the railroad station on our arrival in Italy, he raised me in his powerful arms and kissed me on both cheeks. My wife, who was standing by, received a respectful kiss on the back of her right hand. "Good Lord" she exclaimed, "this is a world upside down! The men get kissed and women are respectfully saluted!" Little did she know what was in store for her to witness! And this was the man Carlotti, whom I thought might be exaggerating!

The fateful evening of the Scala concert arrived at last, and I must confess that, in spite of years of debut routine, my heart was in my mouth. Finally there came the usual "death march" to the stage. Barely a smattering of applause greeted my friend. Although forewarned that this might happen, it was a chilling experience. I suppose the audience went on the assumption that, not knowing this artist, why go to the trouble of a purely hypocritical welcome before knowing what he had to offer? In the midst of a profound silence, Spalding began the opening phrase of a lovely sonata by Archangelo Corelli. It starts with a long sustained note lasting almost two bars, during which the piano performs beautiful modulations. But if the violinist's bow trembles the slightest bit the whole effect is marred. It did not tremble, however; but beginning softly, increased in a beautiful crescendo till the apex was reached and then went on to the magnificent arabesques that follow. Nervous as I was, I could not help but think, "lucky dog, with that beginning!"

Then, apparently out of nowhere, I noticed a murmur rising from the audience. I could, here and there, distinguish a few words such as "E un angelo" (He's an angel) and "Ma, suona benissimo"

244

(My, but he plays beautifully). "Thank Heaven," I thought, "no ripe tomatoes or eggs! Sounds encouraging. If only he doesn't stop. Must go on!" And on he went as if serenely unaware of the commotion he was causing. The concert continued at this rate until intermission time. Having returned to the green room, an avalanche of humanity, mostly male, nearly overwhelmed us, all bent on kissing Spalding on both cheeks. I had my modest share of it myself, but after a few judicial breaths of the aroma given forth by garlic, I judged it the better part of valor to retire to the only room where one can reasonably be assured of some degree of privacy. Emerging from retirement a bit later, after the earthquake had subsided, I met Carlotti who said in choking tones, "He is made in Italy!"

And, truth to tell, "made" he was. He was greeted by hero worshipping crowds wherever he went. This result, however, was not brought about by the usual American "ballyhoo" methods. For the Italians, as a rule, distrust the printed word, and especially that of what we are pleased to call "critics." To be sure, they have critics, but not in the same sense that we have them. Italian critics do not have to meet a deadline. They are generally prominent persons in the respective fields they are to write about and have themselves proven to be masters in their own field of endeavor. They are engaged by a newspaper to give written reports about artists who have become successful enough in the public eye to be worthy of reviews. These reviews are written quietly, thoughtfully, and at leisure, sometimes weeks after the concert in question has taken place. It may be a right or wrong estimate, but never careless or flippant. That does not mean that the Italian public takes much stock in it though, for it is taken as one man's opinion. But it does arouse curiosity, which, commercially, is good.

As I said, the Italians distrust the printed word more than we do. They prefer word of mouth, which is always easier to refute, or at least, to argue. And as Italians love an argument above all, this produces, somewhere along the way, a more rightful estimate than the nonsensical arrangement we have with our newspapers. For how can one give a proper opinion upon hearing a performer once, and generally under unfavorable circumstances, such as extreme nervousness caused by a debut appearance? Besides, newspapers are notorious cowards, for when called to order over some gross injustice perpetrated by one of their writers, they generally hide behind the fact that "this is not necessarily the opinion of the paper, but merely the opinion of the writer." Now what redress can one get under these conditions? When a man errs in an opinion expressed verbally, one can then and there refute him. But newspapers inject their poison in the victim, and then leave the dart in the wound to fester and rankle.

Thus it came to pass that wherever we went on our southern tour, Mr. Spalding's fame preceded him, mostly by word of mouth, and consequently, great enthusiasm greeted him on all occasions. The most climactic one was in Palermo, where the kissing enthusiasts became so aggressive with Spalding that I hid behind a high-backed chair, and from that vantage point watched the vanishing of the last music enthusiasts. Then, with a sigh of relief, I reappeared on the scene, and we all made our escape back to the privacy of the hotel. The Palermo concert being the last on our Italian tour, we took a ship the following day for Naples, where, after a horrible crossing, we entrained for Brindisi.

There we embarked on the good ship *Helouan* for Alexandria, where three days later, we were to make the acquaintance of one of the strangest human beings it has been my lot to meet among the species: "managers."

Chapter XVIII

The entire arrangements for our concerts in Egypt had been made by our Italian manager, Carlotti, in correspondence with an individual vaguely named Lifonti. On our way across the Mediterranean we had rather speculated as to what sort of person this Lifonti would prove to be. Was he honest? Would he be enthusiastic? Would his publicity be adequate? The steamer at last tied up to the dock and we descended the gangplank where we were met by the strangest individual my eyes had ever beheld outside of story books. His trousers were tucked into high boots. He wore an old-fashioned Prince Albert coat under which flourished a flowered waistcoat. He had a long, flowing and fierce-looking black moustache, and his head was topped by a huge black wide-brimmed sombrero. He looked like a combination of a western brigand and the general conception of the ideal confidence man. This character addressed us in French, tinged with a strong Gascon accent.

Being too large a party for one carriage, we had to divide ourselves; and Spalding, in a whisper, urged me to join Lifonti in his carriage, so as to artfully discover what sort of person we were dealing with. For we were both a little appalled by his appearance. So I cautiously inquired what he thought of the financial prospects of our undertaking. He replied that he thought them good, but one never could tell until afterwards. That seemed plausible. So I further inquired as to publicity. His reply was to stop the carriage before a huge poster. "Look," he said. "I have had these printed in letters the size of a man!" "Yes," I replied, "But all it says here is SPALDING and a date underneath; you don't say what he is or what he does! How will people know?" "Ah," he ejaculated,

One of Benoist's snapshots of the main street in Cairo, Egypt, during the 1914 tour with Spalding.

"that's the trick! I don't tell them! People come to the box office and inquire whether this is a juggler, a singer, a dancer or whatnot! In answer, I tell them, 'Just buy a ticket for a sovereign, and you'll find out!' " "Well, do they buy?" I inquired. "Some do," he answered, "but at any rate it has aroused so much curiosity that everybody in Cairo and here in Alexandria is agog!" "Pretty primitive," I thought, "but it may work."

Our financial arrangements, I ascertained, were satisfactory, but whether they would be carried out honestly, I had no means of finding out, at least until one concert was over. His box office arrangements also were primitive. They consisted of a board pierced by two small slots under each of which hung a canvas bag. As a gold piece was handed to him (all seats being priced alike) he slipped it in one or the other slot, giving in exchange a pasteboard ticket entitling the bearer to enter and choose a seat. The concert was scheduled for 9:00 p.m. and we were all sitting backstage waiting for a signal to start. The hall looked hopelessly empty, with just a scattering of people in attendance. It was a dreary sight,

248

and I had given up peeking through the curtain to see how things were shaping up. Suddenly Lifonti appeared, and regretfully said, "I am sorry, ladies, but I shall need your chairs; you can sit in that corner on some of these cushions, if you will allow me." "What for?" inquired Mr. Spalding. "Why I cannot let people stand in the aisles, can I? Just look for yourself." With that we both peeked through the curtains and saw a milling crowd trying to get seated, with more at the doors trying to enter. At last we stepped on the stage, and an "Ahhh. . ." went up from the assemblage, probably denoting either astonishment or delight or both; we would not know until after the first number. It turned out to be both, with a genuine ovation following at the end. But then came the funniest part of the whole enterprise. For our apparent highwayman insisted that the counting up be done forthwith. He came to fetch us,

Benoist's favorite photo, showing Spalding on a donkey. Alice Benoist is seated on the other donkey, while Nannie is shown to her left, seated in the carriage. March, 1914.

holding a heavy canvas bag in each hand, and thus crossed the street to his office where we followed him. Arrived there, he dumped the contents of both bags onto a large card table. These contents proved to be all gold sovereigns and I admit I never saw so much gold assembled at one time and place!

Now our financial arrangements were to be fifty-fifty of the gross receipts, and out of his share Lifonti was to pay all expenses connected with the concerts. His method of division was simple and also primitive in the extreme. From the pile at hand, he counted five sovereigns which he pushed to one side. Then he counted five more which he slid towards himself. And so on, until the heap was divided equally. He put each side in a canvas bag, handed one to us, and took the other one for himself. With that he wished us good night and said he would see us at the next concert. "You see," murmured Spalding, "that's how you can trust appearances. This fellow looks like a highwayman and is as honest as the day is long; whereas managers often look like real gentlemen and are as crooked as a ram's horns!"

The next concert took place in Cairo. I had dreamt of Cairo all my life. It represented all I had read in Phillips Oppenheim novels. Shepheard's Hotel. . . the pyramids. . . carts driven by white oxen that took you to the edge of the Sahara Desert, etc! In other words, my conception of the whole Cairo enterprise was very romantic. The only personage I had left out of my reckoning was the enterprising, international, and extremely beautiful spy-adventuress; and with just cause, for was I not a young man on a honeymoon?

My first disappointment came when I found we had not been booked at Shepheards' Hotel, where all good international intrigues were supposed to be properly started. No, we went to the Savoy Palace Hotel, where, unromantically enough, each room was connected with a very modern bathroom. However, I took my courage in both hands, and went to interview the majordomo behind the hotel desk, who regarded me benevolently but rather haughtily over his spectacles. I unfolded to him my plan to engage a cart drawn by two white oxen to take us to see the pyramids the following day. I noticed his looks changing from condescending haughtiness to deep concern, and he seemed to look around as if seeking help of some kind. I inquired politely whether there was anything wrong with my request, upon which he blurted out,

250

Indoor photography was difficult in those years, but that hardly stopped Benoist from making this posed photograph of his wife, Alice, in Egypt, 1914.

Andre Benoist, 1914.

"What do you mean, wrong? Young man, are you trying to pull my leg, or are you really out of your mind? White oxen, indeed! Who ever heard of white oxen in Cairo? I want you to know that we are a civilized nation and that under no condition will I allow you to make any insinuations to the contrary! Are you sure you haven't been drinking?" "Whence this wrath," I asked in surprise, "What's the matter with you? Isn't my request a perfectly natural one?" "Natural?" he retorted. "Who ever heard of two white oxen treading these asphalted streets? Why this isn't carnival time! People would think you'd gone suddenly insane! Besides where would one obtain white oxen?"

I explained, to the best of my ability, that I had read of such a thing in some of our most celebrated books. But the majordomo just sniffed and said with scorn in his voice, "Celebrated books indeed! You must have been reading fairy tales or nursery rhymes." Whereupon I diffidently inquired as to how one went to the pyramids. "Why," he replied with a chuckle, "you take the trolley

252

car that passes by the hotel and just go. It costs you one piastariff (about a nickel, American style) and that's all there is to it!" Completely deflated, I reported the result of my inquiries to the rest of our party, thereby causing a hearty laugh all around. Murmured Spalding; "Your confounded romantic imagination will someday get you in serious trouble, and then look out! I won't come to bail you out!" And that is the way we went to see the renowned pyramids of Egypt, on a common trolley car! My second delusion!

My third came immediately upon alighting from the vile vehicle that had transported us to the site of dreams. Right opposite the first and smaller pyramid was an English tea room from which issued sounds of revelry. On entering, to fortify ourselves with the usual "spot of tea" before starting on our expedition, the sounds proved to be those of a fairly good jazz band that was entertaining the guests! Shades of Cleopatra! What a descecration! The refreshments over, we started, and we were told by an ubiquitous guide that we would be better off riding around on donkeys, as a camel in motion might make us seasick. This was done, and certainly was not as romantic as camels, which I had secretly hoped we'd ride. But when I looked around at Spalding, I thought I would die with laughter; for up to now, I had failed to notice his costume, engrossed as I was in the contemplation of the historial scene. This costume consisted of patent leather shoes, beautiful striped trousers, and a fashionable "cutaway" morning coat, all topped by a bowler or derby hat. Seated on a donkey with the temperature in the neighborhood of 100 degrees Fahrenheit, I could conceive of nothing more comical. And everybody agreed, including Mr. Spalding, who sheepishly remarked, "I didn't think it was worthwhile buying a straw hat for so short a stay!" "Just for that" I replied, "I am going to take your picture just as you are." This I did forthwith, and I still treasure it as one of the oddities I encountered.

The rest of our musical adventure in Egypt proved as successful as its beginning, and it was with sincere regret that we took leave of our brigand impresario, who had proved to be honest and enterprising, as well as being a genial host.

The greatest of the great pianists, Franz Liszt.

Chapter XIX

Our return to Florence was celebrated with the usual rounds of festivities, copiously enhanced by good music given in the ideal music room of the Spalding Palazzo. This house had an interesting history. From different rumors, I gathered that it had been originally built by some member of the Talleyrand family as a winter pleasure home. All the rooms were stately and vast in size. The whole place reeked of the Napoleonic period, but certain improvements "a l'Americaine" had been made, such as modern plumbing and an excessive number of bathrooms.

Regarding these, there is a story extant that tells of a visit made to the Spalding family by the French composer, Saint-Saens, which lasted several days. He was, of course, lodged in what was called the "State Bedroom." This appellation was given more in a spirit of fun than from ostentation, the reason for this being that the bed, raised three steps above the floor and surmounted by an ornate canopy, was the same as when the original owners were in residence. It all looked very regal; in addition to this, the adjoining bathroom was huge, with the enormous tub in dead center. Anyway, that is where the extremely Gallic, and therefore frugal Saint-Saens spent his first night under the Spalding roof. Upon joining the family at breakfast the next morning, he was politely asked whether he had had a restful night, and whether he enjoyed his bath. Whereupon the old gentleman turned around as if stung by a wasp, and exclaimed, "Bath? Are you joking? Why I would as soon bathe in Carnegie Hall in New York as to bathe in such a sized room!" No one pursued the subject further!

The great two-stories-high music room, where young Spalding rehearsed with Saint-Saens prior to a joint tour of Italy, had once echoed the magic playing of the great pianist-composer Franz Liszt, in the heyday of his glory! In other words, the whole atmosphere reeked of a glorious past.

It is therefore understandable that we left this delightful residence with utmost reluctance. But the time had come for our start back to America. Two recitals in Paris on our way completed our European adventure. This was in the spring of 1914, and everything was peaceful and serene. On the Parisian avenues and boulevards, the fine chestnut trees were burgeoning with their exquisite buds. The flower sellers around the Madeleine were offering lovely bargains in all kinds of posies. The cafes were bulging with foreigners, as well as Frenchmen, sipping their aperitif in the welcome sunshine, after a dreary winter drizzle. In short, "God was in His heaven, and all was right with the world!" In this frame of mind we sailed from Le Havre for New York, little dreaming what an inferno was simmering beneath the apparent bliss.

We were fully compensated for our sudden transition by the joy we felt at being back again on home soil. And all the customary petty annoyances one had to submit to on arrival did not succeed in dimming this joy. It was AMERICA. The magic country of elbow room, of rudeness. Of kindliness combined with roughness. Of resentment at any restraint but minding the law just the same (when convenient). The combination of everything the world had to offer, good, bad, or indifferent. With all this we quickly fell in step again, and loving every moment of it.

It was the end of May, and we had engaged a small cottage at Monmouth Beach, New Jersey, for the summer months, so as to be nearer to my friend Spalding, whose family had its summer home there.

Suddenly out of a clear sky, exploded the appalling news of the Crime of Sarajevo! Of course it left the world aghast, but none of us dreamed what consequences it would have for our future. It was so peaceful here by the seashore! One shrugged one's shoulders, as if to say, "Thank heavens, we have nothing to do with all this mess!" The fateful declaration of war came from Austria, aided and abetted by von Bethman-Holmeg, for Germany; and still one shrugged contentedly. "Them furriners," the workmen would say, wagging their heads, "always a chip on their shoulders! Always fighting! Well, it's none of our business!"

So the comfortable summer went by, and the forthcoming season's repertoire was being faithfully and conscientiously rehearsed, with a copiously booked winter tour ahead. But in spite of our happy and peaceful surroundings, the thunder clap of Germany's ruthless egging-on of Austria in its pursuit of vengeance on hapless little Serbia, with the result of an even more ruthless war being started, had a certain amount of repercussion even in our quiet little village by the sea. Yet all went along as usual—our concert tours, the same as all the rest.

There was, however, an undercurrent of sullen anger in us all, for the way the Germans had initiated this war was something that left even the hardest and most inured of us appalled. Everyone realized the injustice of the cause and the way retaliation was being carried out. Our 1916-1917 tour was drawing to a close when on April 6th, 1917, President Wilson found himself in the position of no longer being able to evade the issue, and so the blow fell. WAR WAS DECLARED ON GERMANY BY THE UNITED STATES OF AMERICA! From that moment on, I found Spalding's usually sunny disposition undergoing a change. He would sit on a train, apparently lost in dreams, which I knew better than to disturb by chit-chat. Thought I to myself, "He's pondering some new composition, and when he's ready, I'll hear about it."

A few weeks later I "heard about it." And when I heard, I thought the man had suddenly lost his senses. "I'm going to enlist," he said out of a clear sky. At first I thought he was joking; but no, he was deadly earnest, and I saw at once that even an attempt to dissuade him in any way would threaten our friendship, a thing I could not have stood. I did remark that we had a heavy season already booked for 1917-18. "Oh that," he answered, "well, what's to prevent us from cancelling those bookings? There's reason enough, I'm sure!" And that was the end of that. Cancel the whole season we did, giving the reason, to which no one seemed to object.

It was a hard blow for his family as well as for myself. For there was a contingency I had never contemplated; that of risking precious hands which had given esthetic joy to hundreds of thousands of listeners all over the world. I timidly advanced this reason for my objection to his decision, but to no avail. The only reply my remonstrances elicited from my friend was to the effect that, "All you say is beside the point and only evades the real issue. In the first place, my hands are no more precious than any other individual's who does his work conscientiously and with loving care.

257

Andre Benoist, 1917.

In the second place, I have no responsibilities except my own, as I am not married, have no children, and my immediate family is able to care for itself. And as for me, I have to live with myself, and could not do this comfortably knowing that other men, be they steam fitters, miners, painters, etc., were going to give their all in the defense of their country, while I, being fortunate enough to have a profession that makes for a comfortable living, stood by and watched them do the dirty work! No! Let anyone who feels that his hands are too precious to risk them in this drama keep out of it. I do not blame them for the thought; but I could never reconcile such a thought with my personal feelings in the matter. Precious indeed! Why everybody's hands and welfare are precious! The rest is all in your minds, so let the matter rest there. Let's have a good dinner and forget it!''

I could not help letting my mind drift back over the last two years of happy association, traveling all over our wonderful country. The warm appreciation shown Spalding everywhere for his art and heart-warming humanity. One of the episodes that stood out was an evening spent in close intimacy at James M. Beck's home, where we had both been invited to a quiet dinner party. Mr. Beck was the attorney-at-law for Ignaz Jan Paderewski, who, that evening, was the guest of honor. I had met the latter several times, but only in a formal way, when he was surrounded by sycophants and autograph hunters. Not a very satisfactory occasion, as a rule.

But this was quite different, for to hear Mr. Paderewski discuss world affairs, music, politics and personalities in a completely informal manner, was a pleasure long to be remembered. His was another of those all-embracing minds rarely met, and his conversation scintillated with wit and understanding. The dinner over, we were sitting in easy chairs over our coffee accompanied by fragrant Havana cigars, when Paderewski, evidently mellowed by the relaxing atmosphere, turned to Mr. Beck and said, "I see that you have a fine Steinway concert grand; wouldn't you like to hear a little music?" The answer was that which the reader would expect: unanimous exclamations of deep pleasure and anticipation. Upon which the grand "gentleman of music" walked to the piano and for one hour entertained us with music by Chopin: mazurkas, waltzes, nocturnes, scherzos. . . It was such playing as one dreams of but seldom hears. Absent was all showmanship. Absent was all self-

A photograph of Albert Spalding in uniform autographed to his "companion in arms of the concert platform, Andre Benoist." September, 1917.

consciousness. There remained only a great artist completely immersed in the music which dripped from his fingers as from a magic fountain. It was an unforgettable evening.

Some comical happenings also come to mind during this retrospecting. For instance, the little old lady in a small southern town who came backstage after one of our recitals. Frail as she was, her eyes were flashing with fervid enthusiasm. "Ah, Mr. Spalding," she exclaimed breathlessly, "you know, I have heard them all, since I was a little girl, and I'll tell you what the trouble is with all of them. They're all technique and no soul, whereas you . . . you're all soul and no technique!" And thereupon, with an air of having done her duty bravely and well, she stalked off with the smile of a somnambulist fixed on her features.

Delving still further into my memory brought to mind the fact that we had booked our last tour from our own office, which we had opened after severing connections with the established management bureaus, owing to some unfortunate experiences. The experiment proved eminently satisfactory. This sort of thing could still be done in those days, for as yet there had not come into existence the peculiar edifice called a *combine of managers*. Not a little of the success of our enterprise was due to an individual named George E. Brown, whom Mr. Spalding had engaged to travel and do most of the booking that could not be done by correspondence.

George deserves a bit of individual description. He was tall, lean, muscular and in his early forties. His face was rugged and bore a habitually grim look. This was apparently to indicate that he was utterly heartless and completely devoid of any sentiment. However, when caught off guard, as when looking at a child or a dog, his face would light up with the sunniest smile imaginable, assuming an almost childlike sweetness. This, in George's eyes, constituted an unforgivable sin of which he was deeply ashamed; for, if caught in the act, he would clear this throat and gruffly say, "Damned nuisances, those kids!" His career had been checkered. He had been a Shakespearean actor (gravedigger in Hamlet, etc.). He had been advance man for theatrical shows. He had even, for a while, been a minister of the gospel. In expansive moments he would confide, "Sure! I still got my makeup in my trunk!"

But he could sell! And to sell a Spalding concert, for him, was no

Albert Spalding in uniform. These are two of Benoist's favorite photographs and they occupied a place of honor in his scrapbook. Albert Spalding Benoist, Andre Benoist's son, called his father a "squirrel" because he saved everything he could get his hands on.

Albert Spalding was of very strong moral and patriotic inclination. When World War I began, he couldn't resist joining the army air force as a volunteer.

trick at all. For, while he was ostensibly engaged by Mr. Spalding, the reverse was true. He had adopted the latter as his one object in life and became his devoted slave. Therefore no work or hours existed for him so long as his efforts were devoted to the cause he had embraced, namely seeing to it that Spalding appeared wherever there were music lovers, and under the most favorable circumstances. This was the man to whom we had to announce Mr. Spalding's enlistment in the army and the cancellation of the really splendid tour for the forthcoming season. On hearing the news, Brown's eyes blinked rapidly and in a rather choked voice, he muttered, "Damn good riddance; artists are a damn nuisance; guess I'll go back to show business, it's easier." But I also noticed that he walked away in great haste, as if wishing to be alone. Yes, George was tough, and "could take it!"

At last came the day we all had dreaded. Mr. and Mrs. Spalding, Sr. had not wished to drive their son to the camp on Long Island where he was to join his regiment, thereby sparing him and themselves the agonies of a last minute leavetaking. They had schooled themselves for that moment which they preferred take place in the privacy of their home at Monmouth Beach. So it fell to our lot, George's and mine, that we should escort my friend to the camp where, after a never ending drive, we at last arrived amidst a drizzly rain. Two sentries stood at the gate. George unloaded the little metal locker trunk from the waiting taxicab, and with the sentry's permission, set it down within. He came out again, we shook hands perfunctorily all around, Spalding crossed the gate, the sentries crossed bayonets, and our friend became a little dot on a dirty road. And that was that! George Brown returned to the taxicab, his eyes very red and his nose running, his voice not very clear either. "Damn nuisance, these damn head colds!" Whereupon he blew his nose ferociously.

Chapter
XX

Earlier I mentioned that in the old days one could book concerts outside the realm of the established managements. I spoke of this because such a thing would be impossible today. For the manager of today is non-existent. There are combines of managers, in the same manner that General Motors Corporation is a combine of automobile firms. And the musical managers' combine sells artists much as automobiles are sold, the difference being that in the automobile business, most of the people concerned do have some knowledge of engineering, or at least know something about an internal combustion engine.

In the artist-selling business this is not deemed necessary. For the managers do not know anything of the art of music. They are mostly swayed by what music critics report. They believe in slogans like "sales resistance," "personality plus," "he or she goes over well," or "he played a lot of encores." The intrinsic merit of the artist in question plays no role at all. Managers in a combine have neither faith nor belief in anything but the question: "Is he or she 'box-office' or not?" At the slightest hint of the latter commodity, the whole promotion machinery is set in motion and if it happens that the artist is really what he is claimed to be, the public is the gainer.

But it often happens that a total nonentity by some fluke of chance is suddenly taken to the heart of an audience, for no reason clearly apparent. The publicity blast is let loose anyway, and then you have an audience asking itself, "That's what you call an artist?" Well may you ask, "But why all the publicity? Doesn't the public flock to hear an artist once it knows he is worthy?"

No, gentle reader, the public never flocks to anything except prizefights, football games, baseball games, or the races. The rest is promotion and salesmanship. For in every town in our dear United States, one combine or another maintains its branches (I almost said tentacles), in the shape of community concerts or civic concerts, which are pledged to buy artists exclusively from this or that combine. Ostensibly, this is for the good of the community in question, so as to safeguard it against any deficit it might incur, should it choose to engage a particular artist of its own choice and manage the concert independently. This part of the story, at least is correct. And to bring it about, the "combine" has a staff of salespeople, politely called "organizers," who take over a town and through various methods of promotion, too long and complicated to go into thoroughly here, arrange for subscriptions to be made by as many people in that town as possible, in order to create a fund that will enable the town to run a course of three or four concerts during the season, according to the sum that has been garnered.

Naturally, the larger the total, the higher-priced artists the town is able to engage. And if the town has a hall with a small seating capacity, it cannot raise enough money to engage the more experienced artists, for it cannot sell more subscriptions than the seating capacity of the hall.

But now comes the amusing part of the story. Assume that the drive for subscriptions is over, the expenses for the said drive have been paid (out of the subscription fund of course), and the net sum left over is in the bank. Comes the meeting of the board. This board is usually composed of the prominent citizens of the town. They must be the possessors of either purse or influence, or both, preferably. It is part of the organizer's job to root out these prominents or purses. Sometimes a few of them know a little about music in general, or something as to the value of certain artists.

There and then takes place what you would expect to take place if you went into a Buick salesroom and asked for a De Soto car. A member of the board suggests the name of an artist he or she has heard with considerable pleasure and would like his fellow townspeople to hear. "I am indeed sorry," comes in dulcet accents from the organizer, "but this artist is not on our list. You each have a booklet at your elbow showing you the artist's list from which you can choose." Or if the organizer is very diplomatic he will call up the office long distance, and return to the table with the sad news that the artist in question is booked for the whole season and has no open date.

In the end, to simplify things and save time and breath, you realize that it is easier to just go over the list and see what bargain you can draw. You find that most of the attractions you want are too expensive for your rather restricted budget, but that if you retrench on three attractions, you can have one of the higher-priced ones. And so it goes. No, dear reader, art has nothing whatsoever to do with the whole business. For do the men who form the combine know anything about the value of an artist? No indeed! They go entirely by what some poor critic says in his newspaper the day after the artist's (I almost said patient's) debut. If the reviews are good, he becomes a possibility, provided he has enough funds to finance some more appearances, so as to "warm his public." But if his reviews are either lukewarm or downright bad, then come standard cliches such as "unfavorable reaction," "sales resistance," etc. And the poor artist can go hang himself. For there is not one chance in a thousand that he can find remunerative engagements without the backing of one or the other combine.

I, myself, have witnessed a manager, being present at a debut recital where the artist had ovation after ovation from the audience, go up to him, embrace him, and declare that never had he heard a finer performance. The next morning the press was bad. And the artist, upon meeting his friend of the night before, had to hear to his amazement the following speech: "What was the matter with you last night? You didn't do so well, what? Too bad!"

Art indeed! The so-called managers of today would sell cattle, fountain pens or automobiles in the same way they buy and sell artists. And how many promising careers they have ruined does not concern them any more than a stock broker is concerned with the stocks he sold to the man who committed suicide the day after the sale. But enough of this tawdry situation.

My friend Spalding's departure for the war left me rather depressed and bitter. Also very lonesome, for I was at a loose end and without much ambition to look for another connection. In this frame of mind I was walking down Fifth Avenue one morning when I was accosted by an old friend, Richard Copley. He was general factotum of the Wolfsohn Musical Bureau which at that time had been taken over by A. F. Adams. Adams was one of the strangest personalities imaginable. He had been connected with a piano concern for years when the idea suddenly came to him that he would like to enter the musical management field. He was short and very thin; and his every movement gave the impression that he was strung on wires. Every word he uttered (with a strong New England twang) was accompanied by voluble profanity. He was capable of real enthusiasm for any artist he believed in and never undertook such management unless he did. He carefully concealed such enthusiasm under the role of the hard-headed business man.

When the old impresario Henry Wolfsohn died, Adams saw his opportunity and bought out the firm including its most valuable asset, Richard Copley, who had been with the bureau from its very beginning. In fact, he would jokingly remark that he was its bottom drawer. The latter was the man who had accosted me on Fifth Avenue.

"Why," he exclaimed on seeing me, "the mournful look? You act as though you'd lost your best friend; what's the matter?" All I could answer was, "That's right; you guessed it." "What do you mean?", he rejoined, "Aren't you with Spalding any more?" "No," I said, "not for the time being; he's just joined the army." Copley looked at me in surprise and exclaimed, "Why, that's fine! Nothing could be better! Come along with me!" Now I was thoroughly angered and with a parting word, "You heartless brute," I started away from him.

But he held my arm, remarking, "Now calm down; I didn't mean it was fine to be rid of your friend Spalding! I only meant that the circumstances seem to fit in so well."

"What do you mean by circumstances?", I replied.

"Why," came back from Copley, "I want you to come to the office with me now and sign up with another violinist immediately, now that you are at a loose end. That way you will not lose any time!"

"Listen carefully," I said, "I don't want to sign up with anybody right now; I want to forget about the whole thing for awhile, and now that the concert season is over, I can do that at my leisure."

"Oh, come now," replied Copley, "this is different. It's a young Russian violinist you've been trying to foist on us for the past five years, but we wouldn't take him on because he was a boy prodigy.

The Benoist family before the arrival of Albert Spalding Benoist. Circa 1916.

But now that he will listen to reason and come over here wearing long pants, we've signed him up and he is coming over early this fall."

"What?" I exclaimed, "That can only be little Jascha Heifetz!"

"You guessed right the first time," came the rejoinder, "that's the fellow, so come along and we'll talk things over on the way to the office. You wouldn't let an old friend like the Wolfsohn Bureau down, would you?", asked Copley with the trace of an Irish brogue.

What could one do in the face of such subtle but persuasive flattery? So along I went, still feeling a bit disloyal to my old friend, but nevertheless touched by the cordiality of the offer before me.

The business arrangements were soon over, since "Pop" Adams, as he was affectionately called, was, under his crusty exterior, no haggler. Thus it came to pass that I was to have one more strange experience in a not-uncheckered career.

That summer, again, my wife, two daughters and I spent at our cottage in Monmouth Beach, New Jersey. This little house looked very much like an English manor viewed through the wrong side of opera glasses. It was all beams, gables and rough hewn walls. The center of the living room was taken up by a huge stone fireplace that occupied the whole north wall. The place had been built by the actor Oliver Dodd Byron with his own hands, out of wood taken from the old Whitney racing stables. And he had worked most artistically. Thus, the summer went slowly by, between preparing myself for the coming enigmatical season, and visits to Mr. and Mrs. Spalding, Sr. whose neighbors we had become.

Along the middle of August my telephone rang one morning. It was Copley at the other end, wishing to know whether I could come to New York the following week to meet the new virtuoso, who was to arrive from Russia any day now.

The appointment being made, I again settled into my old routine, awaiting what was to come with no little curiosity.

Chapter
XXI

I met the Heifetz family in a small inexpensive hotel on East 32nd Street. The modesty of their surroundings did not surprise me; for I knew that, while young Jascha had been, financially as well as artistically, successful during his comparatively short European career, they had been unable to take along much of their worldly goods when they had to practically flee from Russia when the Red Revolution was at its height. Having introduced myself as Jascha's prospective accompanist, and having reminded Mama and Papa that I already had the pleasure of meeting their son in Professor Auer's class in St. Petersburg, I awaited further developments.

There was, for a while, an embarrassing silence, during which I was being steadily examined through fishy and suspicious eyes by both Mama and Papa. Jascha sat in a neutral corner. His personality was as enigmatic as when I first saw him as a young lad of twelve. Physically he had developed into a finely set-up young man. He was as handsome as ever, but his features naturally had matured. No one spoke English, so I cautiously tested them in my somewhat wobbly German. This immediately elicited a voluble response from Papa in a mixture of Yiddish-German. Mama, however, remained silent, still evaluating and weighing me in her mental scales. Finally, Jascha took out his violin and we ran through a few pieces that were standard in the violinist's repertoire.

The result must have been satisfactory, for Mama, who up to then had not opened her lips, suddenly pronounced one word in Russian which in English pronunciation sounds a little like *harrasho,* literally translated, "O.K." Then everybody loosened up,

This photograph was taken at the dinner given by the American Guild of Violinists in honor of Leopold Auer on April 14, 1918. 1. Professor Auer. 2. Frederick Stock, conductor. 3. Jascha Heifetz' mother. 4. Jascha Heifetz. 5. Andre Benoist. 6. Eddy Brown, violinist. 7. Louis Gruenberg, composer.

DINNER GIVEN TO PROF. LEOPOLD AUER
BY AMERICAN GUILD OF VIOLINISTS'
ALEXANDER LEHMANN PRESIDENT
APRIL 14, 1918.
KUNTZ-REMMLERS   CHICAGO, ILL.

A closeup of just a few of the famous music-world personalities present at the testimonial dinner given to Professor Auer in 1918 by the American Guild of Violinists. Left to right: Jascha Heifetz, Andre Benoist, Eddy Brown, Louis Gruenberg.

even to Jascha's lovely young sisters, Paula and Elsa, who came running in, bobbing and smiling; and the ice was broken. Mama even went so far as to offer tea!

It took a good many days before I was able to break through Jascha's natural crust of distant coldness; but when I did, I found a boy with the nature of the friendliest puppy: shy, but full of fun, pranks and practical jokes. Of course, he played the violin like a young god, but never referred to it in action or conversation. Conceit was so foreign to him that I believe he did not know the meaning of the word. In playing together we got along from the very first. His playing was so clean, so sane and sound, and throughout so rhythmical, that there was no difficulty in accompanying him. . . except when he would suddenly take the bit in his teeth and start on a spurt of staggering speed. But even then his rhythm never faltered.

I soon discovered that his management was more worried about his playing than he was, for as the date approached for his first appearance they would ring me up on the telephone to find out what I thought his effect would be on his audiences. They had never heard him play and had only brought him over on his great European reputation. And they were beginning to worry.

At last came the momentous day of the young virtuoso's American debut at Carnegie Hall in New York. Now anyone at all in the know, is aware that, no matter how inured one may be to such occasions, it is almost impossible to remain entirely indifferent to them. I must confess that, in spite of many experiences of the same kind, I felt a bit aflutter myself. But when I reached the old Green Room at the hall, I found Mama and Papa sitting about, as calm and unconcerned as if they were about to witness a Christmas party. As for Jascha, he ran up to me in high glee and said, "Look! Look! Fine long pants! Fine cutaway coat! Fine new necktie! I look fine, no?"

I allowed he did, but I added that there was something else to think about for the present, than his beautiful new raiment. For, even making allowances for the fact that up to now he had appeared in public in boy's knickers and short jacket, this was a queer state of mind on an occasion when so much was at stake. But that did not seem to impress him very much.

Came the moment to begin the concert, and as we approached the little door leading to the stage, Papa's last injunction, which I hesitate to translate was, "Jaschinka, erinnern dich! Du kanst auf alle spucken!" (Remember, little Jascha—you can spit on them all!) Instead of answering his father, Jascha turned to me and asked,

Jascha Heifetz' first calling card. This is the card he handed to Benoist when they first met in New York. The Russian merely states his name.

"Look, is my necktie all right?" And thus the lad embarked on his "great American adventure!"

Came intermission, together with an avalanche of well-merited congratulations. He remained immovable. Nothing seemed to stir him until Leopold Godowsky, who had been sitting in a first tier box, came running backstage. He informed us that he had a priceless story to tell, and Jascha's eyes lit up. I can still see the drafty vestibule where we stood in a huddle not unlike a football team, our heads together so as not to be overheard. The story Godowsky told is by now so old and worn that it hardly bears repeating. It tells of Mischa Elman who, being a guest in the Godowsky box, suddenly loosened his collar, exclaiming that it was terribly hot. To which the great pianist wittily replied, "Yes, for violinists, not for pianists!" But what none of us had noticed was that a lady critic for a prominent morning paper, standing nearby, had overheard the story and, promptly running to a nearby telephone booth, had retold the story to her friends, with the result that all the next morning's papers carried this bit of gossip.

The concert proceeded to its end, when pandemonium broke loose. Useless to describe a scene when New York suddenly grows hysterical and goes berserk. But Jascha, still unruffled, suggested it was time for tea, and that was the end of it. Of course, the boy's career was assured, with a lucrative tour in the offing.

We were quite a little troupe traveling together. There was always Mama or Papa, and sometimes both. At some important appearances little sisters Paula and Elsa would join us. And almost invariably, Jack Adams, son of the owner of the bureau, came along. On tour Jascha became irrepressible, one prank taking the place of the last one; and it often took two of us to hold him quiet a few minutes. But once on the stage, he became the sphynx-like creature the public knew. Poor Jack would threaten him with direct reprisals if he didn't smile, but when the moment came he would not or could not do so. He claimed that to smile in public made him feel foolish and as if he were courting the plaudits of his audience. He also hated to play encores, saying it was inartistic, until one day, at a Chicago recital, Jack Adams bodily shoved him back on the stage with me following and blocking the way back. With that the ice was broken and we seldom experienced any further difficulty with that matter.

As a young man Heifetz was a happy, fun-loving person. Shown here with Dagmar Godowsky on his right and Charlie Chaplin on his left. Next to Chaplin is Samuel Chotzinoff. He became Heifetz' accompanist and brother-in-law when he married Heifetz' older sister.

But, try as we might, we could never break him of his bad stage manners. Overwhelming ovations—storms of applause, cries of "BRAVO," and in response, the sickly nod: right, left, and middle. As a result, rumors began to spread that this was due to overwhelming conceit.

Nothing was further from the truth. His behavior was simply the result of circumstances. He had never known a reverse; never had an adverse criticism, except from his father, who was his most severe, though just and loving, critic. His success dated practically from his babyhood, and what he beheld was simply what he had always seen and consequently expected. Had the contrary happened, he would simply have been bewildered, and not understood. His reaction would have been that of an intensely clever puppy, who, having performed an exceedingly difficult trick, received a kick in the ribs for his pains instead of a pat on the head. But to speak of conceit in connection with Jascha Heifetz is simply laughable. Even to this day there is no more sincere and self-effacing artist, and music is practically the only god he bows to.

The same speculation was rife regarding the so-called "miracle" of his technique. As a matter of fact there was nothing miraculous about it, according to Mr. Heifetz, Sr.'s explanation. One thing was certain: the boy, from the outset, loved music, and especially the violin. In addition, he had an inordinate aptitude for mastering the instrument. But all this had happened before in a good many cases, and while it delighted the tot's family it did not seem unduly extraordinary to them. As a matter of fact, the father explained this to himself as his pre-natal influence on the boy, coming from his own frustration, he having become a very good violinist in spite of being thwarted at every stage of endeavor in his attempts to become a violinist of parts. However that may be, it is true that with anything we learn in the ordinary, routine way (that is, by having a lesson once or twice a week from a teacher for whom this lesson must be "prepared"), we are obliged to do the most useful but at the same time the most dangerous part of the work, practicing, entirely alone and without any supervision. And consequently, for each step we take forward, we take three steps backwards. For we practice mistakes also, and these must be "unlearned," alas! And that takes time and patience.

This did not take place with young Heifetz. He was never allow-

278

The pianist and composer Leopold Godowsky gave this to Benoist
on New Year's Eve, 1924. His daughter and Heifetz were friendly.

Telephone Calls:

6204
6205 } GREELEY
6206

...WOLFSOHN...
MUSICAL BUREAU

A. F. ADAMS, Proprietor

1 West 34th Street

CABLE ADDRESS:
"LABIATED," New York
CODE A. B. C. (5th Edition)
AND WESTERN UNION

1919
NEW YORK, 4th June.

Dear Ben,well Ben I got your long letter O.K.and of corse it supprized
me to here from you so soon but I know how it is Ben with you strong
arm pianoists who spend the summer putting up the screens and looking
over the dolls on the beach to see if they are bow legged or flat
chested. I suppose you just got tired screening and looking; and now
you want somebody to some down and help you. Well Ben you picked the
right guy all right and I appreciate the invitation and the time table,
but I guess you forgot to enclose the RR ticket. But that's all right,
I'll collect the fare when I get down there, including Pullman and
taxi. It's so d-amm hot up here that I got to take a taxi and I guess
that will be O.K. with you. Probaly you and the wife is doing the big
society stuff in the tin wagon by this time, so you can meet me at the
station and it will be all the same to me although of corse I am accustomed to these cars with real leather seats and a ten gallon tank tacked
on behind. But I'll tell you Ben how it is; it's like this. I am kind
of up against it right now with family troubles and I dont know when I
can get away from the torrid city so to speak. You see I am trying to
get settled in a place called Flatbush,out near Brooklyn on Long Island,
and it's a heluva proposition take it from one who knows all about
checking trunks and ordering hotel rooms. I have brought my sisters
down from Palmyra and we are going to make a home for ourselves as soon

A comical. . . though typical. . . letter from Charles N. Drake about
Heifetz' gift of a watch. Heifetz was very generous in his younger
years.

Telephone Calls:
6204
6205 } GREELEY
6206

...WOLFSOHN...
MUSICAL BUREAU

A. F. ADAMS, Proprietor

1 West 34th Street

CABLE ADDRESS:
"LABIATED," New York
CODE A. B. C. (5th Edition)
AND WESTERN UNION

NEW YORK,

as the d-amm furniture comes down by freight and I can bribe some of
these millionaire truck drivers to cart it up four flights of stairs
to our top floor six rooms-and-bath-southern-exposure-sixty-bones-a-
month-godamit. Right now the three of us are giving my brother a nice
social time showing him how to run a hotel and keep a maid with three
extra grafters horning in on the meals and washing. Maybe you did not
happen to hear of it, but I received the saddest jolt of my life by
losing my precious mother the last week in April, and naturally it upset things very much in Palmyra. We closed the house and got rid of
the things we didn't need, and now I have just returned from a booking
trip. Got back day before yesterday and between the junk in the office
and the settling of a new apartment I am up to my neck in trouble and
in debt for the next nine years. Aside from these things, everything is
fine.

But yesterday and today some sunshine came along: your souvenir
and one from a violeen-playER by name of Jasky Heefizz. Yours you know
about so I will not repeat it, but maybe you would stir up a flicker of
interest over the news that the poor fish we used to travel with and
swear at went completely out of his mind and bought me a watch! It's
the swellest goshdarn thing you ever seen - I mean saw,- and since I
have worn it I keep loooking over my shoulder on the street for fear

281

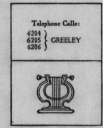

Telephone Calls:
6204 ⎫
6205 ⎬ GREELEY
6206 ⎭

...WOLFSOHN...
MUSICAL BUREAU

A. F. ADAMS, Proprietor

1 West 34th Street

CABLE ADDRESS:
"LABIATED," New York
CODE A. B. C. (5th Edition)
AND WESTERN UNION

3

NEW YORK,

George Gould or J.P.Morgan will tap me on the arm and say I swiped it

off them or something. It says from Jasky Hoefizz inside and it has a

whale of a monogram all over the back and it's solid gold gemacht mit

fiele juwelen in the works inside and everything, y'understand. A

regular swell article which it should ought to be worn in a transparent

pocket. Class is what it calls it; I'll tell the world it is and anytime

you want to know the exact time just go ahead and call up Greeley 6204

and ask for the bottom bureau drawer.

So you see how it is kid; I got a family to look after and a
                                                       to look
new watch to look at and a Long Branch time table through and no sum-

mer suit and no straw hat and no low shoes. But you can't have every-

thing at once. My San Antonio Chop Suey Suit is gradually becoming

thinner, and within a week or two it will probably be light enough for

the rest of the summer, especially in the seat. My right foot is al-

ready on the ground so I cant kick about ventilation, and if I don't

feel like it I don't have to wear any hat at all. So what the hell.

I intended to say before that if I can arrange to get away from

my duties I will certainly whizz down to the Beach and sample your

famous eggs and roast chicken. You'll hear from me later about it. In

the meantime give me best wishes to the wife and family, and don't ne-

glect your practice. You know there a few spots in the Mendelssohn.

Truly urine.....c n d

Telephone Calls:
6204
6205 }-GREELEY
6206

...WOLFSOHN...
MUSICAL BUREAU

A. F. ADAMS, Proprietor

1 West 34th Street

CABLE ADDRESS:
"LABIATED," New York
CODE A. B. C. (5th Edition)
AND WESTERN UNION

NEW YORK, Aug.21,1919

Mr.Andre Benoist

Monmouth Beach,N.J.

Dear Madam;

     A cablegram from Odessa informs our agents in Essex Street that the crop of pretzels is 800,000,000 pounds shy of salt. You can readily understand what a complication this is, particularly since the milk barons here seem to ignore the fact that more than one million milk bottles are lost or destroyed every thirty days.

     However, we have just wired the privy council in Omsk that we can do nothing about the matter until Monday when Mr. Drake returns from his visit to confer with you. We trust you will have all the necessary papers ready so that the conference may open on Saturday as soon as Mr.Drake arrives.

     He will leave New York on his small yacht at 12;30 noon, run on the rocks at Atlantic Highlands and then board a freight due in Monmouth Beach at 2:32 P.M. He will travel incognito, in a light check suit,vintage 1916, a mottled straw hat (Kaufman),clean union suit (slightly shrunk by laundry), a natty but modest tie, no gloves. Probably clean shaven.

     Respectively and posiTIVLE yours,

     PRETZEL MOULDERS UNION.

     J. Schleickhoffenberger.

283

ed to take his little violin in hand except in the presence of his father, who taught him his first steps. He was never allowed to play one note out of tune. He was never allowed to hold or use his bow, even for a fraction of a second, in the wrong way. When his practice time was over, the violin and bow were immediately taken away from the child and locked out of his reach. The consequences were, of course, that he never had an opportunity to undo any benefits he had gained from his practice time. The upshot also was that he never took a step backwards; and each step being steadily forward, he progressed by leaps and bounds, and by the time he was nine years old (having started at three), he was a finished virtuoso. It seemed to me a very logical explanation. For if animals can be trained to do apparently impossible things, why should it seem miraculous to teach a gifted and intelligent child the principles of an art of which he is already deeply fond?

Alas, by the time most artists realize themselves and all that life contains, the first bloom of their technical mastery, which is really their means of expressing themselves, has already begun to wane. But when both are in full bloom, as has happened in some few historical cases, then we experience moments of artistic and spiritual ecstasy which rarely fall to our lot. As the French poet once said: "Si jeunesse savait! Si vieillesse pouvait!" (If youth but knew; if age could!)

Jascha made quite a few records during the first season for the Victor Talking Machine, as it was then called. That they were superb, we all know. But while on this subject I must mention one instance that I do not believe any other instrumentalist has or ever will duplicate.

We left New York at 8:00 a.m., which necessitated much earlier rising, on our way to Camden, New Jersey, where the Victor Studios were located. It was obviously impossible for the boy to have had time to warm up his fingers or his violin beforehand. Soon after our arrival at the studio, following a few moments of desultory conversation, Mr. Childs (liaison officer between the artists and the company) suggested that Jascha start warming up. The boy, by this time, had picked up quite a little English, and characteristically replied, "What you want I play?"

"Well," said Mr. Childs, "last time I spoke to you, you mentioned *Moto Perpetuo* by Paganini, but isn't that a little too strenuous for a beginning?"

284

To the splendid accompanist and my dear friend André Benoist in remembrance of our first American tour. Jascha Heifetz. N York May 15th

For an answer, Jascha went to his fiddle case, opened it, took out his violin, and after passing his bow over the strings and tuning them, stood before the recording horn and said, "I am ready."

I could see on Mr. Childs' face the same misgivings I felt. I could almost read his thoughts: "What? Does that kid think he can get away with that?" Nevertheless, he gave the signal to start. My heart was in my mouth, for while the piano part is really quite simple, I knew that the slightest deviation from the rhythm, or hesitation on the part of the accompanist, could throw the violinist off his balance in a piece which is inhumanly difficult.

The boy played the piece, including the first repeat as indicated, without a flaw. He was totally unruffled while I was bathed in perspiration.

"Bravo," said Mr. Childs, and he continued rather timidly this time, "When you are completely rested, we shall have to make another one just like this."

Came the same reply from Jascha, "I am ready." The same performance was duplicated; flawless, perfect. But this time instead of sitting down, the boy queried, "Would you like more?"

"Oh yes," came in fainting accents from Mr. Childs, who appeared ready to drop from nervous exhaustion, "If you will."

"I will," came the prompt reply, and he did, just as beautifully as the other times! And he made other records that same morning, which he called, "little nothings"! I have witnessed instances of great endurance in many artists, but never anything that even approached what this boy of barely seventeen accomplished that morning.

The tour came to an end in the spring of 1918 and the summer following showed me a new Jascha. It was a "lord of the manor" Jascha. He had purchased a beautiful villa at Narragansett Pier and there held forth in all his glory. Mama and Papa were there, as well as his beautiful little sisters and a quantity of near and far relatives, probably attracted by this new splendor. Also there was a newly acquired Marmon automobile that was guaranteed to do 120 miles an hour. On my first visit to the new home I was taken for a ride in the new shining car by Jascha, who had already learned to drive. When we arrived at a speed of 90, I threatened to jump out, which was the only way I could think of to make him reduce to a snail's pace of 55!

286

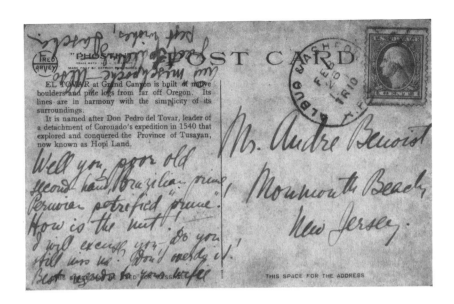

An adorable postcard from Heifetz: *"Well you poor old second hand Brazilian prime Peruvian petrified 'prune!' How is the nut! I will excuse you—Do you still miss me? Don't overdo it! Best regards to your wifie and mischpoche (the Yiddish word for 'family')—Also greet Spalding. Best wishes, Jascha."*

NARRAGANSETT PIER. R.I.

August 20th, 1913.

To Baby Albert S. Benoist

with compliments of

Mrs. Anna Heifetz.

Mrs. Anna Heifetz, Jascha's mother, sent Benoist a gift for his newborn son which reads: *"To Baby Albert S. Benoist. With compliments of Mrs. Anna Heifetz."*

Heifetz' "Love Letter" to Andre's wife:

*O, Alice—my sincere greetings, deep appreciation, affectation (?)
amication—friendation—heartation—ambition—buruation—ukelele
—ability—excelcior and all best wishes from "the great mogul"—How
is baby "Candy at 2"?—Hope you and rest of the menagerie are well
and shining.*
*For the love of Mike, don't mind my absence or I shall burst up my
tour and come at once—Let me know how you feel about it— won't
you?*
Well—good bye, o, maiden—God bless and pickle you—so long—

Yours shortly,
(signed) Jascha

February
  Twenty fifth   *Per Secretary*
    Nineteen Hundred and nineteen

O, Alice — my sincere greetings,
deep appreciation, affectation(?)
amication — friendation —
heartation — ambition —
burnation — ukelele — ability —
excelcior and all best wishes
from "the Great Mogul" —
How is baby "Candy N 2"? —
Hope you and rest of the
menagerie are well and shining?

289

For the love of Mike — don't
mind my absence or I shall
burst up my tour. and come
at once — Let me know
how you feel about it —
wont you?

Well — good bye, o,
maiden — God bless and
pickle you — so long

Yours shortly

Jaseba

February
Twenty fifth
Nineteen Hundred and nineteen — Per
Secretary!

Jascha also took my older daughter, Louise, for a ride in his fancy new Marmon motor car, and when they returned, she was quite upset. Later, I asked her what had happened. She replied that they were driving down a romantic, isolated country road and she said to Jascha, the great mogul:

"Jasch, can you drive with one hand?"

"Of course," he said.

Fully expecting that he would do as other teenage drivers, and drive with his left hand, thus leaving his right hand free to drape her shoulders, she was much surprised when he put his left arm on the car door and drove with his right. She never went for a ride with him after that.

Barnetta and Louise, being typical teenage girls, then concentrated their attention on how they would marry Albert Spalding, another very attractive young man.

Jascha, in addition, was a proud possessor of a typewriting machine, on which he would, with the help of a special slang dictionary, write me long dissertations on nothing at all, but worthy of George Ade at his best. He would also write long love declarations to my wife, all culled from lurid novels he had been given to read to facilitate his use of the new language. What a "real boy" he was, until he picked up his fiddle!

In the early fall of 1918 our second tour began. All through the past summer I had been hoping for an early cessation of hostilities in Europe. But in none of the rare letters that came from my friend Albert Spalding could I detect such optimism. All I knew from him was that he was alive and well.

I had been discussing my hopes with Jascha a good deal, but at every suggestion that the war would be ended by Christmas he would chuckle and reply, "You don't know the Germans nor their Kaiser if you think that!"

One November morning we were rehearsing the Brahms *D Minor Sonata* in Jascha's new apartment on Central Park West. The weather was so balmy and mild that we had opened the window. While playing I could not keep my thoughts from straying towards this hope for peace. Suddenly, out of nowhere, bells began to peal, shouts came from the streets, and steam whistles blew. I stopped dead, and turning to the boy exclaimed, "It's peace!"

"You're crazy," he chuckled. "Let's go on!"

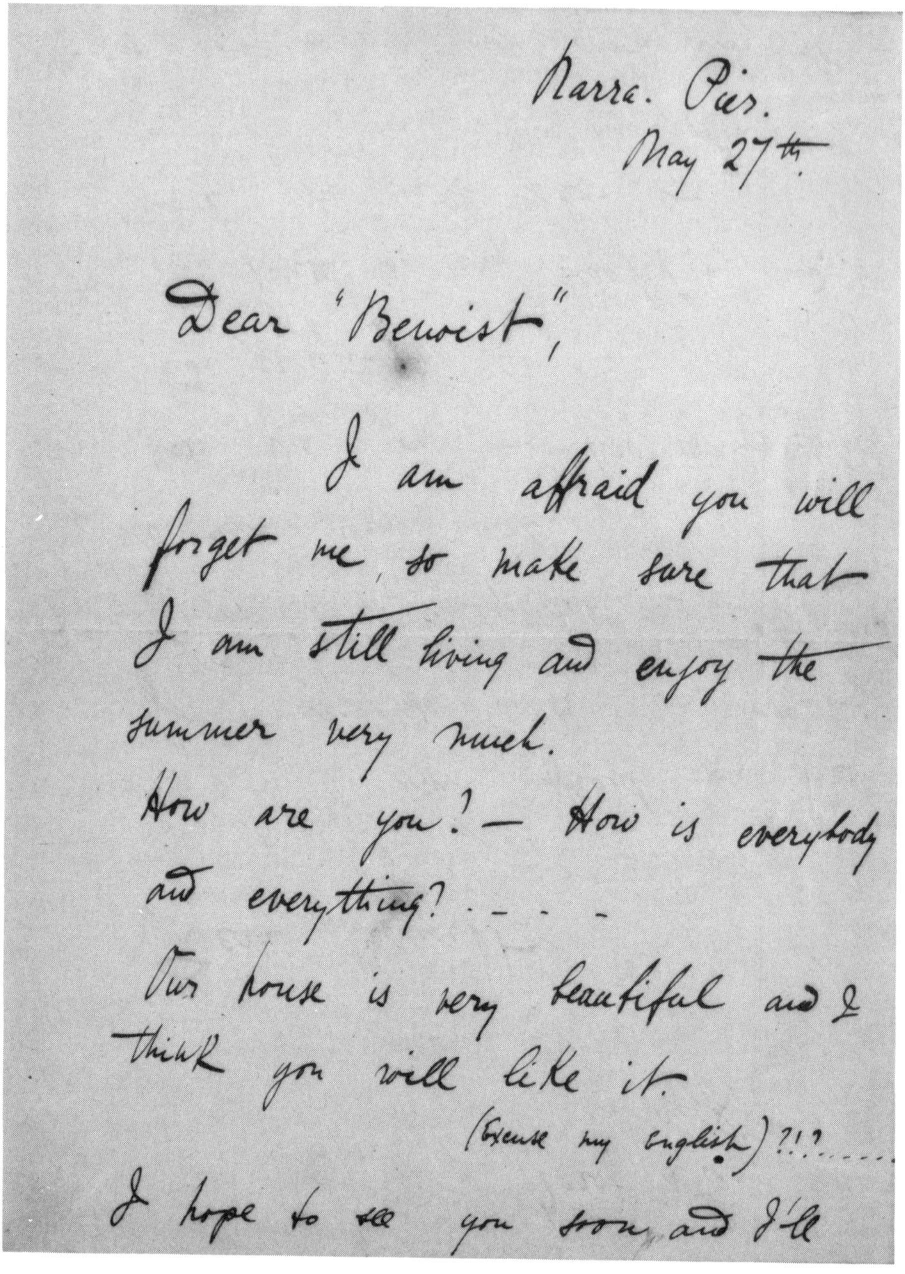

Narra. Pics.
May 27th

Dear "Benoist",

    I am afraid you will forget me, so make sure that I am still living and enjoy the summer very much.
How are you? — How is everybody and everything? ____
Our house is very beautiful and I think you will like it.
(excuse my english) ?!?.........
I hope to see you soon, and I'll

let you know in advance when
to come.

If you have any mails for me,
kindly send it to me immidiatly.

The address is:

To me.

Box № 432.

Narragansett Pier, R. J.

[This is my private address.]

Write to me as soon as you will
get this letter (in generally too) and
let me know about things........
With best regards to you all,
Jascha.

Narragansett Pier, R.I.
July 16, '18.

Dear "Ben-Oyster",

Thank you for your kind
favor, which was received... a month
ago... (about the truth!) _ _ _ _
You are cordially invited to join us..
Come up next week and we will
have some fun and music, of course_
Let me know exactly when you
think you can come and I'll meet
you at the Kingston station.
How _is_ you, sweetz? - ___

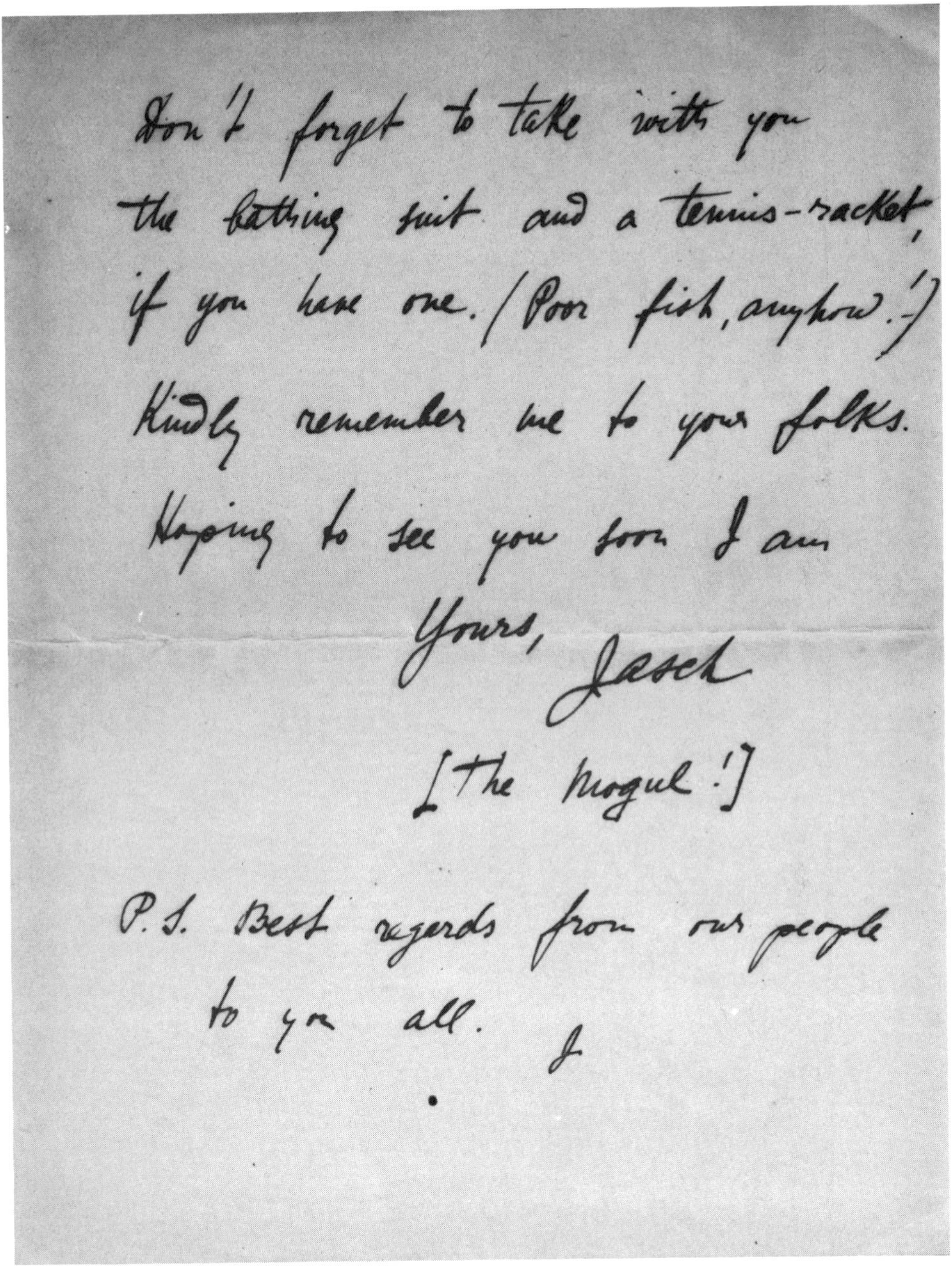

Don't forget to take with you
the bathing suit and a tennis-racket,
if you have one. (Poor fish, anyhow!)
Kindly remember me to your folks.
Hoping to see you soon I am

Yours,

Jasch

[the Mogul!]

P.S. Best regards from our people
to you all.

J

Narravansett Pier, R.I.
June 9, 1919

My dear Ben, the Self-Appointed Vice President of Accompanists;

I received your wail for recognition, and praise your good judgment that among the swells of Narragansett it is difficult to remember little things even those with a shining moonlike shape on the top.

Of course I regret that amidst the brilliant stars that flock to the vicinity of your abode, it would be impossible for me to distinguish the lonely spot on which some rays of light would find a playground, and that the reflections from your noble dome would vainly vibrate endeavoring to pierce the thick veil of darkness that surround the memory of the past...

But how should I forget the happy moments of our partings, our farewells, our staying asunder ?

Now as I was trying to cut the loaf of love that you had sent to the whole family , nothing but the crumbs were left for the mother. However, she has a strong constitution , and having lived through the shock, she as well as the rest of the recipients of your donation, wish to acknowledge to you their sincere appreciation.

Yours till the next letter
Jascha Heifetz.

P.S.
Tell your two sweet little chickens to think of me well, if they do not get too swell.

J.H.

How do you like my entrance into the profession of typists ? Fine, eh ? Wadda ye say ?

J.H.

P.P.S. I also wish to announce that I expect to be at your place around July or August and so Au revoir,

J.

Narragansett Pier, R.I.
July 16, 1919

Mr. A. Benoist,
Mammonth Beach, N.J.

Honorable B.H.M.,

I was very glad to receive the evidence that you were still alive, and ready to think and to do. But why should y you persist in telling stories of trivial matters, always talking about me; why not undertake the discussion of subjects of great international import, something that would astonish the world, why don't you speak of yourself, Ben?

I wonder what changes did your former boss find in you since he left you here ; does he appreciate the ennobling effect that was brought upon his slave who was fortunate to follow the idol of modesty , the innocent, and the saint , who for two long seasons was in constant company of the Great Mogul.

You need not be surprised at the fact that I am not particular with whom I appear on the pages of Musical American, why, was I not seen with you in public, and nobody ever noticed me blush on such disgraceful occasions ?

I do not know when fate will throw me again within the reach of your vision, but if through some premonition , I would feel that the misfortune was coming upon me, to you as my faithful friend, I would impart the information, and I am sure in your noble heart you would find sympathy for the miserable wretch who cannot dodge the hard knocks of Destiny.

With my best wishes to you and your lovely chicks,
I am as you used to know me,

Jasch

Jasch

Balboa, 2009 East Bay Front,
September 2nd. 1936.

Dear Andre:

It was so nice hearing from you
and also to receive your composition. Since
you are asking for praise rather than criticism, I would like to give you all the praise
that you deserve.

The composition is interesting,
melodious and well written but unfortunately
it is not the kind of piece that I could
use in concert. Nevertheless many thanks for
having sent it to me.

I hope that you and your family
have enjoyed a very pleasant summer vacation
and upon my return to New York I hope to
have the pleasure of seeing you and your
wife.

All are well here and send affectionate greetings to you all.

Cordially,

Jascha

P.S. Excuse the typewriter - but I've been
pulling ropes all summer - All the best. -

. J. -

During the summer of 1918, when Benoist was 38 years old, Heifetz was a 17 year old giant. Heifetz often visited Benoist and they had fun together as these photographs show. Unfortunately Heifetz got cut off by the photographer, namely Benoist's older daughter!

Alas, he was right! That was the premature announcement of November 9th! But Jascha, wishing to show me how sure he was that there would be no peace by Christmas, said: "I tell you what I will do. If we should have peace by Christmas, I'll buy you a new Ford car!" On this we shook hands and let it go at that.

On November 11 we were rehearsing the same Brahms sonata, under the same conditions, when the hullabaloo previously heard, was renewed, only even more strenuously than before. But this time, not trusting rumors, I at once rang up the *New York Times* office, and there heard the news definitely confirmed that an armistice had indeed been signed. Thereupon I turned to young Jascha and told him that the car was to be mine, and would he please accompany me downtown to help me select one. "Oh, no!" said he, "This is not peace at all! This is only an armistice, and you're not entitled to the car unless a definite peace treaty is signed by Christmas!" And on that technicality he stood and nothing ever was able to budge him from that stand.

However, armistice or no armistice, our work went on, and young Jascha continued to indulge in pranks of all sorts, such as tying our overcoats into knots and hiding them under Pullman seats on the trains, or tying up his finger in a rag smeared with red ink, thus frightening us half out of our wits. But one little story stands out in my mind. In Chicago we were invited, one evening, to join a party of artists that happened to be there at the same time as we were. It was to be a gala performance of *Carmen,* and I knew Jascha was particularly fond of it. The star was to be a prima donna renowned at the same time for her glamor and her daring and the boy had heard a great deal of both items. When the lady appeared on the scene I could see the lad with an opera glass glued to his eyes contemplating the prima donna with a hypnotized stare. He would only leave off gazing raptly to nudge me once in a while and remark in a hushed whisper, "I've got to meet her; I must know her. Do you know her? Will you introduce me to her?" etc., ad infinitum.

I informed him that I had the honor of the lady's acquaintance, and that if he were really set on knowing her, I would pilot him back stage at intermission and introduce him. However, I thought it best to inform him that at close range the effect would not be all he hoped it might be. Of course, he did not believe me and I soon saw that there was nothing for it but to submit gracefully. So at the entrance we meandered through the corridors that led to the mysterious regions back stage, and after gaining admission thereto, arrived at the prima donna's dressing room door. In answer to my knock came the rather impatient inquiry as to who was there. Of this I informed her, adding that I had brought with me a very nice young man who was anxious to make her acquaintance, and congratulate her at the same time on her wonderful performance. She

300

Benoist and his daughters. His older daughter Louise (on Benoist's left), like almost every other girl that met Heifetz, was infatuated with him and tried very hard to be "the one." Unfortunately, when Heifetz took her for a ride in his new car, her request *"Can't you drive with one hand?"*, didn't end up quite as she expected; she wouldn't talk to Heifetz again.

said, "Who is the fellow?" I answered, "The young violinist Jascha Heifetz."

No sooner had the words left my lips than the door flew open and the lady stood before us. What I had predicted had been mild compared to the sight that greeted us. There she was, clad in rather doubtful undergarments with grease paint spots here and there. Her hair was disheveled, and the perspiration had made her make-up run all over her face. She was awesome! But her eyes, smoldering and glaring in turn, were fixed on Jascha, who with this hypnotic stare upon him was edging slowly away. Then suddenly the lady ejaculated, "Come here, Heifetz, and kiss me!" And with that, panic seized the boy, who suddenly retreated to the front of the house, leaving me to get out of the dilemma as best as I could!

An historic photograph of the "big three" violinists. From left to right: Jascha Heifetz, Efrem Zimbalist, Mrs. Alma Gluck Zimbalist and Fritz Kreisler. Circa 1919.

Chapter
XXII

In the meantime I had heard from Spalding, advising me of his now probable early return to America. And while I had thoroughly enjoyed my association with the "boy wonder" very much, I could not help looking forward to resuming barnstorming with so close a "companion in arms." It was a great joy indeed to meet again, and to be present at his wedding, which took place shortly after his return, and at which I had the honor and pleasure of officiating at the organ, while our dear mutual friend Jacques Thibaud played exquisitely on the violin.

The honeymoon over, we began rehearsing together, preparatory to the forthcoming concert season, which, for Spalding, was to open with an appearance as soloist with the New York Symphony Orchestra. The concerto was the *B minor* by Saint-Saens, and I surely expected that the artist would be greeted by his audience with some display of pleasure at seeing him again, safe and sound, after his ordeal. For what happened I shall quote William J. Henderson, who, at that time, was music critic on the *New York Sun*: "*The reception accorded Mr. Spalding as he stepped onto the podium, would have been proper had he been an alien reserve officer from the enemy army.*" I must admit, however, that while the applause on his entrance was perfunctory, it was much more enthusiastic after he played.

But I cannot help but reflect that Americans are like that. The imported article always wins out over the domestic. And especially with instrumentalists. Some prima donnas such as Clara Louise Kellogg, Lillian Nordica, Emma Eames and Sybil Sanderson did win their spurs, but always via Europe. Even Nordica, whose real

303

name was Lilly Norton, had to "foreignize" her name to gain the proper recognition. Let an instrumentalist end his name with "itz," "sky," "ich," or "off," and with the least talent, he is immediately acclaimed! Americans cannot admit that a real he-man can have artistic ability. Ergo, Americans being notoriously he-men, how can a dyed-in-the-wool American be a great artist? No! Artists are reared in certain soils, like grapefruit and pineapples! They must be effete, temperamental and sickly if possible!

Another requisite is that the artist be born in lowly circumstances, preferably in the slums. No one can be a great artist if he has been accustomed to living in a normally clean room and eating three good meals a day! One must suffer and bleed! The American is at heart terribly romantic, especially about fallacies. And he is very much ashamed of this romanticism, which often leads him astray in his judgment. To cover this up, he is oft times rude, which he calls "being a he-man." As a matter of fact, that judgment is made for him by all kinds of devices and diverse ballyhoo. Consequently, he believes that a play, an artist, or a fashion in dress or architecture is good if he hears that fact repeated often enough. For this reason, he is afraid to trust his own opinion in matters artistic. And for this reason also do Americans dress, eat, and act about in the same manner. In their innermost hearts, their motto could go as follows: "Thou shalt be as all others are; for if thou art not as all others are, then thou art queer." And to be "queer" is mortal sin!

Nevertheless, in spite of this strange beginning upon his re-entry onto the American musical stage, the critical profession, to our intense surprise, suddenly discovered that Spalding was indeed a great artist. They vied in proclaiming him this and that with the most flattering epithets. I was, of course, delighted with the turn of events, but my friend only said that, for better or for worse, he would continue to play as he thought violin music should be presented. At the height of his success, he remained, as always, sincere, simple, unaffected and kindly. That sums up the man.

We usually spent half the season in Europe, and the other half in America. All this necessitated quite a little crossing back and forth. Sometimes we had to cut it rather finely, as on one occasion, when,

Spalding's wife, Mary.

304

owing to a sudden change in sailing schedules, we arrived in Christiana (Oslo today) on the very morning that our first recital there was to take place; thus driving poor Rulle Rassmussen, our Scandinavian manager, nearly to the verge of insanity. But we were on the stage in time and all ended well.

One year I happened to cross on the old *Rotterdam*, of the Holland-American line, on my way home. On the same ship there was a boisterous mob of men returning to the United States from a "hotel-men's" convention that had taken place in Switzerland. There were managers, chief clerks, assistant managers, vice presidents and even some presidents. Life on board was made hideous by their behavior. At night one could not sleep owing to their drinking revels, noise making and shouting until the wee hours of the morning. In the daytime it was almost impossible to escape their back-slapping hospitality. However, I had discovered a very private card room where I usually retired after breakfast to play solitaire or read.

I was congratulating myself on having found this little haven of peace, when, one bright morning, on looking up from my card game, I was dismayed to see a strange character sitting at my table and watching me with a speculative eye. He was an elderly man, wearing heavy-lensed spectacles, and having kindly, pronounced Semitic features. For a long time he watched me play in silence. Presently, evidently not being able to stand the silence, he inquired whether I minded his watching me play. I replied that I did not, provided there be absolute quiet. This was granted for another interval, when he suddenly broke into an inimitable Yiddish-English accent saying, "Say, you ain't no hotel man, is you?" I said, "No," and that it was the reason that I wished quiet. To this he replied, "Bet I know what you are," which somehow intrigued me. I foolishly encouraged him by asking, "Well?" Came the answer, "You're ah musician ah betcha!" I allowed I dabbled in music and hoped the conversation would end there. But no, it did not. What I heard with failing hope was, "My wife is ah musician too; she's ah sing-ger, but she don't sink no more." With that my hopes revived. I would not have to hear her sing! "Maybe you hoid of her," continued my living cartoon. "Her name uset to be Clara Louise Kellogg."

By then I was persuaded that I was dealing with a gentle lunatic,

Benoist took this photograph of Robert Strakosch and his wife Clara Louise Kellogg aboard the ship "Rotterdam" enroute to the United States. Circa 1920.

for I was sure that great lady had died years ago; but to humor him I said, "That's nice, I would enjoy meeting the lady." I was a bit staggered when he answered: "O.K. frendt, ve vill meet you in the shmokink lounge after dinner tonight und ve vill talk!" With that he arose and with an old world bow proffered me his visiting card on which I read what suddenly opened my eyes to the situation, for neatly engraved were the words, "Robert Strakosch!" Of course! The Strakosch brothers: Maurice, Max and Robert, the most famous musical impresarios of their time! Seeing my non-plussed appearance he suddenly burst out with the following priceless gem, "You know, it's ah fonny tink, eferpotty on dis boat tinks ahm ah Jew! Ah ain't no Jew at all! Ahm ah Roman Ketlick!" And after I heard the entire story I realized how I had misjudged the strange creature. The simplicity of it all was baffling. He had naturally managed the great Kellogg's early career, had fallen desperately in love with her, but as she was a Catholic, he was obliged to embrace that religion in order to marry the prima donna.

That same evening my wife and I were thrilled to meet this relic of a glorious past, Clara Louise Kellogg. She proved to be a charming little lady who confessed to the age of 77 and was very sprightly. To our surprise she asked if we would be shocked if she smoked her little after-dinner Havana cigar! Naturally we vowed that this was a most normal procedure, to which with a sly wink she replied, "Oh no! Not so normal, but I like it so much and only indulge myself after dinner with my demi-tasse." She held forth with most amusing anecdotes from the past, and confirmed everything Lillian Nordica had already told me of her kind heart and generosity.

The episode I refer to, I have hinted at earlier in these reminiscences. When Nordica first came to Russia she was very poor. So much so, that for her first appearance she had neither the clothes nor the jewelry needed to do justice to such an occasion. It seems that Kellogg had heard of the young American newcomer, while she herself was creating such a furor as had seldom been seen in the Russian capital. Thereupon, she went to call on Nordica, and asked if there was anything she could do to help her in any way. Touched by her kindness, Nordica asked her if she knew of a dressmaker who would supply her with a gown on credit. Whereupon Kellogg replied, "But my dear, I have more gowns than I know what to do with, and you shall come with me immediately and choose whichever suits you best!" This was done at once. Then when Mme. Kellogg saw Lillian in all her young loveliness, she told her that her appearance would not be completely successful without jewelry, and proceeded to deck the young singer in her finest gems, including a priceless tiara. The overwhelming success that greeted Nordica amply repaid Mme. Kellogg for her generosity, and Nordica never forgot it. I think it is the touching story of a great soul.

The friendship that sprang up between the dear little old lady and ourselves made the rest of the voyage home an unalloyed delight, and we were able to forget the turmoil surrounding us, as we were so enmeshed in charming conversation.

At last we arrived home, and after going through the usual annoyances pertaining to running the gamut of the customs, shipping luggage, etc., we settled again into routine living. The winter was almost over and one could feel that spring was imminent. New York looked its best: brilliant, hard and angular, but lovable withal. For where else could one find central heating, running hot water, elevators that were equipped for service, and a dainty piece of fresh soap in every bathroom? Only in the United States of America!

Our American tour commenced almost at once, and shortly thereafter I was introduced into a new and bizarre world: that of radio. I admit it ill behooves anyone to speak against radio; for in many ways it is a blessing. Its news bulletins, its forums and a small modicum of its entertainment are delightful. It is also true that, to enjoy all this, one has to wade through meaningless blaring fanfares, beer-voiced females who were originally intended to sell fish, coy comediennes typed after the renowned Hildegarde, who make your flesh creep with the falseness of their mirth, crooners and bleaters of the male line whose real vocation in life should be to sort sundry papers in offices, and so on, ad nauseam.

However one can always get rid of those by turning a dial or disconnecting the machine entirely. There is still plenty of good entertainment to be had via the radio. But the unfortunate situation is that radio is run by and for advertisers and it is the power of their money coupled with the inane judgment of the advertising agencies they patronize that makes radio a world akin to an insane

Spalding and Benoist performing for a CBS radio broadcast. Circa 1940.

asylum. The advertising agency will, of course, tell you that they have their fingers on the "public pulse" through the medium of so-called polls. The truth is, that they gather a completely erroneous idea of the public taste, for "polls" are nine times out of ten, wrong. The agencies, like a good many manufacturers, furnish the public mostly with what THEY think it should have.

Another factor entering the case is that everybody connected with the advertiser, be it employee or family, seems to have a voice in what the artists engaged for a broadcast should perform, and how. And these voices, however remote and indirect their influences, still have a certain potency. It does not seem to matter how ignorant their possessors may be; they are heard. And being heard, they shed ideas, no matter how ludicrous these are. The result is often as follows: The advertiser engages the services of a well-known artist to appear as guest on one of his programs. He pays this artist a fabulous fee, which he is obliged to do to tear him away from his legitimate pursuit. Arrived at rehearsal, the guest finds that he will be allowed to play or sing four or five minutes and some seconds. He is then faced with the problem of either performing a couple of inconsequential little salon pieces, each lasting approximately two minutes, or cutting up some major work to such an extent that it no longer bears any resemblance to the original.

Does this procedure give the public any idea of the artist's capability or the full pleasure it ought to enjoy from his performance? Not at all! But the comedian or crooner whose hour this is, must remain the star of the occasion, and the really great artist must remain classed as the hired assistant! Of course, the artist himself is often at fault for allowing himself to be tempted by the huge fee involved, when he already earns quite lavishly in his legitimate field; but he hopes, in this way, to keep his precious name constantly before the public. What he does not realize is that in reality he cheapens him or herself, and that he is appealing to the grosser elements of the population, which would not appreciate him one way or the other.

Naturally, all this has its exceptions, as all things have. We have some legitimate hours on the radio, which present programs of the utmost beauty; but why should they be so rare? The trouble is that the advertiser himself, being quite ignorant on the subject of music, assumes that most of the public follows suit; in that he is

It wasn't often that recitals (violin and piano) could fill Carnegie Hall, but Spalding and Benoist did it regularly.

completely wrong. Excepting the bobby soxers and callow youths, the poor maligned public is quick to sense real value, in art as well as anything else. But this same public is also rather naive, and when you feed it drivel, aided and abetted by clever propaganda, it will, sometimes reluctantly, accept it.

And it is not always that the deepest appreciation comes from those high on the social scale. Far from it. Their appreciation often consists of a thin layer of "culture," augmented by glib phrases and cliches; whereas the love of true beauty is imbedded deeply in the hearts of those less blessed with worldly goods.

I call to mind the example of a letter received by Mr. Spalding after one of his broadcasts. It was written by three miners who had listened to him through a receiving set, below the surface of the earth. The letter, while not worded quite grammatically, expressed deep gratitude for Spalding's performance of the *Ave Maria* by Schubert, and exuded such real sincerity as to be touching in the extreme.

But, useless to continue on this subject. Mine is only one voice in the dark. And so long as the power that "pays the piper" is paramount, so long shall we have to put up with the vagaries of radio!

The Benoists' second home in Monmouth Beach, New Jersey. This same house is now occupied by Andre's son Albert and Albert's wife Joan.

Chapter
XXIII

Spalding's American tour went on uneventfully, with 'his usual success. He was now greeted as "The Great American Violinist" which often made him smile. Here and there I met people who asked me if "Mr. Spalding was not a foreigner?" I hastened to assure them that he was not, but that he was a dyed-in-the-wool genuine American. "But," would come the reply, "He speaks like a foreigner!" "No," I would answer patiently, "He speaks correctly and enunciates his words clearly, whereas you mumble; and that's what sounds foreign to you!" And I would add, as a clinching argument, that Spalding's ancestors came to America in the early 1600's, landing at Jamestown, and that practically made him, being born in Chicago, an American! One would think this would be the end of it. Not at all! There would come a final under-the-breath mumble, "Can't be American, playing like that!" What "like that" meant I did not exactly know, but I doubt it was meant to be an unflattering implication.

In the meantime I was delighted to see a fine mutual friendship had sprung up between Spalding and Heifetz. It made my life, between two allegiances, so much more comfortable, and it fitted in perfectly with the tentative plans we had all made for our next European venture. We spent the summer as usual at our respective homes. Monmouth Beach, as usual, was my headquarters, where the time went by lazily between study, sea bathing and tennis. We had planned to stay in our country until Christmastime, and to go to Europe to play the rest of the winter and spring, then spend the following summer in Florence, resuming concertizing in Europe until Christmas. Finally, back to dear old U.S.A. to finish the winter season there.

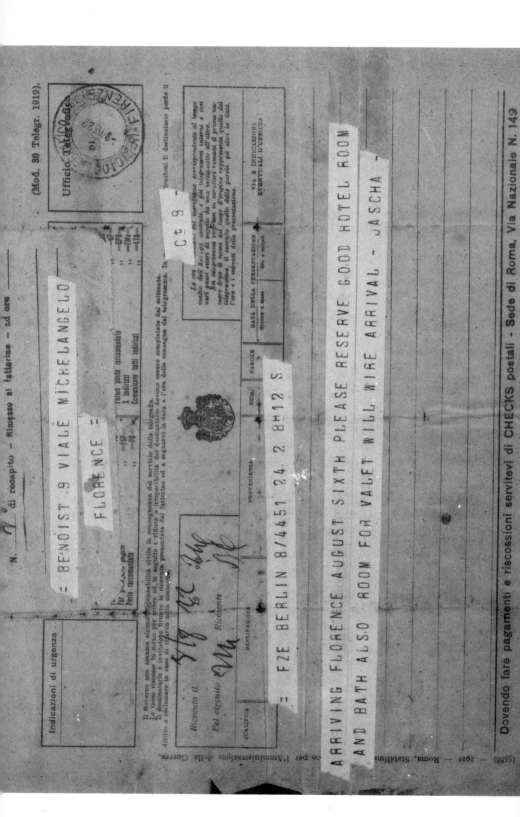

Ufficio Telegrafico

Indicazioni di urgenza

= BENOIST 9 VIALE MICHELANGELO

FLORENCE =

= FZE BERLIN 8/4451 24. 2 8H12 S

ARRIVING FLORENCE AUGUST SIXTH PLEASE RESERVE GOOD HOTEL ROOM
AND BATH ALSO ROOM FOR VALET WILL WIRE ARRIVAL - JASCHA -

Ct 9 -

All went as scheduled. Heifetz had promised he would visit us in Florence during that summer, but I for one had taken that promise with a "grain of salt." I knew my Jascha! And if some heart interest would spring up in the meantime, that would get first priority. In the meantime the Spaldings had taken a charming villa at the outskirts of the city. On the other hand, my wife, young son Albert, and I made ourselves comfortable in another small villa overlooking the city from the heights of the Viale Michelangelo.

I had completely forgotten Jascha's promise to visit us, when one evening, while at a party, what was my surprise but to receive a telegram, relayed by telephone, announcing the young man's arrival with his butler the next day at noon. Of course we were all delighted, but the hour of noon was a dismaying thought. In Florence, the summer mornings and evenings are pleasant. But at noon the temperature is broiling, and usually no one ventures out. The house shutters are kept tightly closed and luncheon is taken in the cool of the shaded house. After which a siesta is in order. As a rule, this lasts until about five, when suddenly everything comes to life again with the coming of the evening's coolness. Was it any wonder we were a bit taken aback on learning Jascha's hour of arrival? However, we prepared ourselves by dressing as near to the fig leaf period as could be done without unduly shocking the natives!

The train, of course, was late, as was customary in the pre-Mussolini days, and perspiration was oozing from our every pore! We were not amused! At long last our patience was rewarded, and the train ground to a standstill. From a first-class compartment emerged a vision I shall not soon forget. It was Jascha in the flesh, but garbed in a regalia that would have made a high-grade Englishman drool with envy! A superb English tweed suit complete with waistcoat and beautiful heavy brogans. A starched collar with silk necktie and heavy capeskin gloves; all this surmounted by a gorgeous pearl gray homburg hat. On beholding this vision, I almost fainted from the heat he must have felt. But the pleasure we all knew at seeing him overcame even the intense heat. I could not help remarking that while his attire was exquisite, I thought he would feel more comfortable in something a bit less conventional. "Oh, no," he said, "I could not think of wearing anything else! Why, I

Spalding, Benoist and Heifetz at the time of their friendly reunion in Florence, Italy. August, 1922.

had enough trouble getting my English tailor to have it ready in time for this trip! Do you think I am crazy?" Under my breath I said I thought he was. However, we got him settled, and when we saw him a couple of hours later, he was minus collar, necktie, waistcoat, gloves, etc., and was wearing only an open silk shirt and a pair of very light slacks. "It is a little on the warm side," he remarked sheepishly.

Jascha remained about a week in Florence, and it was one of the happiest times in my memory. Between showing him the splendors of the Tuscan countryside, playing tennis, ping-pong and MUSIC, the hours flitted by all too quickly.

One evening stands out in my memory as rather amusing. We had had Mr. and Mrs. Spalding as well as Heifetz for a little dinner party at our house, when both artists suddenly decided it would be pleasant to spend the evening playing violin duets, instead of going out. I was commandeered to officiate at the piano. The only audience we had was Mrs. Spalding and my wife. They had made

318

Spalding, Benoist and Heifetz in Florence, Italy, August, 1922.

320

Heifetz was an extremely handsome and successful musician. His first marriage (to Mrs. Florence Vidor) ended in divorce. She was a very beautiful and famous movie star of the silent era. She died in 1977. She and Heifetz had two children. Photo from *Heifetz*, edited by Dr. Herbert R. Axelrod.

themselves comfortable, each reclining on a sofa. Whether it was the effect of the soothing music, or the soft summer breezes being wafted through the open window from the garden, I don't know; but when after a couple of hours we looked their way, both ladies had fallen sound asleep, and when I ironically inquired how they had enjoyed the music, they had the effrontery to say, "Very much indeed!" Love's Labor Lost! But WE enjoyed it!

This wonderful summer ended all too soon and the time arrived when Mr. Spalding and I were to resume our peregrinations. At that time my wife and I had taken a lease on an apartment in Paris, and consequently we made that city our headquarters for our Euro-

Heifetz and Ottorino Respighi. Photo from *HEIFETZ*, edited by Dr. Herbert R. Axelrod.

pean season. We had the pleasure of entertaining some interesting personalities; one especially stands out. He was Ottorino Respighi, the great Italian composer, and with him was his charming Russian wife.

Respighi looked very much like a youthful and debonaire Beethoven, without the latter's reputed irascibility. His wife had the grace, charm and beauty of a Pavlowa. I spent quite some time with Respighi, while he explained to me the intricacy of his, (then new) Concerto Gregoriano, which Spalding was to introduce to America. The great Italian told me how he and his wife had fallen in love while they were both studying with Rimski-Korsakov. A real musical romance!

Mischa Elman and his lovely bride Helen, happening to be in Paris, also came to dinner, but Mischa, being in one of his garrulous moods, did not eat much, with the consequence that later in the evening he became really hungry, and we all adjourned to a nearby cafe where we ended in the wee hours! But what fun in the meantime! For, when at his best, Mischa can be uproarious company.

One of our engagements took us up to Berlin where we were to have a series of three recitals. For this trip I had decided to take my little family, as they had never seen Berlin. The concerts all took place at the Beethoven Saal, and I had noticed that at the end of each session a little old lady would come back to the green room. As she passed me, she would gather her skirts up to herself, as if fearing contamination. Then she would hasten to friend Spalding and extol him to the sky. Never had she heard finer violin playing; he was a great Master, etc., etc. But when she would start for the exit, she would cast a scornful look my way, and again gather herself together as if shrinking from my presence and quickly disappear.

I could only draw one conclusion: Neither my work nor I had found favor in her eyes. At the last concert, I was informing my wife of these incidences, when the little old lady, on passing us, hearing us speak in English, stopped dead in her tracks, and coming to me said with an inimitable Teutonic accent, "Are YOU an American also?" This I admitted, for a good many years at least. "Ach so!" she said, with a grimace of deep distaste, "I thought you were Frrrench, phooey! Ach, you blayed peaudivoolly! Dank you!" And with that she was off. Upon asking an attendant who this eccentric lady was I was informed in hushed reverence, "That is Frau Hans von Buelow." Indeed! The widow of the great conductor and pianist!

Two recitals in London followed by two recitals in Paris about concluded the first half of that season, for we were approaching Christmas and time to sail for home. The twenty-fifth of December was spent at sea, and the celebration of that holy day takes on a new meaning when surrounded by the vastness of the ocean, practically helpless, at the mercy of the elements. It was a typical mid-winter trip, with mountainous waves whipped by gale-like winds. The huge *Homeric* seemed like a cockle shell being buffeted about. But

"To my dear friend Andre from his devoted Mischa." An autograph-ed photograph from Mischa Elman.

on Christmas Day the bad weather seemed to subside and the festive decorations and the tree lent an atmosphere of gaiety in spite of the overcast skies. Copious toasts were drunk that Christmas Eve, but when the ship began to roll again, everyone was glad to adjourn to the privacy of his respective cabin.

Chapter
XXIV

New York again! And almost immediately "on the road" once more. It was on a trip to Chicago that an amusing incident occurred. The dining car being crowded, Mr. Spalding thought it would be a good idea to order luncheon in our drawing-room. He rang the bell for the porter, so as to give our order. No porter came. In the meantime he had been practicing on his violin, and every time he laid the instrument down, he rang the bell. This went on for about a half hour, when suddenly there came a knock at the door. It was the Pullman conductor inquiring as to our wishes. We explained that we had been ringing for a porter to give our order for lunch, but the service was very bad and no one had come. "You've got only yourself to blame," said the gold-braided gentleman, mildly shaking his head at Spalding, as if he were a naughty child, "There are at least ten porters in the next room, with their ears glued to the partition, listening to you; now if you'll just put that damn violin back in its box, they might be encouraged to go back to work and you'll get service again!" Spalding sheepishly did as suggested and things soon became normal.

Another comical happening comes to mind. We were scheduled for a recital in Milwaukee, and on arriving at the hall we found a note urgently requesting an interview, from a man who signed himself as managing a great artist. The concert over, the stage doorman ushered in a character that could have come out of a novel by Mark Twain. He was clad in blue jeans, wore a broad-rimmed felt hat and was meditatively chewing on a piece of straw. After introducing himself as the "manager" who had written the note announcing his coming, he stated that he had heard Mr. Spalding play and had liked it quite well. He would like to engage

From left to right: Jascha Heifetz, Andre Benoist, Albert Spalding, Alice Benoist (seated), and Mary Spalding wearing the dark hat. The other three people are unidentified. Spalding's moustache was shaved off before the end of Heifetz' visit. Florence, Italy; August, 1922.

Spalding as assisting artist for his wife's forthcoming concert tour. The violinist explained that such a thing would be impossible owing to prior commitments. The man kept insisting, saying that he would be willing to pay as high as fifty dollars a week and, of course, traveling expenses. Spalding told him he thought that was very generous, but, he added, "What instrument does the lady play?" "What?" asked the man in an astonished voice, "You didn't know? Why, my wife is the greatest artist in the world on the. . . covered hair comb!" With the utmost seriousness, but with his tongue in his cheek Spalding told him that, flattering as the offer was, he did not feel that his art would measure up to it, and that therefore he must forego the honor. With that the man departed, apparently satisfied.

It is while traveling extensively on railroad trains that one has leisure to cogitate on the idiosyncrasies of people generally, and, in my case, of artists particularly. Why is it that singers, as a rule, are such poor musicians? After all, what is a singer? It should primarily be a musician who, instead of performing on a man-made instrument, does so on one that is God-given. But for all that, it still remains an instrument that should be used with care, taste and understanding. Fundamentally there should be no difference between using a cello, a violin or a voice to make music. The only goal should be to produce music in the most beautiful way possible. To do this it is not sufficient to produce a fine quality of tone and it is not necessary to scratch, pound, or bellow. But it is absolutely necessary to be able to phrase properly and perform within the rhythm indicated by the composer, without the distortion generally used to accommodate either the bow arm of the string player or the breath of the singer. The string player at least reads music at sight and does so, as a rule, in time and correct rhythm.

But the singer? No indeed; all he or she is interested in is the showing of this beautiful instrument they fortunately were born with. They acquire a smattering of music and then it is up to that "rara avis" (rare bird), the wonderful singing teacher. From then on, singing becomes a deep mystery, unsolvable, except by the particular singing teacher in whose hands the singer happens to fall. If he or she is really a fine teacher, he will show his student how to emit his tones easily without forcing, always keeping in mind that music comes first and that the singer is only the liaison between his

Administration :

BUREAU de CONCERTS : MARCEL de VALMALÈTE
45, Rue la Boëtie (Maison Gaveau) PARIS VIII*

Télégrammes : Valmaletav-Paris.   Téléphone : Elysées 06-72

R. C. Seine 311-047

SAISON 1928-1929

MAISON GAVEAU (Salle des Concerts), 45-47, Rue La Boëtie

Premier Concert. — JEUDI 25 OCTOBRE 1928 à 21 heures
(Ouverture des Portes à 20 h. 30)

RÉCITAL DE VIOLON
ALBERT
SPALDING

(Représentant : Dr G. de KOOS)
avec le concours de M.

André BENOIST

Programme

I. a) Sonate la majeur		A. CORELLI
	Grave	
	Allegro	
	Allegro moderato	
	Adagio	
	Allegro	
b) Sonate sol mineur (pour violon seul)		J. S. BACH
	Adagio	
	Fugue	
	Siciliano	
	Presto	
II. Sonate ré mineur op. 121 (pour violon et piano)		R. SCHUMANN
	Lent : vif	
	Très vif	
	Doux simple	
	Agité	
III. Poème		CHAUSSON
Cortège.		L. BOULANGER
Minstrels		DEBUSSY
Tzigane.		RAVEL

PIANO GAVEAU

PRIX DES PLACES : Loges, 40 fr. la place; Parterre, 50, 30 et 20 fr.;
Premier Balcon, 25, 20 et 12 fr.; Deuxième Balcon, 20, 15 et 8 fr. (droits compris)

BILLETS : Maison Gaveau— Durand, 4, place de la Madeleine — au Guide-Billets, 252, Faubourg St-Honoré — Editions Max Eschig, 48, Rue
de Rome — Sénart, 49, rue de Rome — au Bureau Musical, 32, Rue Tronchet. — Roudanez, Laudy, Magasin Musical, etc.

Le 2e Concert aura lieu le VENDREDI 9 NOVEMBRE à 21 heures avec le concours de la célèbre cantatrice
Rosette ANDAY, de l'Opéra de Vienne

A Spalding-Benoist program played in Paris. October 25, 1928.

voice and his listeners. But alas, in nine cases out of ten, the "teacher" knows as little about music as the pupil. All he is interested in is beautiful tone!

Consequently, there comes upon the scene the person who is the musical crutch or prop to the average singer or singing teacher: the ubiquitous "coach." His duty is to see that the singer does not take too many liberties with the music at hand. That he pronounces the texts properly, that his enunciation is clear-cut, that he phrases rightly and observes dynamics. He is the "general maid" of music and does most of the dirty work, while the teacher in his great studio earns the encomiums.

I know, for I have coached some singers of undying fame, and have been surprised by their musical ignorance. They were unable to play four bars of their accompaniments on the piano. As to sight reading, they were unable to do so unless the notes were hammered out on the piano, one at a time. This condition is much less prevalent with French singers, but only for the reason that if they study in the National Conservatory, they cannot study singing unless they also take up the study of an instrument. Their voices may not always be as luscious as those of their warm-climate neighbors, the Italians, but they give greater pleasure to the judicious music lover, for they sing musically, and mostly in good taste.

Another curiosity of our musical life is the star orchestral conductor. Whence comes the hero worship that surrounds him? It is quite true that his is a great art, but it is an art that depends on many factors. Let us assume that Dr. Karl Muck (were he alive) would be given the task of conducting the symphony orchestra of Murfreesboro, Kentucky, composed entirely of amateurs. Would he, by some magic, be able to give the same performance as, for instance, with the Boston Symphony? Decidedly not, regardless of how many rehearsals he would have. No more than could a great pianist give as fine a performance on an inferior instrument as on a great one, or a violinist on a factory-made fiddle as on a Guarnerius del Gesu. Thus we arrive at the crux of the matter. The conductor must have a fine orchestra to work with if he wishes to show his real ability. It is a foregone conclusion that he must also be an able score reader and must have the technique of the baton well in hand. Otherwise, he is no conductor. This latter fact was illustrated by a bitter critic of a renowned artist of the baton. His quip was in the form of a conundrum. The question was: "Why will (so and so) never be struck by lightning?" The answer: "Because he is a non-conductor." Foolish? Yes, and moreover, in this case, not quite true.

Now we have the great conductor in front of a first class orchestra who has, no doubt played the orchestral repertoire under many directors. It knows the pieces backwards and forwards. There can be no deep mystery as to the interpretation, for the composer has carefully indicated in the printed music his tempi and dynamics. What sudden magic happens to make this or that conductor stand out as a new hero? I believe it is a combination of things, none of which has any direct connection with artistic achievement. Being possessed of the routine knowledge his profession requires, he then becomes what an army general is: a leader of men. He must awe and inspire them to do their utmost for his sake. And most of his work is done in the rehearsal room, much as the general's work is done on the training field. To sum it up, it is a matter of technical ability combined with clever showmanship and propaganda that makes the great conductor great, and not some deep mysterious gift from on high.

How affected he was! *"Dr. Karl Muck."* It is unusual for people to sign their photographs with their titles such as "Dr." or "Mr."

Jascha Heifetz and Dr. Herbert R. Axelrod celebrating Heifetz' 77th birthday at the Heifetz home in Malibu Beach, California on February 2, 1978.

Chapter
XXV

Another season came to an end; another happy summer intermission also ended, and off we were to Europe once again! We joined Mr. and Mrs. Spalding in the delightful Shakespearean town of Stratford-upon-Avon, and our stay there is among the happiest of our memories. The charm of these semi-medieval surroundings is gripping, with the musical flow of the tiny river Avon singing its enchanting song beneath one's windows. One of the thrills that confronted us during our exploration of the surrounding countryside came one day while on our way to see Kenilworth Castle.

Arriving on a small rise in the road, our eyes suddenly beheld the American flag floating alone in the breeze atop a fine mansion. It was such an unusual sight to find our flag flying alone in a foreign country that we made inquiries as to the meaning thereof. We were told that this was the only place in England where this exception was made, because that house was the home of George Washington's ancestors: "Sulgrave Manor."

Another great pleasure was meeting one of the former great ladies of the theatre, Mary Anderson, who entertained us one afternoon at tea. She regaled us with innumerable anecdotes of her younger days. At the age of seventy-six, to which she confessed, there were plainly visible traces of her former great beauty, in the fineness of her features, the modeling of her head to which may be added her regal bearing. The hallowed tea time of England engenders so comfortable a feeling that it encourages the great art of conversation, which nowhere else flourishes so well. And this particular "tea" stands out as a rare experience. I gathered that the great actress, at the top of her career, had been fervently wooed by the Baron de Navarro, who persuaded her that the course of love is

SOCIETÀ DEGLI AMICI
S~ DELLA MVSICA

৯৯৯৯৯৯ 5, VIA VECCHIETTI ৯৯৯৯৯৯

CONCERTO

ALBERT SPALDING

AL PIANOFORTE

ANDRÉ BENOIST

SALA BIANCA (Palazzo Pitti)
FIRENZE, 28 Dicembre 1929 - ore 17

PROGRAMMA

I.

VITALI . . . . — Ciaccona

BACH . . . . . — Sarabanda e Giga (dalla partita
per violino solo in re maggiore).

MOZART. . . . — Concerto in re
Allegro - Andante - Rondò.

II.

BRAHMS . . . . — Sonata in la magg. (per piano e
violino)
Allegro amabile
Andante tranquillo - Vivace
Allegretto grazioso (quasi andante).

III.

CHOPIN . . . . — Notturno in sol

ALBENIZ. . . . — Sevillana

BRAHMS. . . . — Berceuse
— Valzer

PAGANINI . . . — La Campanella.

Albert Spalding and Andre Benoist rehearsing at Spalding's home, Aston Magna.

President of the United States Herbert Hoover, who also summered near Monmouth Beach, N.J. was only one of several Presidents for whom Benoist played.

preferable to even the greatest fame. From all appearances there must have been no cause for regret in her choice, for in their advanced years, the two still seemed like lovers; the Baron's attention and devotion, as well as his wife's sweet and gracious acceptance of these, were touching to witness. It was with reluctance that we took leave of them, and soon thereafter, of England.

Again we faced Scandinavian audiences, with their quick reactions and perceptive enthusiasm. By now my friend Spalding had become a prime favorite in these northern countries. This was due as much to his personality as to his art. His unfailing good humor, patience and generosity under sometimes difficult circumstances were quick to gain him lasting friendships, and it was a great source of pride and joy to me to see him appreciated at his true value.

After much "barnstorming," which included Vienna, Munich, Paris, and the Netherlands, came the last week of the European tour for the season 1928-1929. This was spent in Berlin, where we arrived on a rainy Sunday, and where we were to play our seasonal farewell recital the following Sunday at the old Beethoven Saal.

We were surprised and pleased to read in the newspapers that the interim between Sunday and Saturday was to be filled by such a display of artists that even Berlin rarely sees in one week. There were to be heard Elman, Menuhin, Casals, Thibaud, and Piatigorsky. This took care of Monday, Tuesday, Wednesday, Thursday and Friday. On Saturday it was our turn. Of course each artist who was able to remain in Berlin went to the other's concerts and as we were all acquainted, it made for a pleasant reunion week.

This was a time when the bitterness of World War I had subsided, and the relationship between France and Germany was all sugar and honey, at least on the surface. So much so, that the respective governments had arranged for an exchange of artists, as ambassadors of good will. Hence the presence in Berlin of the Frenchman Jacques Thibaud, in exchange for the German Kuhlenkampf, who had gone to Paris.

Under the circumstances, Spalding thought it would be pleasant to give a supper party after our concert, inasmuch as it was the last of that week. He had invited all artists who had been able to remain in Berlin, as well as the local artists and managers. Fortunately Thibaud was able to stay over, and naturally Carl Flesch, the

For Mr. André Benoist from his friend Franklin D. Roosevelt

President Franklin Roosevelt was a friend of Benoist. This autographed photo was on his wall at the time of his death in 1953.

celebrated German violinist, pedagogue and teacher, was asked to preside over the proceedings. The food at the Furstenhof is known for its excellence, and wine and beer were supplied liberally. Speeches were made, also liberally, extolling the great reconciliation, vowing eternal friendship and the forgetting of former enmities, etc., etc. Almost the last to speak was Thibaud, who expressed his gratification at being back in this country where art had always been uppermost and where he had been so cordially received as good will ambassador from his beloved France. Great applause greeted his remarks.

Then arose Carl Flesch who was to be the last speaker of the evening. To those who never knew him, it might be wise to explain that Flesch was rarely seen to smile. He looked like a combination of a rabbi, The Thinker by Rodin, and a Jesuit priest. Of humor, he was reputed to be entirely devoid. His every utterance was weighty and ponderous, as an important professor's should be.

It must also be understood that Thibaud's reputation as an artist was almost equalled by that as a Don Juan, of which he was secretly proud.

After some introductory remarks, very touching in their admiration for the great Frenchman's art, Flesch went on to say that we were all under the impression that Thibaud had come to Germany only as an artistic ambassador. This was an erroneous idea, quoth he. "No, no," he continued, waxing eloquent, "Such is not the case! Thibaud is more than merely an artist! He is a great and generous soul! He knows by experience the loss we have sustained in man-power, and out of the pity in his heart, he has come, in secret modesty, to help us repopulate our poor denuded country! That is his real mission and we thank him from the bottom of our hearts!"

The howls that came from the guests at the table were tribute enough to one who was supposed to be lacking completely in a sense of humor.

On this happy note, all separated, each to go where next duty called. We were to be homeward bound. On arriving in Paris, I was surprised to see more people than usual crowding the precincts of the American Express Company's offices in the Rue Scribe. There were also ugly rumors afloat as to the state of things in the United States; but I could gather nothing definite, so I paid scant attention, knowing full well what rumors generally amounted to.

Soon after arrival home we were to discover that this time rumor had not been far wrong; all banks were closed, and the bottom seemed to have dropped out of all things economic. Many of my friends who had speculated heavily, and who had strongly urged me to follow their example (advice I had fortunately not heeded), had lost all their possessions in the crash that followed. It looked black indeed for our profession, but somehow our season did not appear to suffer too much from the debacle. In times of stress people seem to have recourse to almost any form of entertainment so as to forget their woes! So we weathered this storm as we had many others, and many happy years of concertizing followed.

However, little did I dream that my friend Spalding would again feel called upon to offer his services for the saving of our country. With the advent of this second cataclysm, I began to lose heart. I tried to point out to him how precious his art was to his admirers, and that it was his duty not to put it in jeopardy, but all to no avail. His only reply was that any man's life was precious from the highest to the lowest, and the more fortunate one's circumstances, the heavier the duty imposed upon him. Mary Spalding, too, seeing the futility of arguing, was heroic. She carefully hid her anguish from him when she saw his decision had irrevocably been made. It must have been a superhuman task, but she was a "good soldier." Spalding was enrolled in the office of War Information and sent to the Italian Front, where, thanks to his perfect knowledge of the Italian character as well as language, he was able to accomplish wonders in conducting the activities of the Italian Underground under the "nom de guerre" of "Major Sheridan." But that is another story better left to one equipped to tell it.

Even this second horror came to an end, and my friend came back, emaciated and rather weak from his experiences, but fortunately unscathed.

After a spring and summer devoted to rest and practicing to get back into form, he at last judged that the time had come to resume his public life. I was surprised and delighted to hear at our first rehearsal how quickly and easily his fingers had reattained all their elasticity. His magnificent tone was glowing again and it was with keen anticipation that our post war tour began. . .

I am presently sitting in a corner of the verandah at our old home in Monmouth Beach. This morning I saw a ball of fire rise out of the Atlantic Ocean on the eastern horizon. It was a glorious sun greeting the dawn. Now it is dusk and this same sun is slowly settling in the West over the Shrewsbury River; it is slightly dimmed by some roseate and mauve clouds, as if reluctant to depart after shining all day.

It is a symbol of life; and the dreamy mood it engenders causes me to review in retrospect the joys and woes that have filled the fifty years of a life mostly devoted to providing background music for the great, near-great and sometimes mediocre. The carefree and

Albert Spalding Benoist with his father.

happy childhood in Paris, the catastrophe so heroically sustained by my parents, the open-armed welcome given us in this generous haven called America.

... Young manhood, romance, elopement, marriage, the birth of two baby daughters, bereavement and widowhood, loneliness, remarriage, the birth of a son, the long and loyal companionship of a wife through struggle and comfort, older years creeping on. . . and at last peace and contentment. Many dear friendships also, among which stands in bold relief the lasting one of Albert Spalding, a truly great man.

Thus turns the kaleidoscope. Watching the human side of celebrities from "backstage," their weaknesses and strengths (Thomas Alva Edison's peculiar habit of constant tobacco-chewing which so ill-matched a brilliant mind?). Playing at the White House and watching different presidential reactions to it. Theodore Roosevelt's impatience with anything not pertaining to his "job." Coolidge's boredom, and pulling out his watch every moment, wondering how long this would go on! Hoover's stolid poker face. And Franklin Delano Roosevelt's ineffable charm and uncanny memory for faces. For, upon our meeting he claimed to have seen me before. I admitted he had, and immediately he came back with, "You played for my Warm Springs Foundation benefit some years ago." He was right!

Came across my mind another picture: The great ballroom at Mr. William K. Vanderbilt's house on Fifth Avenue where I had played a private concert with Bessie Abbott and Hugo Heerman. The assembled dowagers and their stuffed shirted escorts had been enthusiastic with discreet kid-gloved applause. They were peering through their lorgnettes and glasses, gawking at the artists ("So delightfully Bohemian, and quite immoral, my dear!"), when on the floor came a charming-looking lady. Her name, I learned, was Natalie Townsend. She announced that she had just arrived from California, and would like to show the assembly the new dance she had discovered in that state. With that, she and her partner went through a routine (I cannot call it dance) which, for sheer vulgarity and obscene suggestion, would be hard to equal. This terminated, she announced that the name of the dance was the "Turkey Trot."

Albert Spalding Benoist, the son of Andre, took this touching photograph of his mother and father at Albert Spalding's home in Great Barrington, Mass. in 1952. This is the last known photograph of Andre before his death on June 22, 1953.

To my dear André —
With affectionate best wishes —
Jascha

New York — *March 3, 19**

Benoist often told his son Albert Spalding Benoist that *"Heifetz was one of the world's great violinists. . . not the only greatest. Technically, yes, he was the greatest. . . but artistically there were others who were greater in the interpretation of some pieces. Certainly Heifetz could play the notes of the Paganini caprices, but he lacked the daring abandon that was necessary to make them effective. His Bach, too, was far from "musical" except, perhaps, the Chaccone. Music is for artists. . . technique is for computers! This is a protest!"*

Benoist

The guests were duly shocked, but one could readily see that their jaded appetites had been titillated. Needless to speak of how the craze spread.

I had lived through two tragic wars, the advent of surrealism in painting, angular forms of architecture and atonal music. There is no question that the artist of today is the most efficient in the history of art. But is efficiency the goal? Is the function of the artist to depict only the sinister and repellent? Is it necessary to progress to show ugly deformities and cacophony of sound? Is it progress to exhibit the wounds and obscenities of the human race? Has spirituality gone by the boards and out of fashion? Must one be ashamed of sentiment? Is the circle closing and are we headed back to the jungle, or is our path leading upwards to some hitherto undreamed of empyrean?

As the sun is setting in the west. . .

An André Benoist
Discography

by John Anthony Maltese

André Benoist's recording career spanned over thirty years and, in line with his chosen profession, the vast majority of his records were made in his capacity as an accompanist. Despite his long tenure in the recording studio, he collaborated (to my knowledge) with only two gentlemen, Jascha Heifetz and Albert Spalding, both of whom, of course, were violinists. This was only natural, since, notwithstanding early stints with Thibaud, Casals, Nordica, etc., Benoist was Spalding's lifetime accompanist. Heifetz, as one will recall, fitted into the picture during World War I, when Spalding was in the service.

Benoist made his first recordings with Spalding for Edison about 1912. The first selections they recorded were for Edison's four-minute Amberol cylinders, but soon they were making his Diamond Discs (some of which also appeared on Edison's more sophisticated blue and purple cylinders). It is interesting to note that, despite the fact that they were recorded acoustically, Spalding always preferred those Edison recordings above all his others. During an interview with Jim Walsh in December, 1940, Spalding said: "From the standpoint of silent surfaces and absolutely perfect reproduction of tone, those Diamond Discs are the finest that have ever been made. . . I used to play my fiddle on the stage in direct comparison with Mr. Edison's recordings, and not a soul in the audience could tell when I stopped and the phonograph took over except by watching the movements of my bow. Today if I tried to play in direct comparison with my electrical Victor records, everybody could tell the difference—and a big one."

In addition to his accompaniments for Spalding, Benoist made his only commercial solo recordings for Edison's Diamond Discs. And it is noteworthy that in reference to Spalding's remarks about the "tone test" recitals, Benoist's solo recording of *The Two Larks* by Leschetizky was often used during these recitals as an example of the general excellence in piano recordings achieved by Edison.

Anyone familiar with Edison is aware of his rather unsophisticated tastes when it came to music, and so it was that Benoist's first solo recording was of *Old Black Joe* rather than of a Chopin etude, which Edison rejected with a note saying: "Rotten. Ain't got no tune."

With Spalding's entry into the war in 1917, Benoist left Edison for a brief time to record with Heifetz for Victor. His association with Heifetz lasted about one year and included four recording sessions: November 9 and December 19, 1917; and October 3 and October 4, 1918.

These recordings were widely acclaimed and are still available from RCA today. One will note (in Chapter XXI) Benoist's recollection of their recording of the *Moto Perpetuo* by Paganini which, incidentally, was recorded at the October 3, 1918, session.

When the war ended, Benoist returned to the service of Spalding, and together they continued to record for Edison until the demise of that company in the late 1920's. Among these final discs was one especially rare recording, made in 1928, using the electrical rather than acoustical process.

With the end of Edison Records, Spalding and Benoist turned to the Brunswick company and made with them a series of early electrical recordings. Dissatisfied, however, with the sound of those recordings (Spalding later termed them "terrible") they turned to Victor and recorded for them until Benoist's retirement from the side of Spalding in the 1940's.

From these Victor sessions come such major recordings as the Franck sonata, the Brahms "A Major" sonata, and the complete set of Spalding's own *Etchings*.

The Victor recordings represent Benoist's last commercial recordings. However, several private studio discs were made by Benoist with the singer Virginia Mauret in April of 1945. Private tapes (recorded by his son Albert) also exist of Benoist peforming solo works in his home, as well as of accompanying some of his students. These tapes date from about 1949 and cover the early 1950's up until Benoist's death.

The following discography includes only Benoist's commercially recorded discs. Listed in order are the composer, the composition's title, and the collaborator(s), followed by information about the type of recording (cylinders, 78s, and LPs, respectively). Compositions are listed alphabetically under the composer, and if a work was recorded more than once, the different versions are listed in the 1-2-3 order in which they were recorded.

The cylinder and 78 rpm information is listed only for U.S. releases, but the LP information is devoted to issues from all countries so as to encompass several recent reissues outside the United States.

Part II of the discography lists the Duo-Art piano rolls Benoist made of piano accompaniments to some of the major violin repertoire.

A key to record formats and numbers is found immediately following the discography.

Bay Head, New Jersey
June, 1977

350

Discography

ANONYMOUS
Drink to Me Only with Thine Eyes (arr. Quilter). 1. Albert Spalding, violin.
Cylinder: Edison 29046; 78 RPM: Edison 82184. 2. Albert Spalding, violin. 78
RPM: Victor 1703.

BAZZINI, ANTONIO:
La Ronde des Lutins, Op. 25. Jascha Heifetz, violin. 78 RPM: Victor 74570 and
6159; LP: RCA ARM4-0942, Everest 3326, MB-1010, Pearl GEM-109, ZRG-
35.

BEETHOVEN, LUDWIG VON
Chorus of Dervishes (arr. Auer). Jascha Heifetz, violin. 78 RPM: Vic. 64759 and
671; LP: RCA ARM4-0942, ZRG-35.
Minuet in G (arr. Burmester). Albert Spalding, violin. 78 RPM: Edison 82284.
Romance No. 1, in G Major, Op. 40. Albert Spalding, violin. 78 RPM: Vic. 1788.
Romance No. 2, in F major, Op. 50. Albert Spalding, violin. 78 RPM: Vic.
14579.
Turkish March (arr. Auer). Jascha Heifetz, violin. 78 RPM: Vic. 64770 and 671;
LP: RCA ARM4-0942, ZRG-35.

BIZET, GEORGES:
Adagietto (L'Arlesienne) (arr. Kreisler). Albert Spalding, violin. 78 RPM: Edison
82172.
Intermezzo (L'Arlesienne) (arr. Kreisler). Albert Spalding, violin. 78 RPM:
Edison 82046

BOHM, CARL:
Gypsy Mazurka, Op. 102. Solo piano. 78 RPM: Edison 51011.

Andre Benoist's son Albert Spalding Benoist is pictured recently in this photo with his wife Joan.

BOULANGER, LILI:
Cortege. Albert Spalding, violin. 78 RPM: Vic. 1740; LP: MB-1009

BRAHMS, JOHANNES:
Hungarian Dance No. 1, in G Minor (arr. Joachim). Albert Spalding, violin. 78 RPM: Edison 82263.
Hungarian Dance No. 5, in G Minor (arr. Joachim). Albert Spalding, violin. Cylinder: Edison 203; 78 RPM: Edison 82048.
Hungarian Dance No. 6, in B-flat Major (arr. Joachim). Albert Spalding, violin. 78 RPM: 82342.
Hungarian Dance No. 7, in A Major (arr. Joachim). Albert Spalding, violin. Cylinder: Edison 203; 78 RPM: Edison 82046.
Sonata No. 2, in A Major, Op. 100. Albert Spalding, violin. 78 RPM: Vic. M-288.
Waltz No. 15, in A Major (arr. Hochstein). 1. Albert Spalding, violin. 78 RPM: Bruns. 15127. 2. Albert Spalding, violin. 78 RPM: Vic. 1667.

CASSADO, GASPAR:
Danse du diable vert. Albert Spalding, violin. 78 RPM: Vic. 1914; LP: MB-1009.

CHABRIER, EMMANUEL:
Scherzo-Valse (arr. Loeffler). Albert Spalding, violin. 78 RPM: Edison 82168.

CHAMINADE, CECILE:
Serenade Espagnole. Albert Spalding, violin. 78 RPM: Edison 82172.

CHOPIN, FREDERIC:
Fantaisie-Impromptu, Op. 66. Solo piano. 78 RPM: Edison 80408.
Nocturne No. 2, in E-Flat Major, Op. 9. 1. Albert Spalding, violin. 78 RPM: Edison 82062. 2. Jascha Heifetz, violin. 78 RPM: Vic. 74616 and 6156. LP: RCA ARM-4-0942. 3. Albert Spalding, violin. 78 RPM: Bruns. 30124 and 50138; LP: MB-1009.
3. Albert Spalding, violin. 78 RPM: Bruns. 30124 and 50138; LP: MB-1009.
Nocturne No. 8, in D-flat Major, Op. 27 (arr. Wilhelmj). Albert Spalding, violin. 78 RPM: Edison 82212.
Nocturne No. 12, in G Major, Op. 37 (arr. Spalding). Albert Spalding, violin. 78 RPM: Bruns. 50099 and A5102.
Waltz No. 10, in B Minor, Op. 69 (arr. Spalding). Albert Spalding, violin. 78 RPM: Vic. 1703; LP: MB-1009.
Waltz No.11 in G-flat major, Op. 70 (arr. Spalding). Albert Spalding, violin. 78 RPM: Edison 82316.
Waltz in A-flat Major. Solo piano. 78 RPM: Edison 50309.

COTTENET, RICHARD
Chanson Meditation. Albert Spalding, violin. 78 RPM: Edison 82206.

CUI, CESAR:
Orientale. Albert Spalding, violin. 78 RPM: Edison 82064.

DE BERIOT, CHARLES:
Concerto No. 2, in B Minor, Op. 32 (2nd move. only). Albert Spalding, violin. 78 RPM: Edison 82250.

DEBUSSY, CLAUDE:
Minstrels (arr. Hartmann). Albert Spalding, violin. 78 RPM: Vic. 1881.

DELIBES, LEO:
Passepied (arr. Gruenberg). 1. Albert Spalding, violin. 78 RPM: Bruns. 15211. 2. Albert Spalding, violin. 78 RPM: Edison 82192.

DRDLA, FRANZ:
Souvenir. Albert Spalding, violin. 78 RPM: Edison 82154.

DRIGO, RICCARDO
Valse Bluette. 1. Albert Spalding, violin. 78 RPM: Edison 82192. 2. Jascha Heifetz, violin. 78 RPM: Vic. 64758 and 673; LP: RCA ARM4-0942.
Serenade (arr. Auer). Albert Spalding, violin. 78 RPM: Edison 82263.

DURAND, AUGUSTE:
Valse in E-flat Major. Piano solo. 78 RPM: Edison 50292.

DVORAK, ANTONIN:
Humoresque No. 7, in G Major (arr. Wilhelmj) 1. Albert Spalding, violin. 78 RPM: Edison 82047. 2. Albert Spalding, violin. 78 RPM: Edison 47005 (electric).
Indian Lament (arr. Kreisler). Albert Spalding, violin. 78 RPM: Edison 82239.
Slavonic Dance No. 10, in E Minor (arr. Kreisler). Albert Spalding, violin. 78 RPM: Edison

ELGAR, SIR EDWARD:
La Capricieuse, Op. 17. Jascha Heifetz, violin. 78 RPM: Vic. 64760 and 672; LP: RCA ARM4-0942.

FOSTER, STEVEN:
My Old Kentucky Home (arr. Spalding). Albert Spalding, violin. Cylinder: Edison 28236; 78 RPM: 82105
Old Black Joe—With Variations (arr. Benoist). Solo piano. 78 RPM: Edison 50292.
The Old Folks at Home (arr. Zimbalist). Albert Spalding, violin. 78 RPM: Edison 82215.

Mrs. Grace
Coolidge, well
known as a
patroness of
the arts,
presented this
inscribed pho-
to to Benoist
after a White
House per-
formance in
December of
1924.

To Mr. André Benoist to thank him for his
part in the musical program of
December 18, 1924.   Grace Coolidge

FRANCK, CESAR:
Sonata in A Major. Albert Spalding, violin. 78 RPM: Vic. M-208.

GLAZOUNOV, ALEXANDER:
Meditation. Jascha Heifetz, violin. 78 RPM Vic. 64769 and 676; LP: RCA ARM4-0942.

GLUCK, CHRISTOPH WILLIBALD:
Melodie (arr. Ries). Albert Spalding, violin. 78 RPM: Edison 82206.

GODARD, BENJAMIN:
Canzonetta (2nd move. from *"Concerto No. 1, Op. 35"*). Albert Spalding, violin. 78 RPM: Edison 82212.
Mazurka No. 2. Solo piano. Cylinder: Edison 3578. 78 RPM: Edison 80408.

GRANADOS, ENRIQUE:
Danza Espanola ("Andaluza") (arr. Kreisler). Albert Spalding, violin. 78 RPM: Edison 82194.

GRIEG, EDVARD:
Butterfly. Piano solo. 78 RPM: Edison 50200.

HANDEL, GEORGE FREDERICK:
Ombra mai fu ("Largo") (arr. Spalding). Albert Spalding, violin; R. Gayler, organ. 78 RPM: Edison 82239.
Sonata in E Major, Op. 1, No. 15. Albert Spalding, violin. 78 RPM: Vic. 14029.
Sonata in E Major, Op. 2, No. 9 (2nd move. only). Albert spalding, violin; William Primrose, viola. 78 RPM: Vic. M-838.

HARRIS, ROY:
Poem. Albert Spalding, violin. 78 RPM: Vic. 8997.

KETTEN, HENRI:
Caprice Espagnola (arr. Loeffler). Albert Spalding, violin. 78 RPM: Edison 82154.

KREISLER, FRITZ:
Caprice Viennois. Albert Spalding, violin. 78 RPM: Edison 82067.
Liebesfreud. Albert Spalding, violin. 78 RPM: Edison 82323.
Minuet (In the Style of Porpora). Jascha Heifetz, violin. 78 RPM: Vic. 64856 and 673; LP: RCA ARM4-0942.
Schon Rosmarin. Albert Spalding, violin. 78 RPM: Edison 82046.
Sicilienne et Rigaudon (In the Style of Francoeur). Jascha Heifetz, violin. 78 RPM: Vic. 64917 and 674; LP: RCA ARM4-0942.

Top, left: Paul Sladek, composer and string pedagogue; top, right: Virginia Ralston with Andre Benoist; below: Valeska and Jaime de la Fuente with Andre Benoist and his new 1934 Buick Roadster.

LACH:
Valse Arabesque. Solo piano. 78 RPM: Edison 50980.

LESCHETIZKY, THEODORE:
The Two Larks. Piano solo. 78 RPM: Edison 50200.

MASSENET, JULES:
Meditation. Albert Spalding, violin. Cylinder: Edison 28102; 78 RPM: Edison 82043.

MENDELSSOHN, FELIX:
On Wings of Song (arr. Achron). 1. Jascha Heifetz, violin. 78 RPM: Vic. 74583 and 6152; LP: RCA ARM4-0942, Everest 3326, Pearl GEM-109. 2. Albert Spalding, violin. 78 RPM: Bruns. 50066; LP: MB-1009.
Spinning Song. Piano solo. 78 RPM: Edison 50309.
Spring Song, Op. 62, No. 6. Albert Spalding, violin. 78 Edison 82135.

MOSZKOWSKI, MORITZ:
Guitarre (arr. Sarasate) 1. Jascha Heifetz, violin. 78 RPM: Vic. 64823 and 672; LP: RCA ARM4-0942.
2. Albert Spalding, violin. 78 RPM: Bruns. 15107; LP MB-1009.

MOZART, WOLFGANG AMADEUS:
Minuet (from K. 334) (arr. Burmester). 1. Albert Spalding, violin. 78 RPM: Bruns 15127. 2. Albert Spalding, violin. 78 RPM: Vic. 1667.
Sonata No. 28, in E-flat Major, K. 380. Albert Spalding, violin. 78 RPM: Vic. M-819.

OPENSHAW, JOHN:
Love Sends a Little Gift of Roses. Albert Spalding, violin. 78 RPM: Edison 82308.

PAGANINI, NICOLO:
Caprice No. 20, in D Major. Jascha Heifetz, violin. 78 RPM: Vic. 64833 and 670; LP: RCA ARM4-0942.
Moto Perpetuo. Jascha Heifetz, violin. 78 RPM: Vic. 74581; LP: RCA ARM4-0942.

PIERNE, GABRIEL:
Serenade in A Major. Albert Spalding, violin. 78 RPM: Edison 82184.

QUILTER, ROGER:
Three Poor Mariners. Albert Spalding, violin. 78 RPM: Edison 82192.

Spalding and Benoist signing autographs for the troops during World War II.

A mon cher ami et collègue
André Benoist
votre bien dévoué

Rodolphe Ganz

1916.

Rudolphe Ganz autographed this portrait to Benoist in 1916: "To my dear friend and colleague Andre Benoist, your devoted admirer."

360

RAFF, JOSEPH:
Cavatina. 1. Albert Spalding, violin. 78 RPM: Edison 82047. 2. Albert Spalding, violin. 78 RPM: Bruns. 50136.

RANDEGGER, ALBERTO:
Pierrot Serenade, Op. 33, No. 1. Albert Spalding, violin. Cylinder: Edison 28241; 78 RPM: Edison 82105.

ROGERS:
Prelude—Arabesque. Solo piano. 78 RPM: Edison 50200.

RUBINSTEIN, ANTON:
Melody in F (arr. Spalding). Albert Spalding, violin. Cylinder: Edison 28285; 78 RPM: Edison 82135.

RUST, FRIEDRICH:
Gigue. Albert Spalding, violin. Cylinder: Edison 28241; Edison 82105.

SAINT-SAENS, CHARLES CAMILLE:
Le Cygne (The Swan). Albert Spalding, violin. Cylinder: Edison 28185; 78 RPM: Edison 82316.
Introduction and Rondo Capriccioso, Op. 28. Albert Spalding, violin. 78 RPM: Edison 82043.
Prelude (from *"Le Deluge, Op. 45).* Albert Spalding, violin; R. Gayler, organ. 78 RPM: Edison 82172.

SARASATE, PABLO DE:
Carmen Fantasie, Op. 25. Albert Spalding, violin. 78 RPM: Edison 82245.
Danza Espanola, Op. 26. No. 2. Albert Spalding, violin. 78 RPM: Edison 82062.
Habanera, Op. 21, No. 2. Albert Spalding, violin. 78 RPM: Edison 82095.
Introduction and Tarantelle, Op. 42. 1. Albert Spalding, violin. 78 RPM: Bruns. 50099 and A5102; LP: MB-1009. 2. Jascha Heifetz, violin. 78 RPM: Vic. 74626 and 6154; LP: RCA ARM4-0942, Rococo 2025.
Malaguena, Op. 21, No. 1. Jascha Heifetz, violin. 78 RPM: Vic. 74569 and 6154; LP: RCA ARM4-0942, Everest 3326, Pearl GEM-109, Rococo 2025.
Romanza Andaluza, Op. 22, No. 1. 1. Albert Spalding, violin. 78 RPM: Edison 82342. 2. Albert Spalding, violin. 78 RPM: Bruns. 50136.
Zapateado, Op. 23, No. 2. 1. Jascha Heifetz, violin. 78 RPM: Vic. 66097; LP: RCA ARM4-0942, Everest 3326, Pearl GEM-109, Rococo 2025. 2. Albert Spalding, violin. 78 RPM: Bruns. 15211 and A8854.
Zigeunerweisen, Op. 20. Albert Spalding, violin. Cylinder: Edison 290; 78 RPM: Edison 82192.

SCHERTZINGER, VICTOR:
Marcheta. Albert Spalding, violin. 78 RPM: Edison 82316.

SCHINDLER, KURT:
Souvenir Poetique. Albert Spalding, violin. 78 RPM: Edison 82323.

SCHUBERT FRANZ:
Ave Maria (arr. Wilhelmj). 1. Albert Spalding, violin obbligato; M. Rappold, soprano. 78 RPM: Edison 82258. 2. Jascha Heifetz, violin. 78 RPM: Vic. 74563 and 6152; LP: RCA ARM4-0942. 3. Albert Spalding, violin. 78 RPM: Bruns. 50066; LP: MB-1009.
Horch! Horch! die Lerch (arr. Spalding). 1. Albert Spalding, violin. 78 RPM: Edison 47005 (electric). 2. Albert Spalding, violin. 78 RPM: Vic. 1667.
Serenade (arr. Remenyi). Albert Spalding, violin. Cylinder: Edison 29070; 78 RPM: Edison 82222
Sonatina No. 3, in G Minor. Albert Spalding, violin. 78 RPM: Vic. (unissued) (Note: Single-sided Victor test pressings numbered 050574-2, 050575-1, 050576-2, and 050577-2.)
Valse Sentimentale (arr. Franko). Albert Spalding, violin. Cylinder: Edison 29058.

SCHUMANN, ROBERT:
Abendlied (arr. Wilhelmj). Albert Spalding, violin. 78 RPM: Vic. 1727; LP MB-1009.
Gartenmelodie. Albert Spalding, violin. Cylinder: Edison 217.
Romance No. 2, in A Major (arr. Kreisler). Albert Spalding, violin. 78 RPM: Edison 821268.
Schlummerlied. Albert Spalding, violin. 78 RPM: Edison 82284.
Traumerei. 1. Albert Spalding, violin. Cylinder: Edison 29050; 78 RPM: Edison 82188. 2. Albert Spalding, violin. 78 RPM: Vic. 1727; LP: ME-1009.

SIBELIUS, JEAN:
Valse Triste (arr. Franko). Albert Spalding, violin. 78 RPM: Edison 82322.

SINDING, CHRISTIAN:
Fruhlingsrauchen. Solo piano: 78 RPM: Edison 50309.

SPALDING, ALBERT:
Alabama (Plantation Melody). Albert Spalding, violin. 78 RPM: Edison 82095.
† *Etchings, Op. 5.* Albert Spalding, violin. 78 RPM: Vic. M-264.

---

† Consists of 13 selections: Books; Cinderella; Desert Twilight; Dreams; Fireflies; Games; Ghosts; Happiness; Hurdy-Gurdy Waltz; Impatience; October; Professor; Sunday Morning Bells.

Mrs. Eleanor Roosevelt inscribed this photograph to Andre Benoist after one of his performances at the White House.

Joan Field, a famous violin prodigy and close friend and associate of Andre Benoist. Other students who became well known were Virginia Ralston and Paul Sladek in Pittsburgh, Jaime de la Feunte, Rita Perez and Julius "Buddy" Katchen.

From the Cottonfields, Op. 7, No. 3. Albert Spalding, violin. 78 RPM: Edison 82222.
Hurdy-Gurdy Waltz (from "Etchings, Op. 5"). Albert Spalding, violin. 78 RPM: Edison 82250.
Sunday Morning Bells (from "Etchings, Op. 5"). Albert Spalding, violin. 78 RPM: Edison 82250.
The Wind in the Pines (Prelude). Albert Spalding, violin. 78 RPM: Vic. 1881.

SUK, JOSEF:
Burleska, Op. 17, No. 4. Albert Spalding, violin. 78 RPM: Vic. 1740.

SVENDSEN, JOHAN: *Romance in G Major, Op. 26.* Albert Spalding, violin. 78 RPM: Edison 82194.

TARTINI, GIUSEPPE:
Sonata in G Minor ("Il Trillo del Diavolo"). Albert Spalding, violin. 78 RPM: Vic. 14139 and 1787.

TCHAIKOVSKY, PETER ILYITCH:
Andante Cantabile (arr. Kreisler). Albert Spalding, violin. 78 RPM: Bruns. 50100.
Chant sans Paroles (arr. Kreisler). Albert Spalding, violin. 78 RPM: 82064.
Concerto in D Major, OP. 35 (2nd move. only). Albert Spalding, violin. 78 RPM: Bruns. 50100.
Serenade Melancolique, Op. 26. Albert Spalding, violin. 78 RPM: Edison 82067.

WAGNER, RICHARD:
Prize Song (arr. Wilhelmj). 1. Albert Spalding, violin. Cylinder: Edison 28177; 78 RPM: Edison 82117. 2. Albert Spalding, violin. 78 RPM: Bruns. 30124 and 50138; LP: MB-1009.

WHITE, CLARENCE CAMERON:
Nobody Knows de Trouble I Seen. Albert Spalding, violin. 78 RPM: Bruns. 15107; LP: MB-1009.

WIENIAWSKI, HENRI:
Capriccio-Valse, Op. 7. Albert Spalding, violin. 78 RPM: Edison 82308.
Concerto No. 2, in D Minor, Op. 22 (2nd move. only). 1. Albert Spalding, violin. 78 RPM: Edison 82117. 2. Jascha Heifetz, violin. 78 RPM: Vic. 74600 and 6160; LP: RCA ARM4-0942, Everest 3326, Rococo 2025, ZRG-35.
Mazurka in A Minor, Op. 3 ("Kujawiak"). Albert Spalding, violin. 78 RPM: Edison 82245.
Polonaise Brilliante No. 1, in D Major, Op. 4. Albert Spalding, violin. Cylinder:

Edison 177.

Polonaise Brilliante No. 2 in A Major, Op. 21. Albert Spalding, violin. 78 RPM: Edison 82048.

Scherzo-Tarantelle, Op. 16. 1. Albert Spalding, violin. Cylinder: Edison 29062; 78 RPM: Edison 82188. 2. Jascha Heifetz, violin. 78 RPM: Vic. 74562 and 6159; LP: RCA ARM4-0942, Pearl GEM-109.

Souvenir de Moscow, Op. 6. 1. Albert Spalding, violin. Cylinder: Edison 28102. 2. Albert Spalding, violin. Cylinder: Edison 28163; 78 RPM: Edison 80071.

WOOD, HAYDN:

Roses of Picardy (arr. Spalding). Albert Spalding, violin. Cylinder: Edison 29074; 78 RPM: 78 Edison 82215.

KEY

78 RPM-10" DISCS

BRUNSWICK (Bruns.) (U.S.)
 15000 series (electrics, double-faced, c. 1929)
EDISON (U.S.)
 80000 series (acoustics, double-faced, c. 1912-27)
 47000 series (electrics, double-faced, c. 1928)
VICTOR (Vic.) (U.S.)
 60000 series (acoustics, single-faced, 1917-18) 3 and 4 digit nos. (600 to 1999) (reissues of acoustics and records made electrically, double-faced, pre-World War II) M-000 series (indicates an electrical set; can also denote a 12" set; double-faced, c. 1930-45)

78 RPM—12" DISCS

BRUNSWICK (Bruns.) (U.S.)
 50000 series (electrics, double-faced, c. 1929)
VICTOR (Vic.) (U.S.)
 70000 series (accoustics, single-faced, 1917-18) 4 and 5 digit nos. (6000-19999) (reissues of acoustics and records made electrically, double-faced, pre-World War II) M-000 series (indicates an electrical set; can also denote a 10" set; double-faced, c. 1930-45)

12" LONG-PLAYING DISCS

EVEREST (U.S.)— No prefix; re-channeled stereo
MASTERS OF THE BOW (Canada)—MB series (mono)
PEARL (Gr. Britain)—GEM series (mono)
RCA—ARM4 series (4 disc mono sets)
ROCOCO (Canada)—No prefix; mono
ZRG Records (Japan)—ZRG series; mono

Lily Pons had this photo taken for presentation to Andre Benoist.

Vladimir Horowitz inscribed this photograph to Benoist with his "warmest sentiments" many years ago.

Part II: Piano Rolls

BEETHOVEN, LUDWIG VON:
Romance in F Major, Op. 50 (violin-piano). Piano accompaniment only. Duo-Art 12948.

CORELLI, ARCANGELO:
La Folia (arr. Spalding) (violin-piano). Piano accompaniment only. Duo-Art 12998.

DRIGO, RICCARDO:
Valse Bluette (violin-piano). Piano accompaniment only. Duo-Art 12810.

DVORAK, ANTONIN:
Humoresque No. 7, in G Major (arr. Kreisler) (violin-piano). Piano accompaniment only. Duo-Art 12579.

ELGAR, EDWARD:
La Capricieuse, Op. 17 (violin-piano). Piano accompaniment only. Duo-Art 12778.

GRIEG, EDVARD: *Sonata No. 1, in F Major, Op. 8* (violin-piano). Piano accompaniment only. Duo Art 11798 (1st movement); 11808 (2nd movement); 11818 (3rd-4th movements).

KREISLER, FRITZ:
Caprice Viennois (violin-piano). Piano accompaniment only. Duo-Art 12028.

MENDELSSOHN, FELIX:
Concerto in E Minor, Op. 64 (violin-orch.; arr. violin-piano). Piano accompaniment only. Duo-Art 11488 (1st movement); 11498 (2nd movement); 11508 (3rd movement).

MOSZKOWSKI, MORITZ:
Guitarre (violin-piano). Piano accompaniment only. Duo-Art 12810.

RIES, FRANZ:
Perpetual Motion, Op. 34, No. 5 (violin-piano). Piano accompaniment only. Duo-Art 12398.

SAINT-SAENS, CHARLES CAMILLE:
Introduction and Rondo Capriccioso, Op. 28 (violin-piano). Piano accompaniment only. Duo-Art 12039.

SARASATE, PABLO DE:
Zigeunerweisen, Op. 20 (violin-piano). Piano accompaniment only. Duo-Art 12429.

SCHUBERT, FRANCOIS:
The Bee (violin-piano). Piano accompaniment only. Duo-Art 12579.

SPALDING, ALBERT:
Alabama (Southern Melody and Dance in Plantation Style) (violin-piano). Piano accompaniment only. Duo-Art 12598.

WIENIAWSKI, HENRI:
Polonaise-Brilliante, Op. 4 (violin-piano). Piano accompaniment only. Duo-Art 12538.
Scherzo-Tarantelle, Op. 16. (violin-piano). Piano accompaniment only. Duo-Art 12080.

Left to right: Benoist, Godowski, Sinceheimer and Elman at the Deal Conservatory in Deal, New Jersey.

The Supreme Test!

Thomas Edison autographed this portrait to Benoist around 1915.
According to Benoist, Edison had the "peculiar habit of constant
tobacco chewing which so ill-matched a brilliant mind." Benoist
recorded for Edison for several years

The Music Of André Benoist

by John Anthony Maltese

Aside from his esteemed career as an accompanist, André Benoist was also a fairly prolific composer. Many of his compositions were intended as gifts for friends and collaborators, and one notes in the following list that these people included such famous names as Albert Spalding, Lillian Nordica, Ernestine Schumann-Heink and Alma Gluck.

The following list of his works date from 1895 to 1952, and all except nine have been published. The format is more or less self-explanatory: the title is listed first in bold print, followed by what instrument the work is intended for, the dedication (if there was one), the publisher and copyright date, and finally, any additional information, such as the arranger, author of the words to the songs, etc.

1) **ARIA.** Violin and piano. Dedicated to Albert Spalding, December 29, 1918, Monmouth Beach, New Jersey. Unpublished.

2) **BERCEUSE DE NOEL.** Piano solo. G. Shirmer, Inc., New York, 1938.

3) **BESIDE THE CROSS.** Voice and piano. Dedicated to Ernestine Schumann-Heink. M. Witmark and Sons, New York, 1910. Words by Thomas F. Fallon.

4) **CHANSON D'AUTREFOIS** (SONG OF THE OLDEN TIME). Voice and piano. Dedicated to Lillian Nordica. G. Shirmer, Inc., New York, 1910. Words by Emile Benoist.

5) **CHANT RELIGIEUX.** Cornet and piano. Dedicated to Edwin Franko Goldman, January 21, 1899, New York. Unpublished.

6) **ETOILE D'AMOUR** (STAR OF LOVE). Piano solo. G. Shirmer, Inc., New York, 1897.

7) **FANTAISIE L'AMERIQUE.** Cornet and piano. Carl Fisher, Inc., New York, 1910. Arranged by Edwin Franko Goldman.

7a) **FANTAISIE L'AMERIQUE.** Brass ensemble. Carl Fisher, Inc., New York, 1934. Adapted by J.I. Tallmadge.

8) **THE FREEMAN'S HYMN.** Voice and piano. Carl Fisher, Inc., New York, 1917.

9) **THE GAIETIES OF LOVE.** Voice and piano. Wednesday, June 24, 1908. Unpublished. Words by Thomas F. Fallon.

10) **GAVOTTE ANCIENNE** (PETIT MORCEAU CARACTERISTIQUE). Piano solo. G. Shirmer, Inc., New York, 1911. (In the set: DEUX PETITS MORCEAUX).

11) **IMPROMPTU-GAVOTTE.** Piano solo. Dedicated to Elisabeth L. Hume. G. Shirmer, Inc., New York, 1897.

12) **IMPROVISATION ON THE SECOND PRELUDE FROM THE WELL-TEMPERED CLAVICHORD** BY BACH. Piano solo. Carl Fischer, Inc., New York, 1937.

12a) **IMPROVISATION ON THE SECOND PRELUDE FROM THE WELL-TEMPERED CLAVICHORD** BY BACH. Violin and piano. Unpublished.

13) **INQUIRY.** Voice and piano. G. Schirmer, Inc., New York, 1902. Words by R.C.V. Mapes.

14) **INTERMEZZO-AMERICANO.** Piano solo. Unpublished (signed: Andrea Benoa).

15) **L'HEURE DU SOMMEIL.** Violin, 'cello, piano. Luckhardt & Belder, New York, 1906.

16) **LAUGHING SONG** (FROM "MANON" BY AUBER). Piano accompaniment. Unpublished.

17) **LYS.** Voice and piano. M. Witmark and Sons, New York, 1910. Words by Thomas F. Fallon.

18) **MARLY-LE-ROI.** Violin and piano. G. Schirmer, Inc., New York, 1936. Fingering and bowing of violin part by Albert Spalding.

18a) **MARLY-LE-ROI.** Two Pianos, Four Hands. Unpublished.

19) **MAZURKA.** Violin and piano. Dedicated to Albert Spalding. M. Witmark and Sons, New York, 1910.

20) **MEMORIES.** Voice and piano. Luckhardt and Belder, New York, 1902. Words by Andre Raas.

22) **MENUET DU BON VIEUXTEMPS.** Piano solo. G. Schirmer, Inc., New York, 1909.

22) **MENUET** (BY BACH). Violin and piano. Volkwein Bros., Inc., Pittsburgh, Pa., 1949. (Transcribed and harmonized by Benoist). Violin part edited by Paul Sladek.

23) **TWO MENUETS** (BY BACH: ORIGINALLY **"G MAJOR, NO. 1" and "G MINOR, NO.2"**). Two Pianos, Four Hands. Volkwein Bros., Inc., Pittsburgh, Pa., 1948. Transcribed and harmonized from piano solo by Benoist.

24) **MOODY CHILDREN.** Piano solo. M. Witmark and Sons, New York, 1911. Suite consists of:
   a) THE DREAMING CHILD
   b) THE HAUGHTY CHILD
   c) THE MERRY CHILD
   d) THE THOUGHTLESS CHILD
   e) THE FICKLE CHILD
   f) THE AFFECTIONATE CHILD
   g) THE DETERMINED CHILD

Gregor Piatigorsky gave this inscribed photo to Benoist as a token of his esteem.

Andre Benoist with his second wife and his son, Albert Spalding Benoist, in a photograph taken many years ago.

25) **MORNING.** Voice and piano. Luckhardt and Belder, New York, 1903. Words by John Telfer Coventry.

25a) **MORNING.** Voices (S.A.T.B.) and piano. Luckhardt and Belder, New York, 1905. Arranged by Anthony Richards.

26) **MOTHER'S SONG.** Voice and piano. Dedicated to Alma Gluck. Waterson, Berlin and Snyder, Co., New York, 1909. Words by Andre Benoist.

27) **PERSUASION.** Violin and piano. Dedicated to Albert Spalding. Luckhardt and Belder, New York, 1906.

28) **PIANOFORTE PIECES FOR THE LITTLE ONES.** Piano solo. Unpublished. Suite consists of:
   a) FIRST STEPS
   b) YEARNING
   c) JUMPING JACK
   d) HAPPY-GO-LUCKY
   e) MERRY-GO-ROUND
   f) SCATTER-BRAIN
   g) CAPRICIOUS

29) **PRELUDE IN E-FLAT MAJOR (A STUDY IN CHORDS AND INTERVALS).** Piano solo. Volkwein Bros., Inc., Pittsburgh, Pa., 1949.

30) **PREMIER AMOUR**, FEUILLET D'ALBUM. Piano solo. G. Schirmer, Inc., New York, 1911. (In the set: DEUX PETITS MORCEAUX).

31) **ROSE LEAVES.** Voice and piano. Dedicated to Frederick Hastings. M. Witmark and Sons, New York, 1910. Words by Thomas F. Fallon.

32) **SOUTHERN QUEENS.** Piano solo. M. Witmark and Sons, New York, 1908.

33) **A THEME.** Voice and piano. Dedicated to Lillian Nordica. John Church Co., New York, 1908. Words by Thomas F. Fallon.

34) **THEME AND VARIATIONS IN ROCOCO STYLE.** Two Pianos, Four Hands. Volkwein Bros, Inc., Pittsburgh, Pa. 1952.

35) **THREE LITTLE IMPS.** Piano solo. January 17, 1895. Unpublished.

36) **TOUJOURS (EVERMORE).** Voice and piano. G. Schirmer, Inc.; New York, 1902. Words by Jules Lemaitre.

37) **THE VIRTUOSO'S DAILY DOZEN.** Daily Finger Gymnastics for the Piano. Carl Fischer, Inc., New York, 1924.

38) An unpublished manuscript for Piano solo, in two movements: **ALLEGRETTO** and **ANDANTINO CON MOTO.** Monmouth Beach, June 1917.

Andre Benoist in one of the later years of his life.

INDEX

Bold numerals indicate illustrations.

Left to Right: Jim Spalding, Ruth Norton, Margaret Horn, Leo Kruycek, Viola Mitchell, Sue Spalding, Barnetta Benoist, Alice Benoist, Albert Benoist, Andre Benoist, Wyman Spalding and Mischa Pischach. Students and teachers partook in the Benoist Monmouth Beach family life!

Benoist, Andre
The accompanist...and
friends

SEP 26 84
DEC 5 84
DEC 5 84
FEB 10 89

S 2 0 2 1

S 1 6 0 7
F   2 5 4